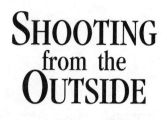

SHOOTING
from the
OUTSIDE

Also by Joan Ryan

Little Girls In Pretty Boxes:
The Making and Breaking of
Elite Gymnasts and Figure Skaters

SHOOTING
from the
OUTSIDE

How a Coach and Her Olympic Team
Transformed Women's Basketball

··

Tara VanDerveer
with Joan Ryan

AVON BOOKS · NEW YORK

Every effort has been made to give proper attribution to quoted
material. Any oversights are unintentional.

AVON BOOKS
A division of
The Hearst Corporation
1350 Avenue of the Americas
New York, New York 10019

Library of Congress Cataloging in Publication Data:
VanDerveer, Tara.
Shooting from the outside / Tara VanDerveer with Joan Ryan.—1st ed.
        p.   cm.
1. VanDerveer, Tara. 2. Basketball coaches—United States—Biography.
3. Women coaches—United States—Biography. 4. Stanford
University—Basketball. I. Ryan, Joan, 1959–   .
II. Title.
GV884.V37A3   1997   97-3231
796.323'092—dc21   CIP

First Avon Books Printing: September 1997

Printed in the U.S.A.

FIRST EDITION

QPM   10   9   8   7   6   5   4   3   2   1

To my "life coaches,"
my parents,
Rita and Dunbar VanDerveer.

I love you.
—Tara

Acknowledgments

I would like to thank my family, friends, and all the people I've been associated with throughout my playing/coaching career, including teammates, coaches, administrators, trainers, staff, boosters, media, fans, and other organizations/individuals who have encouraged and supported me.

From the 7th grade at Milne School through SUNY at Albany, Indiana, Ohio State, Idaho, Stanford, and USA Basketball, I've had the privilege to learn from and work with the best.

A special thanks to Beth, Marie, Nick, Heidi, Helen, Tina, Brooks, Konn, Sam, Toni, Mary, Vicky, Shelly, CJ, Kris, Susan, Gelbs, Weismans, Lewellyns, Ingrams, Manors, Bouchals, Tuckers, Parks, Vikki, Esther, BJ, Fishers, Beth B., Marsha, Bea, Ding, Jorga, Lou, Sami, Carol K., Debbie, Jane, Pat A., Pat W., Linda, Bill, Phyllis, Fred, Mary, Harriet, Nancy B., JD, Kathleen, Dick, Nancy H., Kathy, Bonnie, Don, Pete, Willette, Andy, Eleanor, John K., Peter, Helen, Ted, Cheryl, Tessie, Tim, Karen, Steve R., Beth G., Mark, Fernando, Michael, DeeDee, Pat M., Chris, Dave, Ann, Angela, Marianne, Kate P., Bobbie, Amy W., Kate S., Jamila, Regan, Chandra, Vanessa, Milena, Naomi, Olympia, Christina, Melody, Yvonne, Tara, Heather, Charmin, Kris, Angie, Dave, Marvice, Lindsey, Erica, Sue, Beth B., Rae, Torrae, Phil K., Val, Carol B., Sandi, David, Pat S., Billie, Kay, Theresa, Bob, Pete, Dwight, Charlotte, Steve W., Ann, Candice, Nancy G., Alex, Gwen, Mimi, Chuck, Robin, Carol S., Warren, CM, Susan, Lea, Lynn, Tracy, Joanne, Shawn, Craig, Amy E., Carolyn, Ed, Margie, Jenny, Sandi, Jay, Melody.

Gold Medal Olympic team: Teresa, Dawn, Ruthie, Sheryl, Jennifer, Lisa, Carla, Katy, Katrina, Rebecca, Venus, Nikki, Lori, Gina, Nell, Reneé, Nancy, Marian, Ceal, Carol.

Des—I know you were watching. How about our field goal percentage?

Amy—congratulations on the Pac-10 Championship, Final Four, and UPI Coach of the Year.

Joan—thanks for helping me share my story. You're awesome.

SHOOTING
from the
OUTSIDE

Prologue

Teresa Edwards bent at the waist, head bowed, and felt the wide ribbon slip over her hair onto her neck. When she stood, the weight of the gold medal fell against her chest. Then Dawn Staley bent for her gold medal. Next came Ruthie Bolton, and on down the line to the last of the 12 U.S. players. The 33,000 fans inside the Georgia Dome chanted "U-S-A! U-S-A!" and waved American flags in a pounding tribute to the greatest women's basketball team ever.

I watched from the sideline, by the bench where I had just coached these remarkable women to the highest scoring win in the history of Olympic women's basketball. We had won 59 consecutive games during our year together and now on the final day of the 1996 Olympics in Atlanta, we had won our 60th, a 111–84 victory over world champion Brazil. We had grown from an unproven collection of women, each into her own dreams and ego, to an undefeated power that reclaimed the gold medal the United States had lost in the 1992 Olympics.

From the small college towns where our practices drew thousands of fans, to the drafty court in Siberia where we had shivered on the bench, I had conjured the picture of this medal ceremony in my mind. Every day, I visualized each player rising from a deep bow with a gold medal around her neck. Now I stood on the floor of the cavernous Georgia Dome and watched Lisa Leslie wipe tears from her face and Rebecca Lobo break into her great toothy smile as if they were images sprung from my own mind.

The players held hands and raised them high in the air as the crowd roared. My arms rose, too, as if I were up there with them. Coaches don't receive medals, and I didn't need one. How could a disk of metal hold a dream? How could it begin to capture the many definitions of triumph I had learned during the year?

Even as the noise thundered around me, pictures floated through my head as if in a movie. Dawn Staley's no-look passes to Lisa. Katrina McClain's graceful layups. Teresa's stutter-steps around defenders. Ruthie's long, looping jump shots, smooth as rainbows.

"Please rise for the national anthem of the United States of America!" the announcer boomed, and the Georgia Dome fell silent. From the far end of the court, the American flag slowly began to rise, one end attached to a bar parallel to the floor, the loose end unfurling from the hands of an Olympic attendant. The flags of Brazil and Australia rose on either side.

I could barely breathe, so I sang almost without sound, my eyes roaming from the flag to the players, trying to soak it all in, to wring every sensation from the day. My eyes settled for a moment on Ruthie, who always sang gospel on our bus rides and who had performed the national anthem before many of our games. Now I saw her close her eyes tight and sing as if the words were a final prayer. In many ways, they were.

In a few hours we would go our separate ways, returning to the husbands, friends, and jobs that had been put on hold for a year. But we weren't the same people who had arrived in Colorado Springs for the team tryouts the previous autumn. Our year together had changed us in ways we couldn't have predicted. And more importantly, it had changed women's basketball forever.

1

"As long as you're going to think anyway, think big."
—Donald Trump

5

....

"You're crazy."

Bobby Knight said it without hesitation. No two ways about it. He thought I was crazy and said so. I like that about him. There are no gauzy filters between his brain and mouth prettying up his thoughts before he delivers them. He's honest to the point of bluntness. It's a trait I came to know when I was a student at Indiana and would watch him coaching every afternoon before my own practices with the women's team. I'd sit quietly high up in the stands, sometimes jotting notes about some motion offense he might be teaching, sometimes simply losing myself in the strategy of his drills. Despite his barking and criticisms, he was the kind of coach I liked: someone who understood how basketball should look and did whatever it took to make sure his players understood, too.

I've turned out to be that kind of coach myself. I say what I think, sometimes to the chagrin of my players and bosses. I'm not out to hurt anyone's feelings. In fact, I try to keep in tune with my players' moods and concerns. But being honest is the only way I know, and it's the only way for me to coach. The most direct route between teaching and understanding, as between two points, is a straight line. Don't make your players guess what you're trying to tell them. Lay your cards on the table. Tell the truth as clearly as you know it.

Sometimes this kind of honesty gets me in trouble, as it did on several occasions during the Olympic year. Most times it gets me what I want. This is why most successful coaches are hard-core pragmatists, people who deal as much as possible in black and white: "This is the goal. This is how we get there." Simple. The challenge, of course, is making sure the people around you are on the same page. So the more clearly you state what you want, the greater your chance of getting it. Though, as I found out as Olympic coach, this isn't a foolproof system.

It was October 1995. I was at a basketball clinic sponsored by Baden in St. Louis with Coach Knight and other top coaches from around the country. Seven months earlier I had accepted USA Basketball's offer to be the women's Olympic basketball coach. I had no illusions when I asked Knight what he thought. I knew he would give me a straight answer.

"You're crazy."

I laughed, but I knew he was on to something. The following day, I was flying to the U.S. Olympic Training Center in Colorado Springs with three suitcases to meet with my assistant coaches for the first time. We and the 11 women who had been selected for the "national" team would begin our grand experiment: ten months of living and training and traveling together, culminating in two weeks in Atlanta the following summer. The goal, of course, was gold. Winning the gold medal was the sole purpose of USA Basketball's spending $3 million for this unprecedented program.

"This isn't about bronze. This isn't about silver. This is

about gold," USA Basketball president C.M. Newton told us at our first team meeting.

It was a charge that guided my every thought and action in the ensuing months. I also remembered the words of David Stern, commissioner of the NBA, which had a big stake in our success. The NBA was handling all the marketing and promotion for the team, and it was also mulling over the idea of starting its own women's pro league. Our team would test the market to see if America was ready.

"The only person who can mess this up," Stern told me one day over lunch, "is you."

Those words would wake me up at night sometimes after a bad day at practice or a disappointing game. I always believed we would win, but sometimes I wondered how.

But winning the gold became more than an end in itself. Along the way on this year-long journey, the gold medal took on surprising shapes for me.

It tapped into a patriotism I had not known was in me.

It became a symbol, as we mounted a perfect record against the best American colleges and international teams, of how far women's basketball had come since I had been a young girl in New York with no place to play.

But maybe more than anything, the gold medal became something intensely personal on two counts. It came to represent tangible proof that my confounding, relentless passion for the game wasn't the waste of energy people had told me it was when I was a child.

And two, as the year unfolded, and despite the distance I often had to maintain to push them to do their best, I came to want the gold medal most of all for my players, who had become more than players to me.

To win it, I'd have to do what no other Olympic basketball coach in the United States had ever done: give the team a year of my life. When Knight coached the men's Olympic team that won the gold in 1984, the job took about six weeks. He couldn't imagine taking a year's leave from his job at Indiana for anything, much less to spend it working and living with a collection of professional all-stars for the purpose of winning one two-week tournament, even if that tournament was the Olympic Games.

"You really have to be careful they don't get burned out," Knight was telling me in St. Louis. "I just don't know that it can work, keeping people together for a year."

Duke coach Mike Krzyzewski agreed. "How do you keep them motivated?" he wondered. "How do you keep them from getting bored? Are they going to get on each other's nerves being together day in and day out for so long?"

They were good questions, ones to which I had no answers yet. Some wondered if women could work together for a year without cliques emerging and feelings getting hurt. It turned out we would have not only an all-woman team but an all-woman coaching and traveling staff. I picked two assistants to help me through the training schedule: Renee Brown, who had been my assistant at Stanford in 1990 and 1991, then went on to join the staff at Kansas, and Nell Fortner, who had been an assistant at Louisiana Tech for five years. My sister Heidi, who was the head coach at Eastern Washington, told me about Nell, and I trusted her judgment. If I did anything right during that year, it was bringing Nell and Renee on board. But I didn't know just how critical they would be to the team's success and how much they would teach me.

The fourth key woman on our staff was a former math teacher and high school coach named Carol Callan. Her job for USA Basketball was to oversee every detail of the program, from travel arrangements to uniforms to training schedules. I knew Carol a little bit from traveling to the Goodwill Games together in 1994. I figured she was my kind of person when I heard that she had coached her team to the state high school championship when she was nine months' pregnant. Her son was born a week later. I saw this determination in her all year: she let nothing get in the way of finishing the job.

I never bought into the "women can't get along" theory. In all my years of playing and coaching, I never understood why this perception even existed. It certainly has never been my experience. But I did have other concerns about the year-long program. I wondered how well professional players, each of whom was the star on her foreign pro team and had been a star in college, would accept being role players. And I wondered if these stars would buy into my system and not question me every step of the way, as I felt some of these same players had done on past national teams.

So I wasn't surprised to hear Bobby Knight say I was crazy. Sometimes I thought so, too. I was leaving Stanford, a place I loved, where in ten years our teams had reached four Final Fours and won two national championships. Our 1995–96 squad—the one I'd have to leave in the hands of my assistants—was favored to return to the Final Four. What if Stanford didn't make it? Would I feel guilty for leaving them? And what if I sacrificed critical recruiting time and a year's worth of tending to my college athletes— and the Olympic team didn't win the gold medal? It was almost too nightmarish to consider.

I knew I was risking a lot in taking this job, but I fully supported USA Basketball's decision to train the team for a year with a full-time coaching staff. The United States had always put together its Olympic basketball teams a month or so before the games and expected to win. Basketball was a U.S. game. We had the best players and coaches. We took the silver in 1976, the first year women competed in Olympic basketball, didn't compete in 1980 because of the boycott, then won the gold in 1984 and 1988. Between 1983 and 1991, the U.S. women won 41 consecutive games at international tournaments.

But in 1992, while the men's Dream Team of Michael Jordan and company swept through to the Olympic victory stand, barely breaking a sweat, the women struggled. They lost to the former Soviet Union (the Unified team) in the semifinals at Barcelona and returned home with a bronze. The disappointing finish was part of a disturbing pattern.

The first setback had come on August 4, 1991, at the Pan American Games in Havana, Cuba. The United States lost to Brazil in a preliminary round by three points, breaking the nine-year winning streak by the U.S. women in major international competitions. The team lost again in 1994 at the World Championships in Australia. I was the coach. It was a disaster, probably the worst coaching experience of my life. I have an office filled with team pictures, but I never hung my photo of that 1994 World Championships team. It was a headache from the start, the players blaming the coaches, the coaches frustrated that we couldn't get the players to buy into the program. The players were accustomed to doing things their own way. They were stars on their foreign-league teams and pretty much dictated to the coaches how they would train. So some balked at mandatory running, or at practicing twice a day. They questioned every rule. You can't coach well if each player has her own ideas on how to do things. It would be like taking 12 exceptional soloists and trying to make an orchestra. Unless they're all committed to playing the same music, you have a mess. People on that World Championships team weren't playing the same music.

The same sort of finger-pointing had gone on after the 1992 Olympic loss. So I, and others, told USA Basketball, "It's the system, not the people." The coaches were given too little time to knit their players into a team. We were throwing them onto the court, rolling the ball out there, and telling them, "OK, win."

Women's basketball around the world had progressed too far for us to think we could win on just talent and history. Our international rivals had women's professional leagues, which helped develop their best players. We didn't. They had "national" teams that trained together leading up to the Olympics. We didn't.

While there was nothing USA Basketball could do about the lack of a pro league, it could create a national team program. This was something I had talked about when coaching the national team in the Goodwill Games in 1994, after losing in the World Championships in Australia. I felt we needed a year-long training program, though I figured the coach wouldn't have to be with the team the whole time. She could check in regularly but stay in her real job until after the college season. She could join the Olympic team full-time in March and still have nearly four months to get the team ready.

I had accepted any and all opportunities to get myself ready to be that coach, should I be chosen. I like international basketball, and so I coached developmental teams, then the national team in the World University Games in 1991, the World Qualifying Tournament in Brazil in 1993, and the World Championships and the Goodwill Games in Russia in 1994. During the 1992 Olympics in Barcelona, I was one of about 17 people who bought the pay-per-view telecasts of the women's basketball games. I taped every single game. I watched them, studied them.

"If you want to be the Olympic coach in four years," I told myself, "you better get your ass ready."

In early 1995, USA Basketball offered me the job. But they wanted a full-time commitment. I'd have to leave Stanford for a year.

I sensed there was concern among some people that maybe I wasn't the right choice for this kind of team in this kind of climate. More than the gold was riding on this team. NBA Properties, Inc. was the exclusive marketing representative for USA Basketball. Nobody does marketing like the NBA, and it planned a full-court press. It was going to use this Olympic team to promote women's basketball, sell sponsors' products, and blanket the country with team merchandise. I think some people thought I wasn't a good fit. I was an X's and O's coach, not a performer. They felt I wouldn't buy into the public relations side of things, that I was strictly about hoops, not hoopla.

They were right to a certain extent. I don't like being a dancing bear, and I had concerns that the media attention and autograph sessions might distract the team from preparation and focus. But anyone who says I'm not sensitive to and supportive of public relations doesn't know me. I'm always telling my Stanford players to put out their best effort every single game because somewhere out there someone is watching women's basketball for the first time. We want to give them a reason to tune in again. That's my kind of public relations.

Playing excellent, exciting basketball is how you win people over. It's how you build a professional women's league. It's how you change attitudes so that women athletes are admired for their strength and skill. It's how we turned around a Stanford program that drew a handful of parents and classmates in 1985 to one that draws more than 6,000 a game now.

I felt that all the T-shirts and *David Letterman* appearances in the world wouldn't mean anything if we didn't, in the end, win the gold medal. Chatting with Regis and Kathie Lee wasn't going to do it. We'd win the gold with X's and O's, weight training, scouting, scrimmages, strategy sessions—hard, unglamorous work.

And we'd win it by choosing the right players.

Twenty-four players were invited to Colorado Springs for a week in late May 1995 to try out for the team.

It was, to be polite, a challenging seven days.

2

"A team above all, above all a team."
—*Skip Kennedy, Stanford swim coach*

From up in the stands of the U.S. Olympic Training Center gym, 13 sets of eyes watched the players jostling under the baskets. One player stumbled off with a bloody lip. Another twisted her knee. Elbows flew, striking whatever happened to be in their way. The 24 women had come to Colorado Springs with one goal: make the national team. All were already known to the basketball community— stars in college, All-Americans. Five had their jerseys retired by their schools. Two had Olympic gold medals in basketball. But their resumés meant little now. The players had to prove themselves all over again, show they were still the toughest, the most focused, the best.

"It's survival of the fittest at this point," point guard Dawn Staley told a reporter after one grueling workout.

The 13 people sitting in groups of twos and threes in the stands were members of the USA Basketball selection committee, made up of coaches and administrators from around the country. They would decide which women would return to the foreign leagues to play in relative anonymity and which women would finally taste a bit of the stardom historically reserved for their male counterparts. But there was more riding on these tryouts than stardom. Playing in the Olympics meant they could show American fans that they had not fallen off the face of the earth when they graduated from college. They could show that they were even better than they had been in college, just as men are better after a few years in the NBA.

There was no pro league for women in 1995 and hadn't been since the Liberty Basketball League with its bodysuit uniforms folded in 1982. There was no NBA Championship to solidify their place among the greats. When women finish college, they're just beginning to approach their peaks—and suddenly their basketball careers are over, at least in the United States.

So they go to Italy, Brazil, Sweden, Turkey. They make some money, the top few earning up to several hundred thousand dollars a year. Most don't earn more than $50,000 a year. A chunk of their earnings goes to phone bills and airline tickets to fly friends and family over to see them. They feel isolated; often they are the only Americans on a team of players who speak little or no English. I've heard stories that in some leagues the coaches are physically abusive, shoving and grabbing players in anger, even kicking and punching them. Americans have to include "no abuse" clauses in their contracts. One player I know had to fend off the advances of a team executive who would drive by her apartment at all hours and ask her teammates to keep tabs on her personal life.

The worst part for these women, though, is disappearing from the American radar screen. They'd come home for visits and people would wonder when they were going to get real jobs. Fans who followed them in college never got to see them in their late 20s, when they were strongest and smartest.

In 1995 only the Olympics could get these American women basketball players in front of American fans again.

Playing in the Olympics was the pinnacle of a female American basketball player's career. And the 1996 Olympics in Atlanta had the added attraction not only of being held in the United States but of offering a 20-game training schedule against college teams across the country, allowing players to play at their alma maters in front of the fans who once had cheered them so loyally.

Some at the tryout had tried and failed to make the Olympic team in 1992. This, they knew, might be their last shot.

Jennifer Azzi, who played on our 1990 Stanford national championship team, had been a final cut in 1992, a blow she had felt for a long time. Now she was 28 years old and a veteran of the foreign pro leagues. She was coming off her best season ever, leading her Swedish team to the national championship while averaging 31.6 points per game. Jennifer likes to play ball as much as any player I've ever coached. She looked great at the tryout, but she always does, because as much time as she spends on the court, she spends that much in the gym. She has arms cut like sculptures and legs that can carry her up and down the court all day. One thing about Jennifer—nobody was going to outwork her. She was somebody I could count on when I needed her, and I knew I'd need players like her this year.

Lisa Leslie also looked great. I knew Lisa from her days at the University of Southern California, where she was an All-American her senior year, and from coaching her on national teams for years. In high school, she once scored 101 points in the first half of a game and would have broken Cheryl Miller's high school record of 105 if the opposing team hadn't refused to come out for the second half. She was only 18 years old when she failed to make the 1992 Olympic team, the youngest player at the tryout. The following year, when she helped the United States qualify for the World Championships, USA Basketball named her its female athlete of the year. No one in the country had her combination of size and talent. She was a sure thing.

In my mind, point guard Dawn Staley was, too. The woman can play like nobody's business. She's as tough as the Philadelphia streets that shaped her. She grew up playing against boys and learned, as girls do, to use her guile to make up for her size (she's just five feet, six inches tall). I swear she has eyes in the back of her head. She has all the skills, but what I like most about Dawn is her intelligence and grit. In Colorado Springs, I caught a look on her face of fierceness and concentration that reminded me of a game Stanford played against her Virginia team in 1992. The clock had run out and players had started walking off the court: Stanford had won. But suddenly there was Dawn chasing the ref, insisting there should still be seven-tenths of a second left in the game. She convinced him, and the ref put the time back on the clock, giving Virginia a chance to win the game. Virginia inbounded the ball to Dawn on the far side of the court, away from their basket. Dawn heaved the ball toward the hoop, but it missed the mark, ending the longest seven-tenths of a second in my life. I learned a lot about Dawn from that game. She never gives up, and her head is always in the game. She, too, had been cut from the Olympic team in 1992, and she'd gone overseas to play. She wanted more than anything to show that she now had become the best point guard in the world.

Carla McGhee had walked perhaps the longest and most unlikely road to the tryouts. She had lived with different relatives growing up in Peoria, Illinois. Basketball was one of the few constants in her life. At six feet, two inches tall, she found that the game came easily to her, and she rose to All-American in high school, landing a scholarship to powerhouse Tennessee in 1987. In her freshman year, the Vols won the NCAA championship. She joined the Delta Sigma Theta sorority. She made the dean's list. Life couldn't have been better.

Then one Sunday afternoon in October of that year, on the eve of the new basketball season, she was driving with two friends to a booster's house for dinner. A truck hit their car, setting off a four-car collision. The impact injured her skull, fractured her hip and jaw, broke all but two bones in her face, and tore her voice box. She was in a coma for three days.

When she awoke from the coma, her family wouldn't allow her to look in a mirror. Her face was barely recognizable. She underwent multiple reconstructive surgeries and skin grafts. Doctors told her family she'd never play basketball again. When she left the hospital the week before Thanksgiving, she still couldn't talk, instead communicating by writing on a pad and ringing a bell to summon people. She struggled to brush her teeth. She began to walk with crutches, then with a cane, and finally on her own, limping and dragging her foot.

She returned to Tennessee to attend classes her sophomore year and watched her team on the court doing all the moves that had once come so easily to her, too. She rebuilt her body, slowly learning to run and jump again. Her voice, when it returned, was lower and huskier. She had never known what basketball meant to her until it was gone. She knew then that she would be back, and the following October, she was, wearing goggles to protect her face.

Tennessee won the national championship again. But every game and practice was painful for Carla. She played the following season, but the pain kept her from playing all-out. She decided not to play her senior year and set her sights on graduate school. For her, basketball was over.

But an agent convinced her that playing overseas could pay for graduate school, and Carla agreed to give it a try. The year off had healed her body. She played pain-free, and basketball was fun again. She tried out for the 1992 Olympic team but was cut. Then she played on the World Qualifying team in 1993, and the World Championship and Goodwill Games teams in 1994. After coaching her on all three teams, I had told her that if she wanted to make the Olympic team, she needed to work on her outside shooting. Unbeknownst to me, she spent her spare time during the European season shooting and shooting and shooting.

Then she broke her ankle, putting her out for the year. She returned to the States but still went to the gym nearly every day to practice shooting.

At the tryouts, I couldn't believe the improvement.

"Carla, where'd you get that jump shot?"

"You told me to work on it," she replied.

"I know, but nobody else listens."

Everyone on the floor that week had a story, a history that had led them to this Colorado Springs gym at this moment. As each day passed, the tension and exhaustion seemed to rise like steam from the players' skin. Lives would be changed when the committee announced the team on Thursday.

Maybe no one understood this better than guard Sheryl Swoopes. She had scored an amazing 47 points for Texas Tech in the game that won them the NCAA Championship in 1993, prompting some to call her the Michael Jordan of women's basketball. But between that moment and the Olympic tryouts she had played in only 22 organized games of basketball. Ten were in the Italian League in the fall of 1993, before she abruptly left, reportedly over a contract dispute, and never returned. Eight games were in July 1994 in the doomed World Championships in Australia. And four were in the Goodwill Games in Moscow in August 1994. For the nine months leading up to the tryouts, she had played nothing but pickup games in a West Texas rec center, supporting herself as a spokesperson/teller/publicity assistant at Plains National Bank of West Texas. This Olympic team meant a chance—maybe her only chance—to shine once more.

Val Whiting, another of my former Stanford players,

had delayed admission to UC-San Francisco Medical School to try out for the team. I heard she had lost out on $30,000 in scholarship money by deferring enrollment. For her, the possibility of playing in the Olympics was worth the gamble and the sacrifice.

This, it seems to me, is what truly separated the women's Olympic team from the men's. You had the sense that the men—the Dream Team—were playing as some kind of favor to the country. They were fulfilling an obligation. The women were fulfilling a dream.

But to do so they would have to survive this week. We had them running through drills and scrimmages twice a day in the thin Colorado air. It seemed as if every time you turned around somebody was getting hurt. Few stopped playing, though. They might sit with a bag of ice on their sore knees, but you knew they'd go back out there. If they didn't, someone else might catch the committee's eyes. Better to be limping than sitting.

This team, I knew, would be a combination not simply of the best players but of those who could create a certain chemistry. I didn't disagree with this notion—to a certain extent, anyway. Chemistry was a factor that had sometimes been overlooked in the past. A case in point was the team we took to the 1994 World Championships in Australia, the team that never clicked as a unit. We practiced for three weeks at Stanford before traveling to the tournament. It wasn't enough time to get all the players, particularly the more veteran players, to understand and fully accept what I wanted from them. Brazil scored 108 points to beat us in the championship game. I felt I had put everything I had into that team and nothing worked. I remember being furious when it was over. Since then, I must have watched the video of that Brazil game 40 or 50 times, breaking down every play, freeze-framing individual moments.

After the championship game, we attended a party with the other teams. As it happened, we had to share a bus back to our hotel afterward with the winning team from Brazil. We were down, and they, of course, were exuberant. The Brazilian coach had made a bet with his players that if they won, they could shave his head. So there on the bus, with us sitting there watching, the players toyed with the coach's hair, joking about how they would cut it. I think some of our players didn't even notice. They were listening to music or talking or staring out the windows. But the image of the Brazilian players' faces, so exuberant in victory, stayed with me. I couldn't forget it.

Teresa Edwards, the 31-year-old guard who had played on three Olympic teams and won two gold medals, was on that Australia trip. So was 29-year-old forward Katrina McClain, who might be the best female basketball player in the world. Both were at the Colorado Springs tryouts, and despite their talent, I didn't want them on the team based on my experience with them. I questioned their willingness to accept my way of doing things, which would be different from what they knew from past national teams. This program wouldn't work unless everyone was on the same page. I needed players I could depend on, players I could trust.

I wasn't sure if Teresa and Katrina fit that bill, based on what I had seen in Australia. The two players, teammates at Georgia and on the 1992 Olympic team, seemed intent on winning the games by themselves. They seemed to have thrown away all the sheet music and decided to play their own riffs. They took shots that disrupted the flow. They went one-on-one, trying to overpower everyone. In their defense, they were accustomed to taking over games in their foreign leagues—that's what they were paid to do. But it doesn't work in the long run, especially against the level of competition we faced at the Olympics. A good game is like playing chess. You don't just pull the queen out and try to take all your opponents' pieces. You set things up. You make this move, then that one, maneuvering your pieces to create openings and traps.

Teresa's reluctance to be team captain in Australia did not help our relationship either. The players had been asked to vote by secret ballot for a captain. Teresa, the most experienced player, had been the team's choice. Without consulting Teresa, I announced the result at a team meeting.

"I don't want to be captain," Teresa said.

Strong leadership on a team is vital. The leader is someone who keeps everyone in line, someone committed to the goal, someone others will rally around. A coach needs the strong leaders to support her way of doing things, or else she has a fractured, chaotic team. Teresa should have been that person—and had been that person in the past—but she wasn't in the frame of mind to fill the role in Australia. I was caught completely off-guard by Teresa's rejection. I didn't know what to say. Maybe she was still smarting over the 1992 Olympics, when she was the captain and took undue blame for the loss. Because our training period was only three weeks, I hadn't gotten to know Teresa well, nor she me. So we were both struggling to figure each other out. I was both embarrassed and angry over Teresa's refusal to be captain.

After the team meeting, I asked Teresa, Ruthie Bolton, and Jennifer Azzi to stay.

"If you don't want to be captain," I told Teresa as evenly as I could, "I guess I need to have Jennifer and Ruthie be captains, but I don't think they're ready."

I asked Teresa to reconsider. She relented and accepted the role, but the issue remained in the back of my mind.

Because I never fully understood why she didn't buy into the program, I wanted to be able to count on everyone.

Leadership would be especially crucial on the national team because we'd be together so long. If Teresa and Katrina were on it, the younger players would naturally look to them to set the tone, and I needed their support. Plus, Katrina wavered about playing right until the day before the tryouts. She could make a lot more money playing in Europe, and at one point her agent said she would indeed return to the pros instead of trying out for the Olympic team. Her brother had to talk her into flying to Colorado Springs at the last moment.

Both players worked hard and played well in the tryouts, but then Teresa hurt her knee and couldn't play for several days. She was so stressed out she had fever blisters all over her mouth. She knew how I felt about Australia and pulled me aside one day to talk about it. I listened without saying much. I told her I was going to wait and see what happened. I wasn't ready to put Australia behind me yet.

I told the committee my concerns about Teresa and Katrina. I also emphasized, repeatedly, the importance of versatility and size. Chemistry was important, but chemistry alone wasn't going to win games. Our 1994 Stanford team had great chemistry. They were a joy to work with, but we didn't have the talent to win. I was recalling that lesson during these tryouts. I worried that the committee might get so caught up in piecing together a really terrific group of women that they wouldn't give me what I needed to succeed. We would be facing a Chinese team that had a six-foot-eight-inch center. The Russians were always big, and the Cubans were physical. We had to have big players in the post who could bang with them.

I had put a lot of thought into who ought to be on the team. Before the tryouts, I had written up a preview at each position, looking at the strengths and weaknesses of every candidate. I ranked people according to what I felt I really needed. Right from the start, though, I felt my views had little impact on the committee. I wasn't expecting to hand-pick the team, but I also didn't expect to be treated like some sports festival coach with no credentials. I had committed myself to learning the international game. I had shown that commitment by coaching six national teams already, from the 1991 World University Games team to the 1994 Goodwill Games team.

Most importantly, I was the one who would be working with these players all year. It seemed logical that I should be part of the selection process, as coaches had been in the past. I knew the process from the inside, having been on selection committees including the one that chose the 1992 Olympic team. Basically we had given the coach a list of 16 or 18 players, and the coach pared it to 12. Now the pendulum had swung the other way, with the theory that a dozen minds were better than one, and also as a reaction to the loss in 1992. The coach was basically cut out of the loop in the new selection system. The committee was composed of representatives from all levels of basketball: high school, junior college, National Association of Intercollegiate Athletics (NAIA), National Collegiate Athletic Association (NCAA) Division III, NCAA Division II, NCAA Division I, and the Women's Basketball Coaches Association. USA Basketball wanted to make sure it didn't miss a great player from any corner of the U.S. basketball world.

I was allowed to voice my opinions, but mostly the committee did its work behind closed doors, in a room off the gym. They spent hours and hours in the room, interviewing players, then discussing possible selections. I knew the main debate centered on Teresa, Katrina, and Sheryl Swoopes. They were concerned that Sheryl had not played enough international basketball. I wanted to be in there, hearing the points of view, adding my own. As a college coach I was accustomed to making just about every decision about my team, down to the type of shoelaces we'd wear in our basketball shoes. This time, I felt irrelevant, like decoration.

When I vented my frustrations to Amy Tucker, my long-time assistant at Stanford, she reminded me that when I accepted the job I had agreed to coach whomever the committee picked.

"Now, are you going to coach them or are you going to quit?" she asked me by phone one night. Amy cuts directly to the core of things.

Quitting crossed my mind, fleetingly. But too many forces had driven me to this job. For one, I felt a commitment to a lot of the players, some of whom I had coached on the various national teams for the past eight years. Ruthie Bolton, in particular, influenced me.

Ruthie defines the word "heart," both on and off the court. I loved hearing about her childhood, growing up as the 16th of 20 children to the Reverend Linwood Bolton on a farm in McClain, Mississippi. Ruthie learned hard work early on, feeding the hogs and cows and chickens every day after school, weeding the garden, harvesting the corn, shelling the peas to freeze for winter.

The kids ate in shifts at the counter separating the kitchen from the den because there was no place in the house large enough to accommodate all of them at once. Sometimes, if cousins spent the night, Ruthie would share a bed with four other girls. "We'd sleep sideways, diagonal. Children would be sleeping on the floor. If you got up at night, you had to be careful not to step on anybody," Ruthie said.

She learned to play basketball in her driveway, shooting at a metal rim nailed to a pole. She'd play for hours and hours with her older sister Mae Ola and her brothers and cousins when their chores were finished. It was Mae Ola who was always the star. She was a high school All-American, considered one of the best prep players in Mississippi history. She went on to become a star at Auburn. Ruthie wanted to follow in her sister's footsteps but she was never quite as good. She was All-State instead of All-American. She wasn't highly recruited, and even Auburn didn't immediately jump at her. They took her, but had little hope she could match her sister's accomplishments. But she took over as point guard and became the anchor of the team, leading it to the NCAA Final Four her junior and senior seasons while earning Academic All-Southeastern Conference honors.

Ruthie's whole family sang gospel, so any time I coached Ruthie I knew she'd be singing on the team bus and, because of her stints in the ROTC and Army Reserve, she'd be leading army drill songs during team runs.

When I first coached her, at the World University Games in England in 1991, we got on the bus and realized we had forgotten the trainer's kit back at the dormitory. Ruthie volunteered to run the mile there and back to get it. Then she scored 44 points in the game. She told me afterward that my confidence in her in England had changed her as a player.

"You're the first coach who really, really believes I can be a great player," she said.

I did believe it. Ruthie was everything I could ask for in a player and in a person. She had been cut from the Olympic tryouts in 1992, just as her sister Mae Ola had been in 1988. She was a virtual lock to make the 1996 team, and I knew she was counting on me to coach it. I didn't want to let her down.

The committee kept telling me, as if to allay my concerns, that the 11 women chosen would be the "national team," not the official Olympic team. The twelfth player, and the actual Olympic team, would not be chosen until the following June. The women who made the cut here would be guaranteed only one thing: a salary of $50,000 for the year's work. They were told that the players on the national team would eventually make up the "core" of the Olympic team. Which, of course, could mean anything. Would half the national team comprise the Olympic team? Would all but one or two? I didn't know, and no one else seemed to know, either.

For the final tryout session Wednesday night, the players showed up wearing T-shirts on which they had written "I Survived Hell Week." I think Jennifer and Dawn had started it and everyone followed suit. Afterward, the committee retreated to a conference room and I went out to dinner, trying to guess who would be on the team.

At around midnight, I was handed a list of my 11 players.

It was not the team I had figured it would be.

I was concerned about versatility, and we didn't have a versatile team. I felt we needed size, and I got a team with seven players six feet tall or under. I preferred players with solid international experience, and I got Rebecca Lobo and Nikki McCray, fresh from college. I had hoped for five front-line players and six perimeter players, and got four and five.

And Teresa and Katrina both made the team.

I was pretty upset. I didn't have anything against any of the players personally. But looking at it in May 1995, I felt this wasn't the team that would give us the best chance of winning a gold medal.

That night as I returned to my hotel room, I passed the huge billboard that greets visitors to the Olympic training center. On it were two numbers lit up as on a scoreboard. One was the number of days until the 1998 Winter Olympics, the other the number of days until the 1996 Summer Olympics. When I passed it that Thursday night, with the list of the 11 women in my bag, the Summer Olympics clock said 421. Somehow it seemed both a lifetime away and right around the corner.

There was so much work to do. I wanted to feel more excited, but I was worried about the makeup of the team. And I was feeling a little humiliated by how I had been treated by the committee. Then, piercing through my typical cloud of worry was this sudden and incredible realization that the Olympics were actually going to happen, and I was going to be the coach. The Olympic coach. I resisted saying it out loud.

I would feel this sensation many times. It would come upon me without warning, when I was watching video of a scrimmage or when I saw an American flag outside a supermarket. Just out of the blue I'd be reminded: I am the Olympic coach.

Coaching this team meant as much to me as playing on it meant to the players. Maybe in some ways it meant more. They were not astonished at the crowds and the attention and the money that was being poured into women's basketball for the Olympic program. They had been Title IX children, growing up at a time when federal law mandated equal opportunity for girls in sports. I'm not saying they had it easy. Believe me, girls still have to fight for their fair share and they still have to fight against negative stereotyping and homophobia and the conflicting cultural messages about what is and isn't feminine.

But I grew up among the last wave of girls who had to fend entirely for themselves, for whom few opportunities were available, much less supported by law. When I was a kid, girls aspired to be head cheerleaders, not head coaches. How could I imagine that I would end up in charge of a $3 million Olympic program that was expected to win the gold medal?

And yet somehow, as corny as this sounds, it seemed destined. My grandfather, Ed Hannigan, had been a long-time coach and recreation director in western Massachusetts. As a young man he played for the Baltimore & Ohio Railroad basketball team in the 1920s. My mother has a brittle, yellowed newspaper clipping about him that I love. His team, an underdog, was down by three points with only seconds remaining. He hit a jumper, was fouled, and sank two free throws to win 34–33. He was my kind of player; he had the fundamentals down cold. He scored 26 points that game, including 14 of 17 free throws. When he was a rec director, he coached my grandmother on a girls' basketball team in the 1930s. I can only imagine what those games must have looked like. But in their way, the games—and my grandparents—helped lay the groundwork for what I have been able to do.

But I think my love of basketball came to me not only

through blood but through the air and soil around Spring-field, Massachusetts. That, of course is where James Nai-smith invented the game and where the Basketball Hall of Fame stands today. It is also where my parents met as graduate students at Springfield College. I was born nearby in Melrose, Massachusetts.

In Melrose, my father became the first male teacher in the history of the town's elementary school. Going against convention didn't bother him any more than it would bother me later on. My parents instilled confidence and independence in all their children, encouraging us to navi-gate our way through decisions and prepare for the consequences.

"Have a good strategy," my father always told me. "Nothing pops up tomorrow unless you plan for it."

Of course, I had no plans as a child to be a basketball coach. I had no strategy. I found my way to the job as if on a boat following the currents.

3

"It's hard to beat a person who never gives up."
—*Babe Ruth*

West Hill in New York state was right out of *Leave It to Beaver,* a place of tree forts and tire swings, where children knew their neighbors' kitchens as well as they knew their own. I was the oldest of five children of a school administrator and a speech teacher, bossy from the get-go, acting half the time as if I were one of the parents instead of a kid. I'd change diapers; I'd organize the other children for whatever activity we had planned for the day, and there was always something.

My parents believed one's body ought to be as active as one's mind. We skied, sailed, swam, hiked. Friday nights we went to the local YMCA as a family to swim or shoot baskets. My mother and father centered their lives around us. When I was ten years old, my parents bought me a flute for $1,000, a huge expense on a $20,000 yearly salary. If I wanted a basketball, or new skis, I'd have had to wash windows or clean out refrigerators for my mother's friends in order to earn the money. But my parents bought me the flute because music had a deeper, more enduring value to them than sports. Maybe they saw sports as a means to an end—it kept your body healthy and relaxed your mind. But music was an end in itself.

I took lessons every week and practiced every day. I loved playing the flute. We spent our summers in an extraordinary place called Chautauqua in upstate New York because my father taught reading at their vast educational institute. Basically, Chautauqua is like a utopia where learning is valued above all else. There are symphonies and operas every week, seminars, classes, speakers. It's like no place I know, and my parents, being educators, bought a home there so it could become a part of our lives.

When I was 12, one of the top flutists in the world stayed in Chautauqua and accepted me as a student for the summer. This was a huge deal because he rarely accepted a pupil so young. I responded by practicing two or three hours a day in a "practice shack," one of the plain wooden sheds that were rented out to the many musicians who gathered in Chautauqua every summer. I loved escaping there and losing myself in the music. Part of the joy was mastering complicated compositions. This incredible teacher sent me off each week wanting more.

But as the years passed and I became more advanced, something changed. Back home in West Hill with my usual teacher, I began to get physically ill going to my lessons. No matter how hard I practiced, I could never be perfect. I began to feel I would never be as good as my teacher expected me to be. Maybe with a different teacher, like the one in Chautauqua, I could have pushed through my dread and frustration. But with every lesson, I disliked the flute more.

One day when I was in ninth grade, I came home from a lesson and announced to my parents that I wasn't playing the flute anymore. That was it. I put the flute away that day and didn't pick it up again until I was in college and played for fun. I still take it out now and then and see what I can do.

My response to the flute taught me two things. One, it showed me I am an all-or-nothing person. Either I'm 100 percent committed to something or I don't want any part of it.

Two, I learned how crucial a teacher can be in nurturing or ruining a student's passion. A teacher needs to find the trigger inside each student that will release his or her best work. Some students need to be pushed; others need space. Some need every detail explained, others work better on instinct. I thought back on this often when I became a coach.

My parents didn't fight my decision to give up the flute. They had seen how it was affecting me. They wanted the best for their kids and expected us to make choices for ourselves. I think they felt that if they were around enough, they could give us the values and perspective to make reasonable choices.

When my father got home from work, he'd toss the football around with us outside, or take us skating. He never plopped himself in front of the TV. He had played hockey in college and was still a good athlete years later. Neither he nor my mother was a willing spectator; they'd rather be out *doing*. So we children were the same way. We played dodgeball, football, tetherball, and, of course, basketball in the yards and quiet streets of West Hill, just outside Schenectady. Most families there had a dinner bell to summon their children at nightfall. My sister used to joke that my mother always had to ring it three times to get me to come inside.

The driveway to our house was gravel, so it didn't make sense to have a hoop. I'd go next door to the Fishers. If there were a car parked under their basket, I'd walk down the block looking for another empty driveway with a hoop. There were other girls in the neighborhood who played, but mostly I'd find myself with the boys, who would let me in only if they needed another body to even the teams. I soon learned how to improve my odds of playing. I saved my allowance and bought the best basketball at the store. If the boys wanted to use the ball, they had to take me with it.

That was the game within the game for girls like me in the 1960s.

We waited on the periphery of sports like ghosts, invisible to the boys except when we filled a need, invisible sometimes even to the teachers and other adults in our lives who guided us toward home ec and tennis. My father couldn't have been a more supportive parent, but even he couldn't see the point of a girl playing basketball. This was one of the few instances when my father's vision failed him. He has an uncanny ability to see the potential in things. When he bought our little summer house in Chautauqua, it was a rundown boardinghouse that made others wince to look at it. Now it's a gorgeous inn that shows up in chamber of commerce ads for Chautauqua. One year when I needed a bike and we didn't have money for a new one, he pointed out an old ugly one in a bike shop. I burst into tears.

"No, it will be a great bike," he said. My father paid for it and told the bike shop what he wanted done.

Two weeks later, we picked up a beautiful shiny bike with a new seat and gleaming spokes. I couldn't have imagined what it could be.

But my father couldn't see the potential in basketball.

"Basketball won't take you anywhere," he used to say, summoning me off the neighbor's court. "Come in and do your algebra."

"Algebra isn't gonna take *me* anywhere," I'd mumble, heading toward the house.

As much as his words might have stung, he was speaking the truth of the time, and I knew it. It was foolish to think I'd have a future in basketball. How could there be a future when there wasn't a present? There was no girls' basketball team in my junior high school. There was a so-called team in high school that played all of four games but held no practices. There were no women that I knew or had heard of who made their living in the sport.

In 1971, the year I graduated from high school, just 62,211 girls competed in school sports. The number of boys? Nearly 650,000. People didn't see sports, particularly team sports, as the educational and empowering tool for girls that it clearly was for boys. Boys learned about working as a team, winning and losing gracefully, setting goals, honing discipline. Perhaps most important, sports instilled in them the confidence to lay their talent, skill, and courage on the line and see if they measured up. It's no coincidence that most of the female executives at Fortune 500 companies describe themselves as tomboys as children; they learned how to compete at an early age. I remember listening to boys speak up in class even if they didn't know the answer. They didn't embarrass easily, as most of us girls did. I think sports played a role in this. Sports taught the boys that failing is better than not trying, and that failing isn't fatal. They learned to figure out why they failed, then put it behind them and move on. If there is a greater lesson in how to succeed in life, I don't know what it is. I've seen people paralyzed by their fear of failure, their fear of being less than perfect. If you can't allow yourself the freedom to fall on your face now and then, you'll never know the bounds of your talents.

When I was a child, of course, I didn't love basketball because it might make me a stronger, better person, or because it might provide my livelihood one day. I loved it in the visceral way you love a painting or a piece of music. When I was in Italy with the Stanford team, I saw Michelangelo's *David* for the first time. Maybe this sounds stupid, but I think the passion and reverence Michelangelo had for sculpture is something like the passion and reverence I feel for basketball. His medium was marble; mine is a ball, a court, and five players. I'm not particular about a lot of things—for instance, I'd wear sweats and basketball shoes to the opera if I could, and the inside of my car often resembles a recycling center. But I'm very particular about how basketball should be played, what it should look like.

As a child, I hadn't figured out any of this yet. I wasn't even sure at the time why I loved the game so much. Maybe it was partly because I could play it by myself. I couldn't play kickball or football by myself. Playing in the tree fort was no fun without friends. But I could watch basketball on TV, then go out and spend hours on my own trying to replicate the moves I had seen. And I was good. As when I was playing the flute, I was mastering skills—and nothing is more motivating than success as long as the activity stays fun.

I loved skiing, too, perhaps even more than basketball. But skiing was all skill and sensation. Basketball appealed to the strategist in me. I liked the rhythm and intricacy of the game, the way the players moved around the court like chess pieces in fast-forward. My family always loved card and board games, and bridge became our favorite. Even as kids, my sister Beth and I played with our parents. Maybe basketball seemed a bit like bridge to me. The cards were like your players: You had to work with what you had. The fun was in figuring out how to use the players to the greatest advantage.

I remember sitting in front of the television with my father watching the Boston Celtics and charting their shots in my notebook. It was the first of thousands of notebooks I would keep over the years. Even then, watching the Celtics, it was strategy more than skill that held my attention. My father and I would discuss why the players made the plays they did, though at the time I didn't even speak the language of basketball. I didn't hear, for example, of a pick-and-roll until I got to college. All I knew was that I wanted to play, to be inside the music, and there was almost no place for me to do that.

Title IX of the 1972 Education Amendments, which required schools to provide equal athletic opportunities to girls, was still a few years away. The schools didn't have to give us anything, and for the most part they didn't. In junior high school, the boundaries of the court might as well have been stone walls. The closest I could get to a real game was the sidelines. I loved to watch the boys play against other schools at night, with the bleachers filled with fans and coaches barking their instructions. But the games were 30 minutes from our house at the gym at the State University of New York at Albany, where my father was earning his doctorate and I attended the campus secondary school.

My parents weren't keen on driving me to night games, seeing as how they had four other children to attend to. So I volunteered to be the team mascot, making myself an official part of the team and thus justifying my parents' long drive. The bear costume was too big for me and hot, and I couldn't see out of the eyeholes very well. The cheerleaders would be leading cheers and looking for me to rally the fans, and I would be down on one knee at courtside watching the action, the massive bear head under my arm. I was the worst mascot in the history of mascots. The next season, I was encouraged to find other ways to show my school spirit.

The boys on the team knew I could play because I'd join their pickup games on the playground. They were usually bigger than I was, so I learned how to fake—start one way, and then, when my defender committed to that direction, juke the other. In that way I'd find a clear path to the basket. Only later did I see the metaphor in this. I tell my players all the time: when you're playing against the bigger boys, you're not always going to get your own way. There won't always be a clear path to the basket— or the big marketing account or the graduate degree. But don't give in to failure. Find another way to get there.

That's what I'm always striving to do in coaching. I remember when my Stanford team was playing the University of Georgia in the NCAA West Regional Final in 1991.

Georgia had a phenomenal team, and I didn't have my two post players, Trisha Stevens and Julie Zeilstra. I broke down every tape I had of Georgia, trying to figure out the weaknesses in their players. Then I schooled each Stanford player on the Georgia player she'd be defending. If a Georgia player could drive well to the basket but couldn't shoot, we didn't guard her outside shot. The key was finding all the little things that would add up to something big, something that would compensate for our lack of size. I laid out the situation for our players: people are hurt, so what are you going to do about it? Look at it as an opportunity, I told them. People like challenges, and the players responded. We were down by 12 points in the second half, but rallied and won by eight.

You can't let the obstacles beat you before you even take your shot. You have to have confidence, or at least look as if you do. When I'm out speaking to groups, particularly women's groups, I always say that the most important ingredient for success is believing in yourself—and if you don't, fake it until you can muster the real thing. In life as in basketball, a good fake can be a valuable tool. In the end, no one cares whether you got to the basket through wile or strength. Getting there is what matters.

I was beginning to absorb all these lessons as I stood on the sidelines of the boys' games. As I waited to be asked to play, I dribbled and dribbled, around my feet, through my legs, behind my back, switching from hand to hand. Maybe the boys could keep me from playing, but they couldn't keep me from making myself a better player. I learned from being the underdog as a kid, and I became a good player, even by the boys' standards. I still remember what the best player on the boys' team signed in my seventh-grade yearbook: "You'll go to the Olympics one day."

Somehow this seemed like a reasonable prediction to me at the time. Of course, starring on Broadway and flying to the moon seemed reasonable to my young mind, too. Yet I remember watching the Olympics as a child and, with no hope or plan, seeing myself playing in cavernous arenas in front of huge crowds, not at the Olympics but somewhere. I always visualized what I wanted. It was like putting myself in a movie and directing the scenes. When I was in the third grade, I wanted to water ski on one ski the first time out. So I thought it through, picturing every step: first I'd have to bring the ski back, then slip my foot out, then drop the ski. I thought about it in such detail over and over again that when I got into the water, I did it exactly as I had seen myself do a hundred times in my head already.

I never dreamed specifically about the Olympics. Women didn't begin playing basketball in the Olympics until 1976, a year after I graduated from college. When I was coaching the Olympians, I thought about what it would have been like to watch a team of women like them when I was a kid. I would have been glued to the television set. I wouldn't have missed a single minute. I had heard as a kid that outstanding women basketball players existed, but the only ones I'd ever seen were in my imagination. So I never seriously thought of basketball when I thought about my future. I figured I'd go to medical school or law school, an education befitting the child of a father a dissertation short of a Ph.D. and a mother with two master's.

I was a good student, but not just because my parents stressed academics. School offered a competitive outlet I couldn't find in sports. And school provided a structure and discipline that brought out my best work. I craved that same structure and discipline in sports; I know they would have shaped me into a much better athlete. For me as a child, there was no measuring stick, no accountability, no motivation to push myself in sports. I was always on my own, figuring it out for myself. Trying to learn the game without a coach or team was a bit like being handed a stack of books at the beginning of the school year and being left alone to learn what you could. You would certainly pick up a few educational tidbits here and there, but you probably wouldn't make it to Harvard.

As I grew up, these voids and inequities began to chafe. I resented that boys had Little League and tennis teams and we didn't. I resented that boys had junior high basketball, freshman basketball, junior varsity basketball, and varsity basketball, and we basically had nothing, maybe some intramurals and a few "play days" against other schools.

My basketball career at the junior high school spanned one day. Because I was so keen to play, I was allowed in seventh grade to go with the high school girls on a "play day." I sat in class stealing glances at the clock, counting down the hours until I could join the high schoolers in the parking lot. Without a practice—the boys were always using the gym for practice and we didn't have an official coach, anyway—we boarded the school bus for the game across town. I remember hyperventilating on the way, I was so excited and nervous. We had no uniforms, so we wore our gym suits. I wore Keds. I didn't even know enough to wear two pairs of socks. I returned home with blisters and noxious feet, but I didn't complain. I was thrilled. I had played in a game with referees and a time clock and an official score, though I don't remember now what it was, which is significant. It was perhaps the only time in my life when the score didn't matter.

All I knew was that I wanted more.

The following year I found a women's recreational league that played every Monday night. I was the youngest player by about ten years. We never knew what time our game would be until the schedule was printed in the newspaper Monday morning. I'd rush out to grab the paper as if it were a Christmas package, find my team's name in the small print in the back of the sports section, and announce the time to my father. At night, he would drive me to the small gym for the games. On part of the court, a balcony jutted out just far enough to block a shot launched from the corner. Who cared? I'd rather be scraping the balcony than sitting in it.

I guess I could have pushed to join the boys' basketball team at school, though I hadn't gotten very far doing that the year before when I tried to join the boys' tennis team, but after just a year I departed public school for an all-girls' private school, and left those inequities behind. But I guess I set an example, because when my sister Beth discovered there was no girls' tennis team at her school, she requested a spot on the boys' team. She was an excellent player, good enough to beat most of the boys. With my parents' support, my sister fought and won.

Then my sister Marie asked to join the boys' swimming team because, again, there was no team for girls. She was rebuffed with the explanation that the boys sometimes practiced in the nude. Marie shrugged and said that was fine by her though she would wear a bathing suit. The school relented and let her join.

I found different ways to try to fill my basketball cravings. When I was at the campus school in Albany, I would often have to wait a couple hours for my father to finish up his afternoon classes before we could drive home. He always knew I would either be watching the boys' basketball practice or be reading in the library. One day, the librarian pulled my dad aside. "Tara has read every basketball book we have," she said, amazed and a little concerned. It was a bit unusual, she thought. And I guess it was.

What I remember is that all the books had boys as the main characters. I've always thought I'd like to write children's books about basketball with girls as the heroines, based on some of the players I've coached. What an inspiring thing it would have been to look down at a page and see, looking back at me, a face that looked like mine.

When I watched the boys practicing in seventh grade, I knew I could play better than all of them, partly because they hadn't started to grow yet. I'd sit there and wonder: why do I have to watch? Why aren't I down there? Then I'd get mad at myself. Why do you like basketball so much? Why don't you just get rid of it and then you won't have to feel the way you feel? Every year I would think that the next year I wouldn't like basketball anymore. Then it would come back and I'd be even madder. The eighth-grade boys would be playing, and I was still watching.

Then in ninth grade, the gym teacher wrote in my yearbook: "To the best basketball player, boy or girl." Great, I thought. If I'm the best, then how come I'm up here in the stands?

As I moved into my teens, girlfriends who used to play in the driveway with me wanted to stay inside and listen to records and read magazines. Yet I was still drawn to the court. I knew I was different from other girls my age. I had no interest in cruising Main Street and gathering in the parking lot of McDonald's to sneak a drink of beer. I'd spend weekend evenings at a friend's house playing Scrabble, going to the movies, or staying at home to play bridge with my parents and Beth, which I loved. My dad posted our scores on the refrigerator, motivating Beth and me to read books on bridge so we could beat our parents. I never liked shopping, sewing, or cooking, as my sister Beth did. I studied and read a lot, mostly the classics and historical fiction. I wrote letters to the friends I saw every summer in Chautauqua.

As I hit my teens, I sensed I wasn't supposed to be playing basketball anymore. If I were, there would be girls' teams. There would be more girls on the playground courts. I never thought of myself as a tomboy. All the girls in my neighborhood were just like me when they were seven, eight, nine, ten years old. They changed and I didn't. I still loved games, especially basketball, the way I loved them as a kid. Only now I wasn't supposed to play.

I needed to move on, grow up, leave basketball behind with my other childhood toys.

And for a while I did.

We moved away from West Hill to Niagara Falls when I was 15 and a sophomore in high school. I was upset about leaving my school and my friends, so to cheer me up, my parents said they would buy a basketball hoop for the new house.

"Don't bother," I told them.

I was finally agreeing with my father. So I can block shots and shoot baskets and dribble behind my back. What good was it? I was never going to play on a team because there were no teams to play on. It was painful to love to play so much. So I put away my basketballs, bought a 10-speed bike, and spent my afternoons riding up by Niagara Falls and the Canadian border. I lived on my bike, trying to lose basketball in the blur of the trees and houses.

At my new school, Niagara Falls High, I decided to go out for cheerleading, a notion that sends my players into fits of laughter whenever I tell the story. Cheerleading was the girls' ticket to the court, just as the mascot costume had been. It was what girls did in the 1960s. We were on these rigid tracks: you do this, you do that, you don't do this.

The day of the cheerleading tryouts I forgot my gym suit. Being new, I knew only one girl at the school, and she wore a size smaller than I did. I had no choice but to borrow her gym suit anyway. It was the kind with a dozen snaps down the front. When it was my turn to cheer, I jumped up and shouted, "Go Niagara!" In a great burst of energy and spirit, I thrust my arms out wide—and all the snaps popped open!

Needless to say, I didn't make the squad.

I couldn't wait to get to Chautauqua that summer, after our first year in Niagara Falls. I always knew that whatever my problems were, once the summer began I'd be all right. As soon as school let out, we would pack up the car and drive south on Route 90 to Chautauqua. It was a dream world, with gingerbread cottages, porch swings, and brick walkways leading to a beautiful village green. We could walk out our front door and go half a block down the road, and there was the lake. We skied, boated, and swam with other children who, like us, were lucky enough to spend every summer there. Being at Chautauqua was like opening doors to the best of the human mind and spirit. This was where I developed a lifelong love of opera. I sang in three operas as a child in the town's small opera house, where people would gather on summer nights. There was a different opera every summer, lectures, and three symphonies a week. Because my father worked for the institute that was the driving force behind the cultural events, we got free passes for dress rehearsals. I listened to Ella Fitzgerald, Duke Ellington, Van Cliburn, the Mormon Tabernacle Choir. Chautauquans would tell us stories about Thomas Edison spending his summers in the house down the road and Eleanor Roosevelt coming through to give a talk. It is a place that treasures ideas and the arts, where one can be immersed in academics and conversation or spend the day alone on the lake.

My father spent many of his off hours working on the house. I learned to use a steel saw so I could help him cut the six-foot boards to fix up the hallway. My sisters, little brother, and I painted walls, cut the lawn, cleaned the yard. We helped my parents transform the old guest house into what is now a beautiful lodge. All us kids slept in the long, refurbished attic while the paying guests slept in the rooms below.

I was always happy in Chautauqua and have returned every summer, even as an adult, and still see the same friends I saw as a kid, many now with their own kids. When things get tough in my life, I think of Chautauqua. I know that no matter what, I can always go back there.

I thought of Chautauqua as the week of Olympic tryouts came to a close. It was nearly the end of May. In two months I'd be by the lake again in my parents' lodge. I knew the peace and quiet would help me figure out how to make this year work.

But first I was going to see what we had in this team. Without much preparation, we took the players to Lithuania and Italy for scrimmages against the European teams.

4

"The cards you hold in the game of life mean little.
It's how you play them that counts."
—*Pearl S. Buck*

Nell Fortner, one of my assistants for the national team, had never traveled out of the country. This was going to be a long, trying trip for a novice. The coaches and players had flown to their homes briefly after the tryouts, then gathered at Dulles Airport in Washington, D.C. We flew overnight to Frankfurt and on to Vilnius, Lithuania. By the time we landed the following morning, we couldn't see straight. Our hotel was a seven-story block of gray stone dropped on the edge of an otherwise deserted street. Dim lights caused the small lobby to look even smaller, though we didn't know the meaning of small until we saw the beds. Most of our players had to sleep curled up or their feet dangled off the edge of the mattress.

Most of the older players knew not to expect much from the food, but the rookies were still learning. Nikki McCray walked through the buffet line at breakfast our first day and looked at the runny eggs, the balls of brown meat, and the white gruel that looked like grits but wasn't. (I never did find out what it was.) She returned to the table with an empty tray.

"Go look again," Jennifer told her.

Nikki went back and found toast with jam. At least it was something.

That first day I was already thinking, "When do we leave for Italy?" Nell, however, was standing by the hotel window gazing onto the brown and gray city through the grimy panes. Then she spun around to face me as if she were Mary Tyler Moore about to toss her hat into the air.

"I looooove Lithuania!" she said.

I laughed so hard.

"Wait till you see Italy," I told her.

That's how Nell would be the whole year. She loved everything and everybody. She was 36 years old and had grown up in Mississippi, absorbing more than her share of Southern charm. She made friends like no one I've ever seen. She could talk to a post. Nell immediately buoyed my spirits that day, a gift she would give me many times in the coming months.

When we had boarded the plane in Dulles, I still wasn't sure what to make of this team. That was a large reason we were going to Europe, to take a test drive and see what we had in these players. It was early June. We'd be together for a few weeks, then go our separate ways for the summer. The trip would give the players a sense of what I expected of them when they returned for training camp in October, and how I expected them to prepare themselves over the summer. The trip would set a tone, lay a thin foundation, for the year to come.

I had decided after being so upset with the selections and the selection process that I would wipe the slate clean. I'd let every player define herself anew. We were all professionals. We'd make it work. We had to. This is what I was always telling my Stanford players: No use crying over spilled milk. Deal with the situation at hand. Don't waste time moaning about what *should* be.

On the plane to Lithuania, I found myself thinking about what I hoped to take away from this year. Winning the gold medal was number one. I also wanted to take new knowledge and ideas back to Stanford. I wanted to be sad when it was over. And every time I looked at the team picture, I wanted to feel I had done the best job I could. I knew we had the right staff in place, and that eased my mind tremendously.

At the first team meeting, Carol Callan, the women's team director, had given each player a handout explaining the team rules and the fines for breaking them. Players would be fined for wearing the wrong socks, the wrong shirt, the wrong jog bra. They couldn't bear headbands or any wristbands that weren't USA Basketball's. We wanted nothing that would set players apart from one another and create an atmosphere of 11 individuals instead of one team. Carol would be the disciplinarian, lifting the responsibility from my shoulders and reducing the potential for conflicts between me and the players.

Also spelled out in Carol's handout were what the players needed to bring on the Lithuanian trip and what the traveling rules were. One rule was to wear closed-toe shoes. This is a safety precaution of mine. I'm not the greatest flyer, so I'm always anticipating disaster. I knew we would be safer, should there be a fire or broken glass, in closed-toe shoes.

Rebecca Lobo showed up at Dulles in sandals. And she didn't have any other shoes in her carry-on. I looked at her feet and wondered if she hadn't read the handout or if she was just doing her own thing. Rebecca was the only player on the team I hadn't coached. I had heard only great things about her, but this wasn't a brilliant start. Showing up in sandals wasn't a big thing in itself. But I believed very strongly that adhering to rules and paying attention to details would be critical in melding 11 individual styles and egos into a winning team. Following the rules would be the outward signal that a player had subsumed her own wants for the good of the group. It would also keep chaos to a minimum.

This is something all my players quickly learned about me. I'm fanatical about details. If we're running sprints on the court, for example, I want players to touch the baselines every single time, not just to get close. This is how you create a team "culture." Everybody knows how she's supposed to do things, what is expected.

I wanted Rebecca, and all the players, to understand this from the start. Ruthie Bolton wore the same size shoe as Rebecca and so loaned her the extra pair of Nikes in her bag. The other players teased that they would blackmail Rebecca with photographs: Rebecca had an exclusive contract to wear Reeboks.

Every player had a shoe contract: six with Nike, two with Reebok, and three with Converse. This was an issue that concerned me a little. Not the shoe contracts per se— I had one with Nike myself. But I wondered how much their obligations to their corporate sponsors—whether for shoes, balls, socks, soap, or whatever—would distract and stretch these players. When we gave them a day off, ostensibly to rest, I didn't want them flying off at every opportunity to talk at a Nike event or to shoot a Reebok commercial.

This, of course, had not been a concern on past national teams.

No female basketball player had ever had a shoe named after her, as Sheryl Swoopes did by Nike. No one had a signature basketball as Rebecca Lobo did from Spaulding. Women's basketball clearly was beginning to boom as we set out on this Olympic journey, and I fully understood how crucial our performance would be to pushing it to the next level. I knew this meant not only being successful on the court but being "stars" off it, doing autograph sessions, public appearances, and media interviews.

"If women's basketball is going anywhere," Katrina McClain told a reporter early in our tour, "it will start here."

She was right, and of course I was thrilled to think how

much interest we could generate with this team, how much money and fame were finally trickling into the lives of these great players. But I didn't want outside distractions to pull us away from our primary goal of winning the gold medal.

Rebecca, especially, had opportunities tugging her off the court. She had become more famous than any player in the history of women's basketball. And for good reason. She's smart, down-to-earth, and skilled. And her UConn team went undefeated in 1995, an occurrence that, fortunately for women's basketball, happened within easy reach of the major New York media outlets and Connecticut-based ESPN. UConn's perfect season came on the heels of fantastic national championship games the previous two years. In 1993 Sheryl Swoopes scored 47 points for Texas Tech in one of the most dazzling performances in Final Four history. Then North Carolina won the title with a heartstopping shot at the buzzer in 1994. Those games paved the way beautifully for Connecticut. Fans were primed for something special, and UConn—led by charismatic Rebecca—delivered.

UConn's success helped boost overall attendance at women's games in the 1994–95 season to more than 5 million, the highest total ever, and the 15th consecutive year that attendance had risen. Connecticut's popularity drew a capacity crowd of 18,038 to Minneapolis's Target Center for the championship game. Nearly 250,000 spectators attended the 43 sessions in the women's NCAA tournament in 1995. In 1982, by comparison, just 66,924 attended. The enthusiasm snowballed: Tickets to the 1996 Final Four in the 23,900-seat Charlotte Coliseum sold out nearly a year in advance. ESPN and ESPN2 aired 64 women's games in the 1994–95 season. Local cable outlets such as SportsChannel and the Sunshine Network carried even more. Just a few years earlier, women got on TV only for the postseason, and then only as it fit around the men's schedule.

UConn's popularity proved, I think, what many of us had been telling sports editors and television executives for years. If you tell people about us, they will come to the arenas. But what we kept hearing was: We'll tell people about you when we see more of them in the arenas. It was the chicken and the egg. Not until we won a national championship did the Stanford women attract consistent coverage from the Bay Area media, even during years when the men's local college teams were down.

Suddenly, with UConn's success, people were not only accepting women's basketball but romanticizing it. Columnist Ira Berkow wrote in the *New York Times* that the women's game is "substantially different" from men's basketball because it's a game "in which egos seem to meld into the concept of the team."

Legendary UCLA coach John Wooden agreed.

"To me, the best pure basketball I see today is among the better women's teams," he said. "It's the game as I like to see it played, without so much showmanship."

One reason there's little showmanship, of course, is that women aren't as big or as fast as the men. Those are facts. We don't dunk, or at least we do it only rarely. We play a team-oriented style, with lots of passing and precision, because that's the best way for us to score. We're not taking a moral high ground here in choosing one style of play over another. If women could leap as high as men, believe me, they'd be slamming them in, too. But I admit I agree with John Wooden. Given a choice, I find the women's "pure basketball" more enjoyable to watch and coach than the showier NBA style. But there were times—many during the Olympic year—when I'd have killed for a big ol' Hakeem Olajuwon under my basket.

We'll eventually get our Hakeems in the women's game. We'll see bigger and bigger players because the pool of talent is expanding each year. I recently saw a national survey that found basketball had become the most popular participation sport among females, rising by 19 percent in

1994. The survey said 9.2 million girls and women now play basketball in the United States. What surprised me was how much higher it was than other popular sports: 5.8 million women play tennis and 5.9 million play golf.

The role model for this new generation of basketball players was Rebecca. She found herself pursued by business people with an enthusiasm unknown to any other woman in basketball history. She appeared in the Tom Cruise movie *Jerry Maguire,* playing herself. She published a book with her mother, RuthAnn, called *The Home Team.* She appeared on *Late Night with David Letterman.* She signed deals with Reebok and Spaulding and several New England companies. She had become the face of women's basketball. She had size and a bright, engaging personality. But she was green. She had no international experience, and the international game was more physical and much quicker than what she played in college. It was only much later that I began to understand the subtext of this year-long experiment. USA Basketball wanted a gold medal, but it also wanted a public relations bonanza. Who better to sell women's basketball than Rebecca? The question for me, though, was, could she help us win?

It was a question that wouldn't be answered for many months.

Our first night in Lithuania, we went out together as a team to a street festival. Dawn Staley had a video camera and was taping her colleagues, who mugged like children. Carla McGhee began dancing to the music, joining in the Lithuanian circle dances and immediately picking up all the moves. I couldn't dance if you painted the steps on the floor and threw me into Fred Astaire's arms. But I delighted in watching Carla, who kept insisting I could learn if I'd just loosen up and let myself go.

I'm not real great at that in general, at least with my teams.

Throughout the year, Carol Callan and Renee Brown would tell me I should let the team see the side of me they saw, the one who marveled at the players' talent and personalities, who read voraciously, who hollered like a kid down the ski slopes. I'm not a coach who gets buddy-buddy with my players. I'm not looking to win a popularity contest. A coach needs to keep a certain distance to push her players to be the best they can be. She needs to keep her players on edge just enough to prevent complacency, a real danger with a team as dominant as this one would be during the college tour.

I don't get too involved in my players' personal lives because I can't let my own likes and dislikes get in the way of making the best decisions for the team. That's why my assistants are so important and why I take such care in hiring them. They balance my weaknesses. They're the huggers and listeners. They're sometimes the interpreters between me and my players, communicating concerns and opinions from one side of the narrow chasm to the other. They keep misunderstandings to a minimum. No two assistants could have done a better job in this than Nell and Renee. They would play an especially critical role in stitching together the frayed edges of my relationship with Teresa.

As it happened, Teresa barely played on the Lithuanian trip. She still had the soreness in her calf that had limited her play at the tryouts, so I never had to work her into the rotation of point guards. Dawn Staley was my starter, which had been made clear to Teresa from the start. We had won with Dawn in the Goodwill Games. I felt confident with her running the offense, and I was sticking with the people who had gotten the job done. Teresa practiced as well as she could but spent most of the games on the bench.

"If I have to sit here during the Olympics and never play," she told Jennifer Azzi during a game one day, "I'm going to be the team's biggest fan."

So far I liked what I saw. I wasn't expecting great basketball because we hadn't practiced. But I was pleased with the young players. Rebecca played well, and Nikki McCray was a jet. I still was obsessing about having so few big players. Our post people were going to get very tired this year, and I couldn't help worrying about that. What I wanted to see most of all on this trip was whether the players were as committed to winning the gold as I hoped they were. I got my answer in the first few games. Early on, a Lithuanian player pushed Jennifer out of bounds so hard she went flying into a low bench on the sideline. The impact looked as if it might snap her back in two.

I heard a collective gasp from the players on the bench. They leaped to their feet, genuinely concerned.

"Oh God," I thought to myself, "don't hurt yourself in Lithuania."

As the trainer hurried over to Jennifer, I motioned for Dawn to go into the game. Jennifer slowly rose to her feet as she caught sight of Dawn coming toward her.

"You're not getting my playing time," she said, waving Dawn away. Jennifer jogged back onto the court and continued to play. The next day she had a huge welt on her back where she had hit the bench. She still practiced at full speed.

I sensed a spirit among these women I hadn't seen in Australia. Most of them had been on that trip and, afterward, had received a four-page letter from me that was intended as a kick in the rear before we went to the Goodwill Games in Russia. But perhaps it was still in their minds a year later in Lithuania. In the letter, I told them I didn't care what their reputations were; they had to get the job done. I said I didn't care if they were All-World, All-Europe, or All-American. I needed them to give me a complete effort defensively and play hard every minute.

"Shakespeare said, 'The hungry lion hunts best.' We are surrounded internationally by hungry lions. Our country [and USA Team] is seduced by past glory," I wrote in the letter's conclusion. "As a nation, we are borrowing from abroad to maintain our standard of living—this can only last for so long.

"As a USA Team, we are in denial. We are arrogant and soft. Players from China are taking 3,000 three-point shots per week. The Australians are strong and fit. Brazil has the best offensive perimeter in the world and they played with tremendous emotion to win a World Championship. Who knows what Russia [the defending Olympic champion] has up its sleeve?

"How can we reverse this trend? We need to become 'hungry lions.' Our team will be successful only if we become the aggressor. We have to want it, and want it bad."

I was seeing that kind of desire on this team, and I wondered if we could keep it burning for an entire year. I also sensed the players truly liked one another. They knew this wasn't like other national teams, for which they came together for a few weeks, then scattered again to the ends of the earth. They were in this for the long haul, and they seemed to settle immediately into a comfortable existence.

I couldn't know for certain what the dynamics would be once Sheryl joined us. She was getting married in June and so didn't make the trip. I didn't know Sheryl well, though I had coached her at the World Championships and the Goodwill Games. She had been a superstar in college, landing a Nike contract when few women had done so. I had heard she could be a prima donna, but I had not seen that. Of course, I had never spent a year with her. Would she disrupt the chemistry? I wouldn't find out until after the summer, when the team would reconvene for training camp in Colorado Springs.

On the plane to Europe, I had worked on what kind of defense we would run. That was my primary concern. I knew we could score. We had scored against everybody we played in the World Championships and in the Goodwill Games. But sometimes we had trouble stopping people, as evidenced by the 108 points we gave up to Brazil in Australia. I wanted our players to focus on helping on screens, stopping ball penetration, and playing aggressive, intense defense right from the start.

Three times we beat Lithuania pretty easily on our trip, winning by double digits. But in one game we were down by a point with 20 seconds left. We ran a play to get Katrina an inside shot. She nailed it, and we won by one. Though we hadn't practiced or learned many plays, I still had the players watching videotapes of their performances. I tend a little toward overkill when it comes to watching tape (thus the Nintendo-sounding nickname "Video Van-Derveer"). I also handed each player a notebook, which she would keep for the year. The players would collect information from all their games, meetings, and practices, and they would keep individual and team goal sheets for each game. Until the Olympics, winning wasn't the priority, though of course I always want to win. The important thing was to improve every time we stepped on the court.

We had a good time one night at an American-style restaurant owned by NBA player Sarunas Marciulionis, but I was happy when I boarded the plane to Italy. We landed in Pisa and drove to a seaside resort town called Via Reggio. It was like passing from purgatory into heaven. I had never tasted food like this, though maybe the flavors were enhanced by comparison to the food in Lithuania.

I took a walk on the beach one day with Renee, who was the first African-American woman to help coach an Olympic team. (The national team wasn't officially the Olympic team, but that turned out to be mostly semantics.) We talked about who I should pick as the official Olympic assistants the following spring. Renee and Nell couldn't fill the positions once the Olympic team was officially announced because only college head coaches were allowed to be on the staff. Renee and Nell were college assistants. I asked Renee about other African American candidates for the job. There was Vivian Stringer at Rutgers. Marian Washington at Kansas.

The list doesn't go much further. Although so many of the players are African Americans, few hold jobs as head coaches. One reason is that women's teams in the 1970s—teams that produced most of today's coaches—were overwhelmingly white. There were just two African Americans—both reserve players—on my Indiana team at a time when three of the five starters on the men's team were African American. Many inner-city boys saw basketball as a way out of their poverty. For girls, basketball was a way out to nothing. There was no women's professional team on TV to provide inspiration. There were no women's college teams on TV. Girls mostly played basketball in suburban driveways in the 1960s and 1970s, and so the coaches who emerged from that era are mostly suburban and white.

Another reason that there are so few African-American women coaches is that half the jobs in women's basketball are held by men, thus shrinking the job market for all women. Of the 269 Division I teams, about 130 are coached by men, whereas before Title IX, nearly 90 percent of women's college teams were coached by women. But under Title IX, women's coaches' salaries increased to come more in line with the men's, so more men were interested in coaching the women. Men could make a decent living, and coaching the women could be a foot in the door toward coaching a men's team. Women also once held virtually all the administrative jobs pertaining to women's athletics. Today, women fill less than 31 percent of athletic department positions. According to a 1992 Brooklyn College survey, more than 25 percent of women's programs employ no female administrators at all. Women struck a necessary but mixed bargain with Title IX. To gain greater equality and greater opportunities for female athletes, we gave up control.

*   *   *

Ruthie Bolton became our unofficial guide in Italy. She had played professionally in Italy for three years and, true to form, knew everybody. She was a piece of work. During her stints in Italy, she sang in the local nightclubs, just as her sister Mae Ola had before her. (During her last season in Italy, Ruthie was the lead singer of a band called Anti-dum Tarantula—singing in Italian.) We scrimmaged the Italian and Croatian national teams and the men's junior Olympic team from Italy. Scrimmaging men would become part of our training regimen over the next year. The men pushed us more than most women's teams did. They were generally taller and stronger than our opponents, which gave us great practice in figuring out how to win with quickness and guile. The men toughened us up. If we could withstand their large bodies trying to block us out under the basket and setting screens, we'd have a pretty good shot at standing up to any women's team that came along.

In one game against the men in Italy, we were getting blasted, down by 25 points in the first ten minutes.

"Look," I said during a time-out, "we might be doing to the college teams what these guys are doing to us now. I'll have a lot more respect for the college teams that don't give up."

The players began playing with more intensity and chipped away at the lead. We didn't win, but again it showed me the kind of competitiveness and courage I had hoped to see.

When the trip was over, Renee flew with the team to New York, where they spent a day at the NBA offices taking photographs and talking to the NBA marketing people. Before they left, Jennifer gave me a note and some pictures she had taken. She wrote that she was happy to be on the team and that she appreciated how positive I was during the tour. Jennifer has always been the peace-maker, the one who wants everyone to be happy. In many ways, she would be the glue for this team, bringing to-gether different factions, smoothing over prickly feelings, letting me know when the players felt tired or confused about what we were doing.

When the team left, Nell, Carol, and I stayed to scout teams at the European Championships in the Czech Republic town of Bruno to get a look at potential Olympic opponents. The top three finishers would qualify for the games. Each day we drove in from our hotel in Vienna and watched games all day, getting a first look at some of the teams we might face in Atlanta. Russia figured to be our fiercest competition. They were a young team and big. Their six-nine, six-seven players moved and shot well. But as I watched Russia and the Ukraine and others that we might play next year, I knew that it would not necessarily be the best team that won the Olympics, but the team that could survive the best, that could face the pressures and distractions and fatigue and not be weakened by them.

Carol and I had to get back to the States for other business. Nell, who was in charge of scouting for the team, would have to move into a hotel in Bruno and stay by herself for three days. Then Ohio State head coach Nancy Darsch could fly in to assist her. Nell, still a green traveler, wasn't thrilled to be left behind, especially in a country as unfamiliar as the Czech Republic. She was uncomfortable trying to communicate, so she dreaded going to restaurants by herself, exchanging money, asking directions. She wanted to go home, but we needed the scouting reports.

"Nell, think of the hardest thing you've ever done and remember how you got through it," I told her.

"This *is* the hardest thing I've ever done," she said, only half-joking.

I thought about what Nell said on the plane home. There's something affecting in that phrase, especially for a coach. Whenever I hear it I know I'm about to witness a triumph and a transformation, maybe so subtle as to be almost undetectable. Maybe so great as to change the person forever. I'd hear the phrase over and over, stated in many different ways, during our grueling training camp in Colorado Springs in the fall.

After New York, the players went home for the summer, promising to stick to a strict workout schedule I had tailored for each one. The ones who kept their promise wouldn't suffer so much when they returned in the fall.

The ones who didn't, well, they were in for the hardest thing they'd ever done.

5

*"The gem cannot be polished without friction, nor
man perfected without trials."*
—Chinese proverb

The cinder track sat up on a mesa behind Eagleview Middle School, a few miles from our Colorado Springs training base. The mesa protected the school from the stiff winds that swept down from the Rocky Mountains, but it left the track exposed. When we arrived at 7:30 in the morning, the winds were gusting at about 25 mph, smacking our faces like icy hands.

It was October 4. We had begun practices several days earlier after being on our own for the summer. I had kept tabs on the players' physical conditioning during our four months apart, sending them training schedules that they would return twice a month, verifying their workouts. They knew that when they arrived, they would be timed in a two-mile run. I couldn't control who was on the team or how big they were or how committed. But I could control their preparation, and if I did my job right, no team at the Olympics would be in better condition than ours.

The players walked toward the track slowly, their chins tucked behind the collars of their jackets. I was tempted to reschedule. But the thought left as quickly as it arrived. Things wouldn't always go our way when we traveled to Russia and China. They wouldn't always go our way at the Olympics. Our training needed to be tough enough so the Olympics seemed easy. I've read how fighters have their sparring partners pummel them in training so when the bell rings for the real fight, their bodies have been toughened to the abuse, and, more important, their minds know they can withstand anything. That's what we would do. We wanted to make sure we faced nothing at the Olympics that we hadn't already faced and conquered in training.

The miserable run would begin to establish a tone. The next ten months were not going to be a picnic of interviews and world travel, though an outsider might have gotten that impression from the first day or two of camp. Before I arrived, the players went through a day-long seminar with media consultant Andrea Kirby. She told them to think about how they wanted to be portrayed and taught them how best to communicate it to the press. The players put their media training to the test right away: On our first official day of practice, reporters from around the country crowded around, outnumbering us by about four to one on the court. We couldn't turn around without bumping into another camera and doing another interview. We all felt an incredible buzz in the air, as if the gym were the deck of an ocean liner about to pull away from shore.

When finally we gathered alone at midcourt, I delivered my first real talk as the official Olympic coach. I told them I expected three things from them: attitude, effort, and pride. I felt my throat tightening as I talked. This was the beginning of the real thing. All the "what if" discussions and memos about having a year-long program had, incredibly, crystallized and taken the shape of this Colorado gym and these 11 women.

I put a twist on Andrea Kirby's advice.

"On August 5th of next year," I said, standing before them, "when you write a book about this experience, what do you want the story to be? What do you want people to say about this year? What do you want them to say about you? And about your teammates? What it's all over, what is the story?"

I knew what I wanted the story to be.

I wanted Joe and Mary Public who had never seen women's basketball to watch this team play and not only be proud but feel a connection. I remember how connected I felt to the 1980 Olympic hockey team that beat the Soviets at Lake Placid. I didn't care at all about hockey, but I was riveted. I wanted Americans to be proud of our team as they were of that one, not just in how we played but in how we carried ourselves and what we represented. I knew, and the players knew, we represented more than a basketball team.

People always say sports reflects the values of a culture, and I think that's true on many levels. The greed of team owners and pro ballplayers rises from the same altar at which Wall Street and Hollywood worship. The boorish antics, the violence, the drugs, the arrogance—they thrive in sports because our infatuation with fame and our zeal for winning absolve most every sin. Baseball player Albert Belle can bean a photographer, shout obscenities at reporters, chase children from his house at Halloween, and still be rewarded with what was then the largest contract in baseball history. Dallas Cowboys wide receiver Michael Irvin can be caught in a hotel room with drugs, brag to the police that he's too beloved for the charges to damage his career—and sure enough, draw thunderous cheers upon his return to the football field.

But sports also shows what is best in ourselves. Sports shows us grace and courage, strength and perseverance. It shows us not only what is, but what can be.

I looked around the room at the women who likely would be representing the United States at the Olympics the following summer. I saw eight African Americans and three Caucasians. I saw women of ages ranging from 22 to 31. Some had grown up on cracked blacktop courts surrounded by tenements, others in cheery YMCAs and on driveways with hoops bolted to garages. They were America.

"You have an opportunity, and a responsibility, to represent a kind of hope to the country," I told the players. "You can show that differences don't need to divide people, whether you're black or white or ten years older or younger than someone else, or from a city or from a farm." All the things that could pull them apart, as they pull people in our country apart, could unify them instead.

I wanted them to show, too, what women could do and what they could be. They could play hard, be aggressive, and still cooperate and be supportive of one another. They could have their own Nike commercials and hobnob at Planet Hollywood and still sign every kid's autograph, talk to reporters, visit hospitals, and speak at schools.

They could show America something about itself: that it had grown up, that it was ready to embrace great female athletes who didn't wear sequins, leotards, or tennis skirts. These 11 women could toss another shovelful of dirt on the notion that "athletic" means "unfeminine."

We have come a long way in the past 30 years in accepting women in sports, but a dichotomy still exists. Female athletes still have to establish two identities: the athlete and the female. The athlete who neglects to establish her womanliness does so at her peril. It's funny to think that in the 1970s, when I was playing in college, some women's team wore V-neck uniform tops with bows at the base of the V and kilts instead of gym shorts. The players thought the uniforms were dumb, but the administrators seemed insistent on reminding everybody that even when the athletes were crashing into each other under the hoop, they were still ladies.

The world of sports has come so far since then, and yet in some ways it has not changed at all. Nearly every athlete and coach I know conforms to a greater or lesser extent to fit into the conventional image of femininity. When I was at the World Championships, there was only one other female coach. She was confounded about what to wear at the games. Her concern was not what the public would think of her but what the referees would think. Some of the male refs, particularly from Middle Eastern countries, were not accustomed to dealing with women as equals. What did one wear to make the most favorable impression?

"I think there are two ways," I told her. "You either wear a miniskirt and be sexy, or you wear a long skirt and act like a grandma, because those are the only kinds of women they can accept."

When I was coaching at Ohio State in the early 1980s and started to become successful, two other female coaches at the school asked me to come up and visit with them after practice. I thought it was a birthday party. When I got there, they shut the door.

"You know, what you wear is an embarrassment," one said. "The athletic director won't tell you this, but we will."

I was no clotheshorse, but I wasn't a slob. I usually wore corduroy pants and sweaters, which was too casual and unfashionable for them. In any case, I was more interested in turning the basketball program around than in putting on a fashion show.

"Excuse me, but are you finished?" I replied, anger welling in my throat. "I have more important things to do."

I walked out, furious. Were people coming to the gym to watch me or my players? I wondered if anyone ever criticized Bobby Knight's sartorial choices, or Jerry Tarkanian's. Men in sports, of course, don't need to define the two sides of their lives through clothes or behavior. The act of playing or coaching validates their masculinity rather than calls it into question. A man can say, "I'm an athlete," and he can live comfortably inside that single definition.

Women can't be solely and completely athletes, and the truth is, our lives are probably richer for it. Ten of the 11 women on the national team had college degrees, a statistic few professional men's teams could match. The men are no less smart than the women; they simply have less incentive to finish their education. For the most gifted male players, college is often as much a farm league for the pros as an educational institution. They hone their athletic skills for a few years, then, if they're good enough, move on to the NBA or the Continental Basketball League (CBA). Until last year, women had no such goal. The cheers died quickly for young women who played in front of sellout crowds in college. The three hours of practice every day for four years led to one of two places: the final game of one's senior season or a stint in the overseas pro leagues.

For female basketball players, then, deciding where to play college ball is less about sports than it is about life. One reason I've been successful at Stanford is the quality of education I can offer our recruits. They know they must prepare themselves for a career beyond sports. My players have gone on to medical school and law school, become engineers and teachers and businesswomen. They could stay focused on academics because they had no delusions about paying the mortgage with their jump shots. In my 11 years at Stanford, every player who has stayed on the team for four years has left with a degree.

Female players know, too, that if they want to be wives and mothers, they have to balance their athletic image with a wifely or motherly one. Again, male athletes don't worry about projecting a husbandly or fatherly image to attract mates. For a man, being an athlete is attraction enough.

I read something Jennifer said while she was on the Olympic team that gave me a glimpse into the players' view of the athlete/female dichotomy.

"I am a woman first and a basketball player second,"

she said. "That's been hard for all of us to learn. We grew up taller and having to play against guys. We can show that a woman is a complete person, that she can be anything."

Certainly, the pressure to fit into an acceptable feminine image isn't limited to sports. Businesswomen must be forceful but never unladylike. Their clothes should convey competence but not manliness. As much as I balk at it, I know that what I wear and how I look matters. I'm wearing designer clothes on the court these days, for heaven's sakes. I'd like to think I'm more about substance than style, but no woman in sports can disregard style. In the midst of swatted blocks and fast-break layups, style is the neon arrow pointing to our femaleness.

I'm sensing a shift, however, in the young players arriving at Stanford. They seem less concerned about their images. They seem to feel freer to be who they want to be and say what they want to say. They remind me a little of Dennis Rodman and how he has challenged the boundaries of masculinity in the NBA. The women aren't that extreme, but what they're saying is, "We want to be accepted, but we want to be accepted for who we are, and this is who we are."

Our national team was filled with women who were balancing the athletic and the feminine. Lisa Leslie was a Wilhelmina model when she wasn't playing hoops. Nikki McCray changed her hairstyle as often as she changed her nail polish. When the players dressed for road trips, they looked as if they'd emerged from the pages of *Vogue*.

Yet they were athletes, as gritty and fierce as any I've known.

If I needed any proof, I got it that cold October day at Eagleview Middle School. In the howling wind of the two-mile run, none of the players complained out loud. I would hear very few complaints all year about the workload, though certainly the players must have complained among themselves and to the assistant coaches. Players need to do a certain amount of griping. It's the nature of the coach/player relationship, just as it is the nature of the boss/employee relationship. Complaining about the work, or about the boss, isn't always a bad thing. It can connect workers in a way that fosters loyalty and teamwork, so I never worry much about low-level griping. I do it myself, though I've learned that little good comes of it for coaches. A leader ought to correct, critique, and motivate; general complaining just ticks people off, creates a negative environment, and resolves nothing. I read in *Lincoln on Leadership* that Lincoln would write letters to people who had angered or upset him, never intending to send the letters. He felt better simply venting his feelings. I tried it several times during the Olympic year, and Lincoln was right.

On the day of the two-mile run, Renee, Nell, and I held stopwatches as the players ran eight laps around the track. It was awful. Even Jennifer, who normally runs two miles in less than 12 minutes, ran the course in about 14. As players crossed the finish line one by one, Rebecca, Lisa, and Carla still ran like ragged soldiers, gasping for breath in the thin mountain air. They finished short of their required times.

But I left the track oddly pleased anyway. Even when Rebecca, Lisa, and Carla knew they had blown their times, they didn't quit. They had to hate every step, yet they stayed on that track even as their throats burned and their sides ached. And no one grumbled. Those were good signs. They were committed to the program.

My vision of the year took the shape of a pyramid. Conditioning and fundamentals made up the base, then I would add more team play, out-of-bounds plays, special situations, and so on. But these later elements would collapse unless every player was in top shape.

The conditioning wasn't just for the basketball. We had a long year ahead of us. Being in shape, I hoped, would keep crankiness to a minimum as we waited in airports through delays and hauled our luggage onto the bus for the hundredth time. If they were physically strong, they were more likely to stay mentally and emotionally strong and avoid burnout.

Those who knew me as a player would laugh to hear how fanatical I have become about my teams' conditioning. I was a slug compared to today's athletes. In the late 1960s and early 1970s most female basketball players never stepped inside a weight room. We didn't run much. We didn't pay attention to nutrition. Most of us didn't even have organized basketball until we got to college. Here's what we had: sneakers we paid for ourselves, uniforms we washed ourselves, and a passion we nurtured ourselves.

The boom that would produce Dawn Staley and Sheryl Swoopes was just a rumble in the distance for me, but I could hear it. The women's movement of the 1960s and 1970s was changing the world around me, and sports was changing with it.

In the early 1970s, a typical Big Ten Conference school spent $1,300 on men's athletics for every dollar spent on the women. *Sports Illustrated* reported in a 1974 article that Washington State, for example, spent less than 1 percent of its $2 million athletic budget on women's sports. Into this imbalance came Title IX. It stated that men and women were to receive equal treatment in "educational programs [and] activities" that receive federal funds—which was every school that belonged to the National Collegiate Athletic Association. The amendment promised a new era for female athletes. For the first time, a woman's right to athletic opportunity in publicly funded schools was codified in law.

While women were beginning to find support in the courts, they were generating unprecedented excitement on the playing fields. The same year Title IX passed, Soviet gymnast Olga Korbut captivated the world with her incredible athleticism in the Olympics, and Nadia Comaneci followed in her footsteps four years later. Women's representation in the Olympics was growing: Between 1952 and 1976, it increased from 10 percent to 20.6 percent of total competitors. Women tennis players, led by Billie Jean King, launched a pro tour in the wake of King beating the self-described "male chauvinist pig" Bobby Riggs in what became a seminal moment in the women's movement. The 1973 match drew more than 8 million television viewers and 30,000 fans in the Houston Astrodome. The following year King, former Olympic swimmer Donna de Varona, and others founded the Women's Sports Foundation, an advocacy group that would work to support women in sports and to battle inequities.

Though in some ways sports seemed separate from and trivial to the larger women's movement, they were after the same goals: breaking barriers, expanding opportunities, gaining control. Feminists' fight to legalize abortion achieved success with the Supreme Court's *Roe v. Wade* decision in 1973. They were opening women's health clinics, forming self-help groups, taking self-defense classes. They were discovering—and enjoying—the power in their own bodies, which of course is what the revolution in sports was all about as well.

"By developing her power to the fullest . . . [a woman] will inherit the essential source of human self-confidence—pride in and control over a finely tuned body. That alone would be a revolution," *Ms.* magazine wrote in a 1973 article. By 1978, the sea change in women's sports had reached the mainstream press. *Time* magazine made it a cover story under the headline, "Comes the Revolution." Women were going to college on athletic scholarships. Team sports were gaining greater acceptance—women's basketball debuted at the Olympics in 1976. A women's professional softball league was formed that same year, though it died two years later. A professional basketball league began play in 1979. It, too, soon folded, lasting three seasons. The births of the pro leagues meant progress; their deaths were simply obstacles on what women knew would be a long and challenging path.

But when I was in high school, the revolution had yet to begin. As I said, there was no girls' basketball team at the public high school in Niagara Falls. Before my junior year, I transferred to Buffalo Seminary, a private girls' school 30 minutes from home. The school had few official games, but there was a more progressive attitude about girls playing sports. Sports didn't feel childish there. You didn't have to explain yourself or prove your femininity. I played basketball, field hockey, volleyball, anything I could. Basketball, always, was my favorite. Even in pickup games with the girls at school, I'd be designing plays as my classmates rolled their eyes. "Let's just play," they'd sigh. But I had all these ideas. I was always figuring the angles so my team could win.

In the high school yearbook, each student picked a quote to accompany her senior photograph. I might be the only girl in the history of Buffalo Seminary who quoted legendary Green Bay Packers football coach Vince Lombardi: "When the going gets tough, the tough get going." (It's remarkable, and maybe in some ways disconcerting, how little my life philosophy has changed since I was a kid.)

Buffalo Seminary had made basketball OK again for me, so I chose a college where I knew I could play. I wanted to go to Mount Holyoke, a women's school. But the reality of paying for it set in: I was the first of five children my parents would send to college. I had little access to financial aid, and I didn't want to dig myself into debt. Albany, where my father had studied for his doctorate, was a better financial deal, and the women's basketball coach there had been my seventh-grade PE teacher. The team wasn't very good, but it was a real team. Finally.

My sister and mother drove me to Albany from Niagara Falls for my first day of college. They were hugging and crying in the parking lot as I headed for my dorm room. True to form, I didn't get what the big deal was.

"OK," I told them, "thanks for driving me."

I went upstairs, dumped my bags on my bed, and immediately headed for the place I was most comfortable, the gym. It was filled with young men playing pickup games. No women. I called winners anyway, and soon became a regular. Those men were my first friends in college. I'd play two-on-two with a guy from New York, who suckered men into playing against us. They'd look at me, five feet, eight inches tall and a little blocky. ("You got big bones, Tara," my grandmother always told me. "Grandma, that's not big bones. That's *fat*.") These guys couldn't say yes fast enough. Then we'd blow them away. I think my partner from New York was making bets on the side, though I never saw a dime.

The Albany women's team was not great, to put it mildly. Most of the players were like me in that they had never or only rarely played organized basketball. By contrast, my Stanford recruits have been playing organized ball for a decade by the time they arrive on campus. I jumped center as a freshman and led the team in scoring, rebounding, assists, and turnovers. We didn't win many games. When we got annihilated by Queens College toward the end of the season, I decided I needed more than Albany had to offer.

So in the spring of my freshman year, I talked four friends into taking a trip. We piled into a friend's big Delta 88 with a cooler in the back and an eight-track cassette deck in the front. We drove from Albany to Normal, Illinois, to watch the 16-team Association of Intercollegiate Athletics for Women (AIAW) National Championship. I was there for one reason: to find my next team. I wanted to play real basketball with real practices. I wanted to be in the big time, such as it was in 1972.

The national championship tournament for women was still a fledgling event in 1972. Three years earlier, the basketball coach at West Chester State, a teachers' college in Pennsylvania, organized the first national tournament for women. The coach, Carol Eckman, invited 15 teams to her campus, charging each team a $25 entrance fee to cover the officials and awards. Eckman was a professor of health and physical education at the college. She wanted to bring together women's basketball players and coaches from across the nation not only to compete but to share information. This was a time when women's game results were printed on the society pages in some newspapers. Travel schedules were limited, so most teams had never seen their counterparts from across the country. The tournament bore little resemblance to what we see today. Basketball was still a six-woman game at the time (it would change to five the following year), and the uniforms were as varied as the players. Iowa Wesleyan showed up in shiny purple satin uniforms. West Chester played in one-piece gym suits with white Peter-Pan-collared shirts underneath. The University of Iowa, without warmups of their own, borrowed a set from the men's team; the sleeves hung to their fingertips.

Marian Washington, who would join our Olympic coaching staff in the spring of 1996, played for West Chester in that first championship, and her Rammettes easily beat Western Carolina in the title game, 65–39, before a sellout crowd of 2,000.

"If national competition for women needs justification," the Western Carolina coach wrote to Eckman after the final, "we believe your tournament more than justified it."

But Eckman didn't know if another coach at another school would put in the work to host the tournament the following year. Northeastern stepped up in 1970. Then Western Carolina in 1971. Then in 1972, the year I watched from the stands, the AIAW had come into existence and took over the tournament, ensuring its survival.

I saw almost every game of the tournament, taking notes on each team. My friends got bored and found other entertainment, but, surprising no one, I stayed from 8:30 in the morning to the last game at night. My friends knew I'd be perfectly happy staying in the arena by myself and that any entreaty to join them at the local night spots would fall on deaf ears.

Eventually the choice became clear to me: Indiana. I had never set foot in Indiana in my life. I didn't know anybody there. But I liked the camaraderie and work ethic I saw on the floor. I noticed they played a lot of different people, so I figured I'd get opportunities to play. And they were young. They could become a great team, and I could be a part of it. The school also had a good sociology program, which was my major.

My parents said they would pay a third of the $3,000 I'd need at Indiana. I could borrow a third and earn a third. So I spent the summer in Chautauqua working as a waitress. My sister Beth, who was starting college in the fall, worked at the same little restaurant. People were drunk, calling me princess, and I'd wonder who the hell they thought they were talking to. I spilled a beer on a guy, who confirmed my suspicion: "You are the worst waitress I have ever seen."

On most nights, Beth made twice as much money as I did. We'd both go home from our shifts and our younger sister Heidi would rush for Beth, asking to help count her money.

"What about me?" I asked.

"You don't need help."

I counted down the days at the restaurant. As soon as I made $1,000, I was out of there, back to joining my friends at the movies or the amphitheater. For as focused as I was on basketball, few of my friends in Chautauqua cared much for the sport. I don't think I was labeled as an athlete there. In Chautauqua, you were many things—athlete, student, musician, sailor, skier, daughter. So my friends were as varied as my interests. I never hung out in a group that was narrowly defined as the brains or the jocks. I accepted my friends for the complex people they were, and they accepted me.

Toward the end of summer, I found out there was to be a tryout for the U.S. national team in September. Women didn't play basketball at the Olympics at the time, but they played in other international tournaments. I wrote and got myself invited. I drove to Indiana, where I dropped my belongings, then drove to Parson's College in Iowa with the Indiana coach, Bea Gorton, and two other Indiana players who had also been invited. There were 60 women at the trial. Fifty-nine were better than I was. For those two weeks, I have never felt more out of place on a court. I got a bloody nose my first day from a sharp, flying elbow. The coaches were teaching things I'd never heard of. Players were so aggressive and quick, I couldn't believe I had thought I was something special. And I was so completely out of shape that I was sick to my stomach. I think I put people on the national team just by guarding them.

To be at the tryouts, I was missing my first two weeks of classes at Indiana. I'd be behind in my studies before I even picked up a book, and I was clearly in over my head in basketball on this level. I had also bounced my tuition check to the bursar and had to be readmitted to school. I wondered if the move to Indiana had been a huge miscalculation.

I was so worried about flunking out and failing at basketball that I worked like a maniac. For the first and only time in my college career, I earned a perfect 4.0 that fall semester. (If fear of failure doesn't paralyze you, it can push you to your greatest work. I'd remember this years later with the Olympic team.) I had arranged my class schedule so I could play pickup ball with the guys every afternoon in the gym across from my dorm. I'd go to class, eat lunch, and play ball all afternoon. Then I'd eat dinner, play more ball, then study. I knew I had to get in shape before the season began in January.

The work paid off. I earned the starting guard position,

and we successfully made it through our nine-game regular-season schedule to qualify for the AIAW national tournament in Flushing, New York. National championships for women's basketball were less than a decade old. The AIAW was run by women for women. The majority of coaches and administrators were women. They made little money, especially in comparison to what male coaches and administrators were making as members of the much larger and richer NCAA, which governed only men's sports.

Bea Gorton, the Indiana coach, was a graduate assistant making graduate assistant wages. But she was a great coach. She was smart enough to pattern our style of play and even our practices after Bobby Knight's style of play and practices. I'd sit in on Coach Knight's practices every afternoon to see what we'd be doing later that same day. I rarely saw other students watching Knight's practices, though sometimes local car salesmen and boosters would attend. I sat far enough up in the stands that I was never within range of getting pointed out or yelled at and thrown out. I never sat with anybody or talked to anybody. If you talked, you were gone.

If you watched Indiana's practices, they always looked the same. They look the same today. The players hustle from one drill to the next. Everything is very well-organized. Everything is timed, quick, efficient. There is nothing haphazard about it. I've seen other coaches' practices and you see one guy pulling down another guy's shorts. Forget that at Indiana. It was always all business. There was discipline, accountability. To this day, I remember Knight's zigzag drills, his "deny" drills on defense (keeping the offensive player from making his play), his boxing-out drills (with a shot in the air, positioning oneself between the basket and opposing players to increase the likelihood of grabbing the rebound).

I was majoring in sociology and figured on going to law school. I never thought I'd be a coach, but just hearing the same things from Knight over and over, day after day, and watching, watching, watching, my brain formed patterns for how the game should be played. My practices today are very similar to what I saw when I was 20 years old at Indiana.

But as much as I admired Knight's program, I resented it, too. My resentment had nothing to do with him personally. It was the whole athletic system that valued the men so much more than the women. The men had the gym every day from 2 to 6 o'clock, so we didn't practice until evening. There was never a thought that we could split up the prime practice times between us. Basically, it was steak for the men, hot dogs for the women. It struck me as selfish, hoarding all the good things for themselves. I didn't really understand it. I was coming of age during the civil rights movement, and I was passionate about issues of fairness and equality. Why were blacks treated the way they were treated? Why were women treated this way? No one had any answers. That's just the way it was, though it made no sense to me.

At least we had our own national championships. For decades physical educators had disapproved of such events because the strain of competition might turn us into sterile Amazon women. In 1973 the championship was in Flushing, New York, close enough for my family to come and watch. My mother had never seen me play, except in pickup games or at a Buffalo Seminary "play day." My father had seen me only in the seventh-grade recreation league. In Flushing, we played two games a day, and because of injuries our team rotated just six people. I had one great game: I hit eight of eight free throws and played almost every minute. When we lost to Queens to finish fourth, we were devastated. We were crying in the locker room. When I came out to see my family, my mother tried to cheer me up.

"It's just a game," she said.

I couldn't believe it, though I knew she was trying to make me feel better.

"Mother," I said, incredulous, "it's more than a game."

My family had always been supportive of my basketball, but this was when everyone began to understand how much it meant to me. Maybe it's when I began to understand it myself.

What I remember most from the tournament was how exhausted I was. I thought I had gotten in shape by playing pickup games with the guys those autumn afternoons, but I had fooled myself. I was dog-tired playing game after game at the nationals, and I saw how my skills weakened with the exhaustion. I have never forgotten that feeling, and when I became a coach I resolved that my players would never feel the same way.

In Colorado Springs, players who had not completed their summer workouts got up at dawn every morning to make them up. This group came to be known as the Breakfast Club. The Breakfast Club was an important component of the camp. It set a tone from the start that there would be no shortcuts and that each person would be held accountable for any slacking-off. All but Teresa, Katrina, Dawn, and Jennifer were in the Breakfast Club, which Renee supervised. They went from the Breakfast Club to practice. Then every other day, they had to work out with weights, even on game days. Then we usually had a second practice in the evening, if we didn't have a game. I worked out every day, too, with a discipline that did not come naturally for me. I vowed I wasn't going to make history as the fattest Olympic coach we'd ever had.

Teresa had completed every workout exactly as I had asked during the summer, which was a positive sign. It suggested she had bought into the program. I had called her on her birthday, July 19, exactly a year before opening ceremonies. Teresa and Katrina, the two Georgians, were featured on the cover of *USA Today* that day for a story looking ahead to the Olympics.

"A year from today we'll be walking into Olympic Stadium," I told her. We had a pleasant chat, as we usually did. I never had problems with Teresa personally. Now I was sensing that maybe the wall between us professionally was crumbling, too.

At training camp, I paired Teresa with Rebecca in the weight room. Every player had a partner to work with. I knew Teresa wouldn't hesitate to push Rebecca to her limit. She pushes everybody and expects a lot from everybody, which are personality traits we have in common. She'll get in people's faces at practice if they're dogging it or making mistakes, and no one complains because her teammates respect her so much. That intensity was what I had hoped to see from her, and it was there from the first day of practice.

As Teresa pushed others, I pushed her. I was probably harder on her than anybody, though I didn't realize it at the time. During a scrimmage against the Ukraine during those first weeks in Colorado, Teresa took some shots that brought the bad memories of Australia rushing back. She was going one-on-one with people, trying to win all by herself. I exploded. I hollered at her on the sidelines. I wasn't going to put up with that kind of play. I probably overreacted, something I do a lot. But Teresa just took it. She didn't look away. She didn't make excuses. She took it and moved on. I guess I was still testing her, though she was giving me no reason to doubt her commitment to the program. She's as hardheaded as any player I've coached— you don't accomplish what she has accomplished by being a doormat. She stands up for herself. She believes in herself. She knows what she wants and goes after it. Yet she is also one of the most unselfish players in the sport, on and off the court. When she tries to take over the game, as she did during that scrimmage, I know it is born of her intense desire to win, and I didn't want to discourage that intensity. I simply needed to harness it to the team concept, to truly convince her we had a better chance to win if she followed the plan and didn't shoulder more than her share of the load.

Overall, Teresa set a great example for the team, especially when it became clear that Rebecca, not Teresa, was drawing the most attention from the press and public. Teresa had played in three Olympics and was about to make history by playing in a fourth. No basketball player, male or female, had appeared in four Olympics. And yet Rebecca, fresh from college, inexperienced, and a definite backup player on the team, got the cheers and the front-page coverage. Teresa never showed any jealousy or resentment. Her humility had a profound effect on the team. If Teresa wasn't going to get upset about living in Rebecca's shadow, how could anyone else?

On the fourth day of camp, the entire country came to a stop as it listened to the O.J. Simpson murder-trial verdict. We had a diverse team, different ethnic heritages, economic backgrounds, and political views. I was in a meeting with USA Basketball's executive committee and was just about to address the group when we took a break to watch the reading of the verdict: not guilty.

I knew the players were watching in their rooms or in the gym, and I worried what effect it would have on them as a group. They had talked in the first few days of camp about the trial, and some had very clear opinions on Simpson's guilt or innocence and what message a guilty verdict might send to African Americans and what message a not-guilty verdict might send to women.

Before practice that afternoon, I watched as the players pulled on their basketball shoes and pulled off their sweats. Some exulted over the verdict—one ran around the court cheering Simpson's victory. Others, white and African American, thought it was a travesty and said so.

But once practice began, they were all basketball. They weren't going to allow this to distract or divide them. They clearly understood the guiding principle of the year: 11 individual players were not going to win a gold medal. They would do it together, each playing her part, each pushing herself on the court and in the weight room to strengthen the whole. During the three-month college tour, we would travel 25,584 miles and touch down in 26 airports. We would haul 87 pieces of luggage from airport curbs to buses to hotels and back again. We would travel from Virginia to Colorado to get to Oklahoma because that's the only way United could get us there. We would stay in four-star hotels with 24-hour room service and in roadside motels with clanking ice machines. We would sit in basement laundry rooms late at night, waiting for the spin cycles to finish. We'd sign thousands of autographs and visit dozens of schools and hospitals. We'd watch our bus drivers get lost and our flights be canceled. We would lose players to injuries for stretches at a time. We'd sleep two to a room on the road and at the training center for a while.

And we would miss our families and friends terribly. I missed my three cats. I missed rolling out of bed in my own home, climbing onto the Stairmaster or stationary bike down the hall and watching basketball tapes on my TV. In each new city on the road, I'd have to find a gym and a running route. I missed driving familiar streets and shopping at grocery stores where I knew the cashiers' names.

Bobby Knight should have been right. The stresses of living together for a year, with the inconveniences and aggravations of travel, the pressure of winning, and the strain of fulfilling endless obligations should have cracked this team into fragments. I marveled every day that it didn't happen. For all my misgivings about the selections—and I would carry some of them all year—the committee chose wisely. The players fit together like grooved building blocks. My challenge was to keep them focused and motivated. My assistants and I would come up with different ideas through the year, but none worked more effectively than what we did in Georgia before our first college game.

6

Excellence is never an accident;
it is always the result of high intention,
determined effort and skilled execution.

The players had no idea where they were going when the bus left the Westin Hotel in Atlanta early the morning of November 1. We were in town to play the University of Georgia, the first stop on our 20-game college tour. The bus headed down Peachtree Street, past the midtown square that, by summer, would be Centennial Park. Beyond the park, the Georgia Dome rose from the ground like an enormous white cloud.

Inside the dome, the floor was set up as a football field for the Atlanta Falcons, with goalposts and white yard-markers. We walked across the artificial turf to the 50-yard-line, where the players looked up at the rows of empty seats and the white expanse of ceiling. We had told them nothing about our outing, only to bring their cameras.

"I want you to see," I said when we had gathered at mid-field, "where you're going to win the gold medal."

The facilities director of the dome showed the players where a curtain would divide the dome in half, with the basketball arena on one side and the gymnastics arena on the other. "Here's where the spectators will be," he said, waving his hand toward the endless tiers of seats. "This is where the court will be. And right here is where the stand will be set up for the gold medal ceremony."

On cue, a huge screen in the end zone clicked on. President Clinton, against the backdrop of the American flag, was speaking about the honor of hosting the Olympic Games in 1996. His image dissolved into a collage of wonderful Olympic moments: Jackie Joyner-Kersee flying through the air into the long-jump pit, Mary Lou Retton landing her vault, Bruce Jenner waving a tiny flag on his victory lap, Janet Evans beaming from the pool, Carl Lewis straining across the finish line. We stood as if rooted to the turf, captivated by the heroics that had once seemed so remote from our own lives. When "God Bless America" boomed through the speakers as the video faded to black, Lisa swiped a finger under each eye to catch the tears. Several others were doing the same.

A hard dry lump had formed in my own throat, so I said nothing as Carol pulled a box from her briefcase. Inside were Teresa's gold medals from the 1984 and 1988 Olympics. We had asked her if we could borrow them, though we didn't tell her why.

I wanted the players to see and touch gold medals in the place where they would have the chance to earn them. I wanted to transform our distant Olympic goal—still nearly a year away—into something they could hold in their hands, something real. I got the idea from NASA. I read that NASA had hung huge pictures of the moon in the room where scientists were calculating how to land astronauts on it. Every day they were reminded that landing on the moon wasn't simply a physics equation to be solved but a concrete action. The NASA story clicked with my own belief in the power of visualization. So my staff and I had sent for a highlights video from the

United States Olympic Committee and borrowed Teresa's medals.

If the players had done nothing more than look around the Georgia Dome, watch the video, and look at the medals, the day would have been a success. But, spontaneously, the women began trying on the medals. I had hoped that was what they would do, but I couldn't orchestrate it myself. If you make an outing like this too hokey, it can backfire; no one appreciates having her emotions manipulated. But when the players bent their heads to accept the medals and feel the weight of the gold against their chests, I knew this day would stay with them until they were back on this spot in August, playing for their own golds. The players snapped pictures of one another. Katrina, who also had a gold from 1984, raised her arms in victory when Teresa's was placed around her neck. The women began to hug, many crying, as if hit all at once by the enormity of their quest.

"Don't let anything come between you and the gold medal," I said.

One of the coaches took a close-up photo of the medal itself. We had it developed into eight-by-ten copies. On the back of each, I wrote:

"What your desire is, so is your will. What your will is, so is your deed. What your deed is, so is your destiny."

We slipped the photos into plastic sleeves and gave one to each player and coach and to Carol. We clamped the photos into the three-ring binders we carried, our basketball bibles, which held our daily schedules and training regiments, scouting notes, and play diagrams. For the next nine months, the gold medal would be the first image we'd see when we opened our notebooks every day.

Now that we had left our little cocoon in Colorado Springs, the distractions began. Our first practice at the University of Georgia, two nights before the game, was a circus. The public was invited to watch, and NBA Entertainment had miked me so my comments reverberated like a ringmaster's through the whole arena. If a player wasn't doing what she was supposed to do, what could I say? I didn't want to embarrass anyone. In the middle of drills, an announcer barked out, "Check under your seats for a sticker to see if you won a prize!"

I was not enjoying this. I knew we'd be spending a lot of time traveling on airplanes and buses, talking to students and appearing at basketball clinics. If practices were going to be turned into a sideshow, when were we supposed to get any work done? Open practices seemed to defeat the purpose of training together for a year. If all we were going to do was let them go out there and put on a show, we might as well have waited to assemble the team until a few weeks before the Olympics, because we certainly weren't going to get any serious work done this way.

I talked to Carol afterward.

"I'm not interested in being a dancing bear," I said. "If we let people use us however they like, we'll have nothing left for basketball."

Our primary job was to win the gold medal, not barnstorm the nation like evangelists. If women's basketball was the better for our presence, great. But I wasn't about to risk the gold medal to win a few fans or be a feel-good feature story on the evening news. I was a coach, not a performer or a saleswoman. Carol struck a compromise with NBA Entertainment. We would still have open practices in just about every city we visited, but I would no longer be miked. It gave me at least some measure of control.

When we left Colorado Springs for Atlanta, Lisa still had not made her two-mile time. Because conditioning was so crucial to our success, I had told the players that anyone who didn't finish her summer makeup work in the Breakfast Club or didn't make her two-mile time would not be in the starting lineup. Once a week in Colorado, Lisa would be on the track, usually with Dawn pacing her, urging Lisa to push, push, push.

Jennifer had done the same for Rebecca and Carla. During one morning run, as Rebecca fell behind Jennifer and Carla, I hollered out to Jennifer.

"If you don't go back and get Rebecca, she'll never make it," I said.

"If I don't stay with Carla, neither one will make it," Jennifer shouted back.

Carla made it that day, but Rebecca fell short again. Jennifer went out with Rebecca a few days later, and she failed again. Rebecca also had not finished the conditioning work that she had failed to do during the summer. I knew Rebecca had been busier than anyone over the summer fulfilling the offers and obligations that followed her starring role at UConn. But I couldn't have a separate standard for Rebecca, and she wasn't the type to expect one. I told her if she didn't complete her makeup work, she couldn't go home for the four-day break before the college tour. I knew perhaps no one needed the break more than Rebecca. She didn't know the other players well, so she might have been a bit homesick for old teammates, her family, and her boyfriend. She was definitely tired. Because she had not trained as hard as most of her teammates over the summer, she struggled in training camp, once going through an entire practice without scoring a point. She was a youngster playing with the pros, who were quicker, more skilled, and more experienced than she. I had little patience for rookie mistakes because this was not a team for rookies. We needed her to help us win, so I was blunt in my critiques.

But Rebecca never seemed to get down or frustrated. Her attitude was: I had a bad day today, I'll have a better day tomorrow. No matter how tough things got, her mental strength carried her through. What also helped Rebecca was that she understood the game so well. She was very bright and always had great questions. And she never had any delusions about her role, despite all the hype. Had she been even the tiniest bit arrogant, she might not have been accepted as completely as she was by her teammates. She impressed us all with how gracefully she handled the uncomfortable dynamic of sitting on the bench and yet drawing the loudest cheers.

She finished her makeup work and with Jennifer by her side, she made her two-mile time on her fifth try. Only Lisa was still struggling when we left Colorado. The day before the first college game in Atlanta, Lisa went out to the University of Georgia track with Nikki as her pacer and Renee as the observer. Without the thin Colorado air to hinder her, Lisa ran impressively. She ran so well, in fact, that I rewarded the whole team. I told them at the next practice that we would not proceed with a second round of two-mile tests, which drew loud, relieved cheers. They had shown me they were committed to the training. I didn't need to test them anymore.

On the court before the Georgia game, the coach, Andy Landers, welcomed back his alums, Teresa and Katrina, by presenting them with beautiful new rocking chairs.

"Teresa and Katrina are no spring chickens," he joked to the crowd. "They're going to need a place to rest their bones."

The two players laughed. The truth was, Teresa and Katrina had gotten better with age. I'd watch them warm up before games and pity the other team. I knew they would not lose. I could see it. They had shown the same intensity in Australia, but it had been applied toward their own style of playing, not the team's. Now I was beginning to see the passion and the discipline come together.

Katrina was a marvel, unlike any player I've seen. She's shy, not easy to get to know, not a talker, but she's a bit of a clown. If you're videotaping something, for example, she might walk through the shot with a ridiculous look on her face. As quiet as she can be off the court, she's equally forceful on it. A quiet storm. I've seen her leap into the air as if she's going to lay the ball in on one side of the basket, then switch directions and lay it in on the other side. She can jump higher than the rim for rebounds. She could easily dunk if dunking meant anything to her, but it doesn't. She makes the game look effortless. She's so fluid that watching her is like watching ballet. What Katrina can do a coach can't teach.

In Georgia, Nike drove two busloads of her family members from Charleston, South Carolina, to watch the game. They all wore Katrina's number 12 jersey, so you couldn't miss them in the stands. Some had not seen Katrina play since high school, others not since college. They rose in thunderous applause when Katrina weaved her way to the basket, past her befuddled opponents, and dropped the ball over the rim as softly as water rolling off her fingers. They saw her pull down eight rebounds.

Katrina wasn't alone in playing well that first game. The team scored 21 points to start the game before Georgia got its first basket. I found myself calling time-outs for Andy, their coach, when he had run out of them.

We were leading 56–22 when Georgia pulled a fast one on us.

As we waited for the ref's whistle to start the second half, Teresa was talking with Georgia point guard Saudia Roundtree in front of our bench. Teresa was telling her how Georgia would have a great year, how she shouldn't be discouraged by the lopsided game, and just being really supportive. Under international rules, you begin the game shooting at the basket in front of your own bench. In college, you begin by shooting in the basket opposite your own bench. Then you switch baskets at halftime. We had been practicing and playing under international rules in Colorado Springs, scrimmaging several times against

Ukraine. So when we came out after halftime and saw the Georgia players gathered under the basket by our bench, we didn't think anything of it. Under international rules, that would have been their basket for the second half. Our players lined up with them to play defense as a Georgia player inbounded the ball.

As Teresa talked, Saudia suddenly bolted toward the other end of the court—toward the correct basket. A teammate tossed her the ball and she scored an uncontested two points as our players momentarily wondered what was going on. We had screwed up. Their trick had worked. We got caught defending the wrong basket.

That got our attention. We couldn't forget to pay attention to the little things.

One of those little things was fine-tuning the skills the players already had. Before we left for the college tour, I brought shooting specialist Des Flood to Colorado. Obviously, the players knew how to shoot. Most of them were scoring machines for their foreign teams. Some, like Ruthie, were among the best shooters in the world. I'm not sure what the players thought when I told them I wanted each of them to work with this specialist, but I can imagine what they thought when they saw this frail-looking, white-haired man in his 70s walk into the gym.

Des Flood was something of a mad scientist in basketball, helping to develop a machine that's like a tennis serving machine. It tosses ball after ball to players practicing their shots. He had once been an assistant with the Stanford men's team and had helped one of my Stanford players, Kate Paye, with her shooting. She swore by him. In Colorado, he stayed in the dorms, and even though we gave him USA Basketball shirts and sweats, he always wore his khakis and pullover sweater, never presuming to be part of the team.

I set up appointments for every player, then they could work with him further if they chose. The players immediately took to Des. He was like a wise and kindly grandfather. They listened as he told them to get their elbows up and push up on the ball. To get a good arc on the shot. To use the index finger and middle finger to control the ball. To remember that the shot is all in the wrist. And, most important, to shoot a lot of balls, 200 to 300 a day.

In the mornings, Des would show up at the Breakfast Club, handing out towels and water if that's what the players needed during their workouts. I saw him once in the gym with the wheelchair athletes who were training for the Para-Olympics, held a few weeks after our Olympics. He had them doing drills similar to the ones he was teaching us. During meals, the players loved to sit and talk with Des. He told them how he ran a marathon years ago, and when Nell said she had run one recently, he asked her time.

"Four-18," Nell said.

"Oh, mine was four-19!" he said, genuinely disappointed. He could have told us he had run it faster, but he didn't. He was always so straightforward and honest.

Des stayed for ten days. On his last day, when the team was gathered at midcourt for the end-of-practice cheer, they called out for him.

"Bring Des in here!" someone shouted.

I was surprised. The team had not invited any other visitor into their circle for the cheer. The team circle is something of a sacred place on most teams. No outsiders allowed. On our team, Carol never even came in, though the players certainly would not have minded. But Carol knew it was for team only. When Nell and Renee gave way to new coaches before the Olympics, they no longer joined in the circle when they attended practices. The circle defined the core family.

When we called an end to practice, we'd come together clapping. The clapping would get faster and faster until we were gathered at midcourt. I'd make announcements about the schedule, then comment on the day's practice. Sometimes I would share an inspirational quote I had come across.

"OK, bring it in," I'd say, and we'd press together into a tight knot, our arms reaching to the center like the spokes of a wheel, our hands gripping one another's. Then we'd shout a quick cheer, usually "U-S-A!" or "The goal is the gold!"

The circle brings closure to the day and reaffirms a team's togetherness. So it was the highest compliment when someone was invited into our circle. I guess in retrospect, I shouldn't have been so surprised the players called for Des. In a short time, he had assumed a special place among us.

Des was one of several specialists I called on to help us in Colorado Springs. We brought in a jump-rope specialist to teach us jumping exercises. And we flew in Don Monson, a big, gruff, old-time basketball guy who had coached at Idaho and Oregon. I had watched his match-up zone defense over the years and was now teaching it to the team. The Americans have always played player-to-player defense. We were going to be playing against some very talented offensive players, and I wanted to have a solid zone defense to shut them down if necessary. Don came in to watch how I was teaching his techniques to make sure I was doing it correctly.

"Nell," I said before he arrived, "you've got to help me with Don."

Don liked to have a good time, and I don't drink. Nell wasn't above having a beer, and she knew some funny jokes that he loved. He had a great time, and he helped us strengthen our defense. I didn't know if I'd ever use his match-up zone in a game, but I wanted to be prepared. As it turned out, the work paid off dramatically at the Olympics.

In that first month in Colorado Springs, we also began to work on the basic motion offense that would lay the foundation for the rest of the year. It was a scheme I had seen North Carolina use to strong effect. (It's not unusual for me, or any coach, to steal ideas from other programs. My dad always said, "No sense in reinventing the wheel," and I agree. If a team runs an effective out-of-bounds play against our team in the first half, I might run it against them in the second half.)

I talked for hours and hours with UNC assistant coach Andrew Calder, who discussed every facet of the offense with me. It was a single-post offense, something I had never used before. I wasn't completely comfortable with it for that reason, but the more I talked to Andrew and to Ohio State coach Nancy Darsch, a brilliant tactician, the more certain I was that it was the right offense for this team. Using two post players clogged up the space under the basket. We had better spacing with this offense. We could isolate our post player—Lisa, Katrina or, eventually, Venus Lacey—to get her in one-on-one situations and thus keep her from being double-teamed. Plus, it was an easy offense to learn, which would be important when we brought in our 12th player close to the Olympics. She would definitely be a post player, and she wouldn't have much time to learn a complicated offense. (USA Basketball decided to carry just 11 players on the roster to allow room later to add someone who perhaps wasn't ready to join the team at the beginning of the year, perhaps someone who was playing in college or in a foreign league. USA Basketball wanted to keep last-minute changes to a minimum. If we carried 12 players all year and wanted to add someone who had emerged as a great player, we'd have to remove someone else, which would, USA Basketball feared, disrupt the team chemistry.)

The coaches at Stanford and I decided to implement the same offense at Stanford while I was away. Amy Tucker and I compared progress constantly, discussing what was and wasn't working for each team. I had been out recruiting until a few days before going to Colorado Springs. I'd wake up in the middle of the night thinking about which of our four recruits we might land and which we wouldn't. I felt helpless being so far away when the recruits were making their visits to the Stanford campus, an important step in the recruiting process. Once the recruits had made their decisions, I knew I'd feel less anxious and perhaps would sleep better.

Pat Summitt at Tennessee told me she'd never leave for a year for the Olympics. She'd worry that all her hard work in building a strong program would be damaged, if not ruined, by her absence. I understood how she felt, but I could do it because of Amy. Amy and I worked so closely that I knew she could handle the job. Ever since I first coached her at Ohio State, she's proved that she's the type of person who crosses every "t" and dots every "i." She looks so easygoing, but just try to beat her at something. I don't think she originally envisioned becoming a coach, but when she went on to graduate school at Ohio State, she took a job as a grad assistant on my team. She'd make a suggestion during a game that would solve a match-up problem. She'd see a kid in high school and could tell almost without fail if the kid had potential or not. She'd return from recruiting trips with meticulous notes. I always knew every bit of paperwork or tape editing would be done right.

I knew the paperwork wouldn't defeat Amy as interim head coach, and that she probably could handle the greater challenge—the pressure not only to win but to fulfill the endless obligations to press, boosters, players, recruits, department staff. She's not easily rattled—in fact, she's much more easygoing than I am. She's always had a great rapport with the players. And it turned out she was great with the press and the boosters, who responded to her straightforward and relaxed personality.

So when I felt almost physically ill about being away from Stanford, it wasn't from worrying about the health of the program. It was simply from being separated from a job and a place that had come to define me. So much of who I was as a coach was wrapped up in Stanford. I had become so successful in coaching in large part because Stanford allowed me to be successful. That might sound silly—what school wouldn't want its teams to be successful? But the answer is: More than you'd think. When many athletic departments were simply tolerating women's sports, Stanford embraced them as valuable assets to the university. The administration expected the women to meet the same standard of excellence that the men's programs—and the chemistry department and the law school and the economics department—met.

But I didn't know any of this when Andy Geiger, the athletic director at Stanford at the time, approached me about taking the coaching job in 1985.

It was not an attractive proposition: The Stanford women had gone 5–23 and 9–19 the previous two seasons, and the Ohio State team I was coaching had won four Big Ten championships in a row, compiling an 18–0 conference record in the 1984–85 season. We had just played before the biggest crowd ever to watch a women's game, 22,157 at Iowa. We won 56–47 after being down by 12 at halftime.

I thoroughly enjoyed working at Ohio State and felt a certain loyalty. They had given me my first coaching job when no one else had offered me a chance.

When I graduated from Indiana, I had intended to go on to law school, though I imagine somewhere in the recesses of my mind lived the unlikely notion that I might coach. Why else would I retrieve from a trash can a brochure about a coaching clinic with Bobby Knight and Abe Lemons? In 1975 I took a year off before law school, traveling around the country, visiting friends, crewing for a time on a sailboat in South Carolina. Running low on money, I stayed for a while with my old Indiana teammate Debbie Oing, in Miami. I took a job working with mentally handicapped people, a job in line with my social-work studies. I lasted a day. I discovered that I wasn't cut out to work with people with such severe problems. As a teacher, I respond to highly motivated, upbeat, energetic students. Maybe that says something about me, that I couldn't handle the social-work job, but I had to be honest with myself. I needed a different line of work.

By Christmas I had completely run out of money and returned home to live in the basement of my parents' Niagara Falls house. I spent my afternoons playing chess with my little brother Nick, who was 15 years old at the time. (I was tired of getting beaten, so I bought a book on chess and read a little bit of it every day while he was at school.)

When my parents noticed that sleeping and playing chess were the highlights of my day, they suggested I go help out with my sister Marie's high school basketball team. Marie is five years younger than I am, and by the time she got to Niagara Falls High, it had real teams for girls. Hers was awful. I would get exasperated when girls didn't show up for practice because of hair appointments or dates, but I soon knew I had found something I loved. Teaching was in my genes, passed down from my parents, and coaching was all about teaching. If I have a strength as a coach, I think it's an ability to get players to understand what I want them to do and why I want them to do it. If they understand why they're doing something, they do it as if it's second nature. And when they truly understand the game, they can think for themselves on the floor.

That spring, I decided to scrap law school. I sent letters to the top 20 college teams in the nation, offering to work for nothing while I went to graduate school for a sports administration degree. The offer to work for free wasn't a ploy: no graduate assistants for women's basketball got paid. I was simply letting the athletic directors know that I was well-aware of the situation. I received two responses accepting my offer: one from the University of Southern California and one from Ohio State University. I chose Ohio State because the athletic director wrote me a personal letter. She remembered me as a player at Indiana. The part-time job was as assistant varsity coach and junior varsity head coach.

My parents accepted my decision to trade law school for coaching, despite the dismal job prospects. They always let us make our own decisions and take responsibility for our failures. They knew, too, that even if they said anything. I'd do what I wanted anyway. Once I made up my mind, that was it.

Before I headed to Ohio State, I saw the brochure and went to Bobby Knight's coaching clinic.

There were about 150 people there, 149 of them men. My parents had always encouraged me to sit in the front row at school so I could listen and pay attention better. I figured this was like school, so I went to the front row. I quickly saw I had made a mistake.

"What do we have here?" one of the coaches asked. "Honey, did you get lost?" Bobby Knight himself embarrassed me over one of my questions, but I didn't leave. After the first session, though, I was smart enough to sit a couple rows back.

Also at the clinic was Cal coaching legend Pete Newell, who was one of Bobby Knight's mentors. He had coached Oscar Robertson and Jerry West in the 1960 Olympics, the year after he led Cal to the national championship. I wouldn't meet him until years later when I took the job at Stanford and I sat on the "Big Man" camps he ran there for NBA centers. He would become my most valued teacher and biggest supporter.

I'm still not sure what drove me to that clinic. There were no real coaching jobs for women. But I just had this idea that change was on the horizon. After arriving at Ohio State as a graduate assistant, I remember telling the athletic director, "Someday there's going to be double round-robin play for women, and I'm going to coach in the Big Ten and I'm going to win it."

I don't know where that came from. Maybe I was visualizing it as a way of making it come true, like learning to ski on one foot. I could truly picture the schedule and the season. It was like I lived in a little imagined world. I had such grandiose expectations at a time when I was sharing a trailer with a friend who let me stay for free, living off food stamps, and driving a Volkswagen Beetle with no heat and so many mechanical problems that I once had to drive into a snowy median when the accelerator stuck. My only income was my minimum-wage job checking students into and off the campus tennis courts from 6 A.M. to 2 P.M.

At night I read coaching books, everything I could get my hands on. I had the entire series of the *Medalist Clinic* books, which encompassed several hundred articles about coaching. I kept them under my bed and read one a night. I'd highlight passages, jot notes in the margins.

The JV team became my coaching guinea pig. I tried out everything on those eight players. We played eight games and won all eight, averaging 90 points per game. If I hadn't been hooked on coaching before, I was by the end of the season. I began working at every basketball camp I could during the summer. I was always pestering the other coaches with question after question. What's your favorite drill? What are your out-of-bounds plays? What do you do in practice? I'd drive them crazy.

"Tara, would you just shut up?"

They'd be heading out to drink beer and I'd be sketching some offensive scheme I had seen during the day.

"All you think about is basketball," my friends at the camps would say.

"No, it's not," I'd tell them. "I'm just curious."

But there seemed to be no bottom to my curiosity. I wanted to know everything and try everything.

Within two years of getting the graduate assistant job at Ohio State and earning a master's in sports administration, I was hired by Idaho as a head coach in 1978.

"How are you going to be successful here?" Idaho administrators asked me in the job interview.

"Work," I said.

"Could you elaborate?"

"Hard work."

I was 25 years old and hadn't thought to ask too many questions of my own, such as "How did the team fare last season?" The answer was 2–18. My mother and sister Heidi drove with me to Idaho, and this time—unlike when they delivered me to college in Albany—I was the one in tears when they left. I felt as if I had been dropped at the end of the earth. I was gripped by panic: am I ready for this?

Fifty people showed up to watch my first game in November 1978, a 75–50 exhibition loss to St. Kilda's Fighting Saints of Australia. Idaho did not have a grand tradition of women's basketball, but that was no reason to accept mediocrity. When the local paper ran a preseason story about the men's team, I called the writer and asked for equal time for the women's team. If the paper purported to cover Idaho University sports, then it ought to cover all of them. The writer obliged and began giving us better coverage. And we began winning, going 17–8 the first season and 26–5 the second, and increasing attendance to more than 2,000 a game.

I left after that second season to return to Ohio State, this time as head coach. A year after I arrived, we won the Big Ten championship. Amy was a junior on that team, then began coaching with me. In my five years at OSU, our teams won four conference titles, including the first three double round-robin conference championships for women, just as I had envisioned. We moved up to number seven in the national rankings in 1985.

That's when Andy Geiger came calling.

My friends thought I was crazy for even thinking about leaving Ohio State after building the program into one that could win the national championship. But Andy was persistent. He sensed, correctly, that I was ready to move on, in particular to a place with good weather where I could enjoy life beyond basketball. I had grown up with such a balanced life, with music and art and time for friends, and I was feeling as if my life was being consumed by basketball at Ohio State and yearned for a bit of what I had at Chautauqua.

But before I could make the leap to Stanford, I needed to know from Andy that he was as committed to winning as I was and that I would have the budget to recruit players from around the country. Andy assured me he was and I would.

He had been an oarsman in college, and he so valued the experience that he had promised himself he would fight to give all athletes the opportunity to compete, whether their sport could support itself financially or not. The value of the athletic experience was the same for all athletes, whether they competed in front of 90,000 fans or nine. He said he didn't want a women's program. He wanted an athletic program, all under one roof, equal and united. But he knew he had to come up with the money to pay for it.

The Buck Club at Stanford was the major fund-raising group for athletics, and it had declined to support women with its money. So Andy started the Cardinal Club. In the beginning the Cardinal Club raised only enough money to fund one scholarship for a female athlete. But in 1983

Geiger and his staff organized an auction that went down in history as the most successful ever for women's collegiate sports.

They held it in the Crystal Ballroom at the San Francisco Sheraton and had teleconference hookups to hotels in New York, Washington, and Denver, where Stanford alums and boosters could bid for items. Former Stanford quarterback John Brodie served as master of ceremonies, offering incredible items such as a ten-day hot-air balloon trip through the Loire Valley in France, which went for $26,000. In four hours, the auction raised more than a million dollars.

The men's complaints about giving up money to the women went out the door with that auction, as Andy clearly pointed out in his sales pitch to me. He also showed me the list of top women's teams already at the school: tennis, volleyball, swimming. When I hired Amy as my assistant at Stanford, I told her that this team, which couldn't win even ten games the year before, would someday soon win a national championship. I truly believed we would, not because I thought I was some coaching wizard, but because Stanford and Andy Geiger had made a genuine commitment, financially and politically, to building the program. That's the difference between the great teams and the also-rans.

For example, I don't think it's a coincidence that Pat Summitt, the head coach at Tennessee, makes more than either the men's basketball coach or the men's football coach and has won four national championships, building the most successful women's college basketball program over the last 20 years. You get what you pay for.

Universities are supporting women's basketball these days as never before, not simply because Title IX has forced them to, but because with support and promotion, women's basketball can become self-supporting and even a moneymaker.

Connecticut's success in 1995 translated into $1.18 million in revenues for the 1996 season—25 times as much as the team generated five years earlier. The school signed a three-year $2.28 million TV contract centered on the women's basketball team. Illinois, with its average attendance of 633 in 1995, hired 1992 Olympic coach Theresa Grentz from Rutgers to turn the program around, which she's in the process of doing. Then Rutgers snapped up Vivian Stringer of Iowa. The demand for top coaches, and the willingness to pay them the salaries and perks that go with winning records, are promising signs that schools are getting serious about their women's programs.

But in 1985 only a handful of schools were making such commitments. Stanford was one of them. I kept saying I was sure we would win, but so many people, including my parents, worried about my decision, that I had second thoughts. My first week on campus I attended a school sports banquet, and all the coaches introduced one All-American candidate after another, swimming, tennis, on and on. With each one, I sunk lower in my chair until I was nearly on the ground. I wondered if we would ever have players that good.

We went 13–15 that first season. I had never coached a team to a losing season before (or since). We were getting blown out by 25 and 30 points. A victory to our players was losing by less than 20. We had so few fans, maybe 50 a game, that we didn't even pull out the end bleachers.

My assistants—Amy, June Daughtery, and Julie Plank—worked with me day and night identifying recruits around the country with whom we could build a championship team. With Stanford's high academic requirements, our recruiting lists weren't long, so it was imperative that we landed as many of those recruits as we could. If we didn't get the players on our short list, there were no second and third choices. Either we got those players, or we went through the year without anyone. My assistants were, and are, excellent judges of talent. They scour the nation for high school players who are also great students. In their senior years, I write to recruits once a week and call once a week. I send postcards from Italy and Hawaii, wherever we're playing a tournament, and tell them I hope they can someday join us.

Our first signings in 1985 were two young women who turned out to be even more remarkable than we had expected, women who ten years after their first Stanford game would be playing again for me on the Olympic team.

One was Jennifer Azzi, a scrappy point guard from Oak Ridge, Tennessee.

Jennifer had always assumed she'd go to the University of Tennessee, just 20 miles from her home, but Tennessee showed little interest. Ohio State and Vanderbilt were wooing her, but Stanford's academic reputation impressed her mother, a high school English teacher, and her father, a department head in a home furnishings store. Jennifer was as intense as any high school player I'd met. Her junior high teams had never lost a game, going 50–0. In four years of high school, her teams lost just 11 of 96 games. I made sure Jennifer never saw our team practice and never saw game films while she was making her decision. I feared that if she saw our ragtag team, she'd go running off to a more established program (such as my old program, Ohio State).

We knew she loved to shop, so when she flew to Stanford for her campus visit, we arranged a shopping trip to the Esprit outlet in San Francisco. She was scheduled to fly out the next day and she still hadn't committed to Stanford. Her flight was before dawn. When she walked through the still-dark hotel lobby on her way to the airport, there were Amy, Julie, June and I smiling and wishing her a safe trip home.

The academics might have sold the parents, but I think

all of our warmth and caring went a long way in selling Jennifer.

She became a cornerstone of our rebuilding, though initially she didn't much like Stanford. She was far away from her Tennessee home. Her roommate didn't like basketball. We were losing. And her $150 ten-speed bike had been stolen from outside the gym her first day on campus.

Katy Steding was the second important building block. She was from Lake Oswego, Oregon, and had been the Oregon prep player of the year, setting the state high school rebounding record. I had seen her play in a summer tournament and decided to recruit her without Amy's input. Katy was a great student, so Stanford was a logical choice for her. She signed on with us early in her senior year; Amy still had not seen her play. So she went to watch Katy at the Oregon state high school championships.

"How'd Katy do?" I asked a little nervously. Amy was the talent expert, not me. I had stuck my neck out signing Katy on my own.

Silence. My stomach began to churn.

"How many points?"

"Two."

"Did she rebound well?"

"Three."

It turned out that Katy had played wonderfully. Amy was just making me sweat it out.

When Katy arrived at Stanford, I sensed she wasn't convinced we could win, but basketball was her ticket to a great education. In her freshman year, she played the low-post, near the basket, a position she had played in high school. But the following year, we had recruited some bigger players, so we needed Katy to move outside, become more of a shooter. She resisted the change, which is understandable. She ended up screening a lot for Jennifer. She began to feel like furniture, and her attitude reflected her frustration. The Olympics wasn't even in her vocabulary. In fact, when she tried out for the U.S. Olympic Festival team—which features up-and-coming players who might one day make it to the Olympics—she was one of the first players cut.

"Weak and slow," said the scouting report.

Katy became my project. I remember one morning inviting her into my office, where we ate muffins and talked. She told me more about herself, how her parents' divorce when she was young affected her. I told her what I saw in her. I knew she could be a great player if she would commit herself completely to becoming one. Stop complaining, stop resisting change, stop using excuses. By her junior year, Katy had become one of our star players, and she was still improving.

We installed an up-tempo offense that used Jennifer's quickness and endurance. One look at Jennifer's lean, muscular legs and you knew she was born to run. The 1986 team, with Katy and Jennifer starting as freshmen, went 14–14, not exactly what I hoped. But I knew that the following year, 1987–88, we would be better. By then, Jennifer and Katy had a year's worth of seasoning, and we had landed two more top-drawer recruits to add to the mix. Guard Sonja Henning, from Racine, Wisconsin, was the state's "Miss Basketball" and was considered the best player ever to come out of Wisconsin. Plus, by taking advanced courses, she had a 4.3 grade point average in high school on a 4.0 scale. Forward Trisha Stevens came to Stanford from Philomath, Oregon, outside Corvallis. She was president of the National Honor Society, had won the state high-jump title four years in a row, and had an uncle who had played basketball at Stanford in the late 1960s. Trisha averaged 27.2 points per game and 16.4 rebounds in high school, the kind of numbers that keep coaches awake at night.

Even with this impressive crew, I never expected our 1987-88 season to begin the way it did. With a starting five of one junior, two sophomores, and two freshmen, we reeled off 14 consecutive victories. We lost to Pac-10 power Washington, then won 11 more games. We lost three of our last four conference games to finish tied for third in the Pac-10 with a 26-4 record. It earned Stanford a trip to the NCAA tournament for the first time in six years. We beat Montana in overtime by two points for the first postseason victory in the team's history. But our inexperience caught up with us against Texas in the Midwest Regional semifinals. We lost by 21 points.

The following year, 1988–89, we went 28–3 overall, 18–0 in the Pac-10. Sonja Henning played point guard, perfectly complementing Jennifer at shooting guard. Katy was blossoming at small forward, developing an outside game that made her one of the best three-point shooters in the country. We won our first five games, then ran into top-ranked Tennessee's buzzsaw. They blew us away, 83-60, knocking us back to earth.

"I'm not sure we'll ever beat them," I told friends after the game. "The top looks so far away for us."

In the NCAA tournament, we advanced to the final eight by beating number eight Iowa; it was the longest any Stanford team had ever stayed alive in the postseason. Then we lost to third-ranked Louisiana Tech. The finish was good enough to put us at number four in the final Associated Press rankings and to earn me the Converse national coach of the year and Pac-10 coach of the year awards.

But what stayed with me from that season was the 23-point loss to Tennessee. I pinned the box score to the bulletin board in my office. I wanted to remind myself of how much work was yet to be done.

We continued to add great recruits. We had signed six-foot-three-inch center Julie Zeilstra the previous season, so going into the 1989-90 season, she had a year's experience and moved into the starting job. We had two outstanding freshmen coming in: Molly Goodenbour, a point guard from Iowa, and Val Whiting, a six-three center from Wilmington, Delaware.

I first saw Val at the tryouts for the Olympic Festival when she was just 15 years old. She didn't make the team, and I saw her crying her eyes out in the car afterward with her mother. At Stanford, Val added a fierce presence on a team that had a reputation, before I arrived, of being the nice girls with the ponytails. Val was aggressive. She helped shore up our post position as the first player off the bench.

It was the autumn of 1989, nearly five years after I had arrived at Stanford. I knew we could win the national championship. I did something coaches almost never do. I all but predicted it in public.

"The ingredients are here," I told the press. "We have the talent, the depth, and the experience to go all the way."

We were ranked number three in the preseason polls behind defending national champ Tennessee and Louisiana Tech. I was talking one day to our women's swim coach, Richard Quick, whose teams have won many national championships.

"The first step to winning is being comfortable with winning. You have to see it. You have to say it," he said.

I printed up a sign that read, "Get comfortable with it. 1990 National Champions" and posted it on the locker room door. Visualization. *What your will is, so is your deed.* If they could accept the championship as a reachable goal, they could achieve it.

We would know early on how realistic the goal was: Our fourth game of the season was against Tennessee.

Nearly 5,500 fans packed into Maples Pavilion on the Stanford campus for the game, the biggest home crowd in the team's history. We got off to a 22–12 start in the first eight minutes and took a 38–31 lead into halftime.

"We've got to work harder," I said in the locker room. "You can do this."

Early in the second half, though, Tennessee closed to

within a point, 45–44. Then Sonja Henning made a spectacular play that broke Tennessee's back. She drove to the basket on Carla McGhee, who played forward for Tennessee. As Sonja tossed the ball up toward the hoop, Carla batted it away and grabbed the loose ball. But Sonja yanked it out of Carla's hands and dropped it in for a layup. Tennessee would never get close again. When time ran out, the scoreboard read Stanford 85, Tennessee 71.

The players fell into one another's arms. The crowd roared and clapped to the booming drums and trumpets of the school band. It was as if the season was a huge mountain we had to climb, and this victory had given us a glimpse of the peak.

We moved up to the number two ranking behind Louisiana Tech. Tennessee fell to number three.

After Tennessee, we won our next seven games with little problem, but we knew Pac-10 rival Washington, ranked seventh in the nation, was not likely to roll over. We played them at Maples before more than 3,500 fans. Our team played brilliantly, making 64 percent of our shots from the field and 73 percent from the free-throw lines. We won by an unlikely 40 points, 102–62.

It was one of the worst losses in Washington's history, so we expected them to be primed when, several weeks later, we played them on their home court in Seattle. We were 20–0 and still ranked second in the country. We were winning by double digits in nearly every game.

We arrived in Seattle in less than top form. We had played Washington State a few nights earlier in Pullman, which had turned into a travel nightmare. We got caught in a blizzard driving to Pullman from the airport in Spokane. We reached a town called Colfax, about 20 miles from Spokane, and discovered the highway into Pullman was closed. Then the road back to Spokane was shut down, too. It was about 9 P.M. We holed up in a cafe in the middle of Colfax, eating pie as we waited out the storm. There was no hotel for us to spend the night, so we wanted to get to Pullman. But by midnight it was clear we weren't going anywhere until morning. So the folks of Colfax opened the high school gym and laid wrestling mats on the floor. There was no heat, so we bundled up in our sweats and covered ourselves with blankets from the Whitman County jail. The next day, we beat WSU by 26 points.

When we arrived at the Hec Edmondsen Arena in Seattle to play Washington two days later, the place was sold out with 7,704 screaming Huskies fans. We played Washington close, but we lost by three points, falling for the first time that season and sending the arena into a frenzy. I was still stewing about the loss a few days later when I ran into Dick Gould, the Stanford men's tennis coach whose office shelves were loaded with NCAA championship trophies.

"That's the best thing that could have happened to you," he said. "You don't want to go into the NCAA championships undefeated."

He was right. Losing one game relieved the pressure, allowing us to relax and play a little looser.

In our seven remaining games, no team came within 28 points of beating us. Then we sailed through the NCAA West Regionals to advance to the Final Four in Knoxville, Tennessee.

We had expected our toughest opponent to be Tennessee, a perennial power that would have the added advantage of playing the championship games on its home court. But Tennessee had been upset in overtime by Virginia in the East Regional final and didn't make it to the Final Four. So our opponent in the semifinal was Virginia, ranked 12th in the nation. In the other semifinal, number 1 Louisiana Tech would play number 9 Auburn.

The talk in the hotel lobbies at the Final Four was the University of Oklahoma's plan to drop women's basketball. I was extremely upset, as were many of my colleagues. I thought back on the day when I had no place to play and now here I was coaching in the Final Four. I looked at the faces of my players and saw how much basketball meant to them, how it was shaping them as people, and, frankly, what a great time they were having. Every girl ought to have the opportunity to experience what my players were experiencing. We couldn't let administrators try to push us out of the gym.

In small groups and across dinner tables, women's coaches and administrators speculated about the repercussions of Oklahoma's decision and tossed around ideas for protests. Armbands during the games? A press conference with all the top coaches? We decided to wear red ribbons on our lapels so the TV announcers would have to explain them to the viewers.

Fueling our anger was the comment from Oklahoma governor Harry Bellmon that appeared in the newspaper.

"It doesn't bother me," he said of the university's plan. "[The women] will still have intramurals, won't they?"

Oklahoma men's coach Billy Tubbs chimed in that funding the women's team was "money down the drain."

Even in the 1990s, 20 years after the passage of Title IX, Oklahoma was not alone in its attitude toward women's sports. Money has often been used as a reason to eliminate women's teams, and yet it is rarely used as a reason to eliminate men's teams. We couldn't help noticing that Oklahoma was not calling for the elimination of every college team that didn't make money.

And it surely wasn't advocating dumping all those football teams around the country that don't support themselves. There's a myth that football is the sugar daddy for the rest of the athletic department. But according to a 1990 NCAA report, only 9 percent of all college football programs make enough money to pay for themselves. Even in the large football universities, 45 percent of the football programs lose money, and no wonder. Most Division I football teams fund about 75 scholarships, support a large coaching staff, and pay huge bills for training, travel, insurance, and support staff. The cost to field a football team can exceed the cost of all of the school's other teams combined.

There's no question that a successful football team, even if it loses money in operating expenses, can create enthusiasm among alumni and fans who are then inspired to contribute money to the school. And in that way one can argue that football pays for itself. I would agree. I would hate to see the elimination of football at Stanford or any university. Anyone who cares about amateur athletics wants to see as many young people as possible competing in as many sports as possible. But when it's time to pare budgets, why is it that women's sports are usually more expendable than other nonrevenue sports? The Oklahoma governor's remark goes a long way in answering that question. He couldn't see that the athlete's heart, with its hunger for excellence, beats as vibrantly within women as it does in men. Intramurals won't cut it for driven, gifted women any more than it would for driven, gifted men.

The uproar at the Final Four and on the Oklahoma campus forced the school to reverse its decision.

Before the Final Four, my mother sent me Sun Tzu's *The Art of War*. She saw, accurately, the connections between war and sports: strategy, motivation, discipline, preparation, leadership. One of the precepts is that battles are won before they're fought. If we were going to win the NCAA title, we would win it on the strength of our three-hour practices, our video work, our scouting, our drills. We'd win on Jennifer Azzi's discipline, Katy Steding's outside shooting, Sonja Henning's intelligence, the post play of Julie Zielstra, Trisha Steven, and Val Whiting, and also our role players, Stacy Parson and Molly Goodenbour.

We played Virginia in the first of the two semifinal games, played back to back on a Friday. I sensed the crowd was eager to get our game over with so they could watch "the real game" between Auburn and top-ranked Louisiana Tech. We beat Virginia, 75–66. Dawn played for Virginia but was hampered by leg cramps most of the game and couldn't dominate as she normally did.

Then in a huge upset, Auburn beat Louisiana Tech. The stars were in alignment for us. Every higher-seeded team we were supposed to face lost before we played them, helping to smooth our way to the championship game.

The game drew 16,595 fans, breaking the championship game record of 15,615 set in 1987 in Austin, Texas, when Old Dominion beat Georgia. Auburn was playing in the championship game for the third year in a row. It had lost the previous two and didn't want to go for a hat trick.

Auburn's pressure defense frustrated us early on; we went eight minutes without a field goal and turned the ball over on five consecutive possessions. But we scored nine straight points before the half to tie the game at 41 going into the locker room.

"Forty-one was my college number," I joked to Amy on the way into the locker room. "Good sign."

For the whole game, I could feel we were going to win, even though the score was so close. At halftime, I knew I didn't need to motivate our players. I just had to keep them focused.

"OK, we've gotten this far," I said in the locker room. "These are the things you need to do: handle their press better and play tighter defense. We have 20 minutes to accomplish something we've worked all year for."

After the half, Katy hit a three-pointer and began a nine-point run that gave us a solid lead. This was the last Stanford game for Jennifer and Katy, and they played ball that day as if they might never play the game again. Katy had six baskets from three-point range, Jennifer had four. Katy scored 18 points, Jennifer, 17. Each had five assists. Sonja was unflappable handling the ball; we had just two turnovers in the second half. We were up 70–57 when Auburn began chipping away, closing the gap to 70–64 with six minutes left. Then Sonja and Katy hit back-to-back three-pointers, and in the final 72 seconds, Sonja went to the foul line four times and hit seven of eight shots to send Auburn home as runner-up again. Final score: 88–81.

If I had died on that court at that moment, I would have had no regrets. Nothing in my life had come close to the pure joy I felt as we swarmed all over each other. Nothing in my life would ever replicate that feeling, not even winning the Olympics. Winning the Olympics brought with it a different joy, maybe even a deeper sense of satisfaction, but as with anything in life, first times are special. We had proven ourselves as a team. We had risen from a losing record four years earlier to become national champions, with just one loss in the season. What I had visualized when I took the job at Stanford was unfolding before my eyes, only the reality was much more fun than the dream.

Jennifer's parents had a party for us at their house in Oak Ridge, a suburb of Knoxville. The Stanford band came along with us, and I sat in on drums for a set. We stayed up all night, got the newspapers just before dawn, and read the stories out loud.

Fans packed Maples Pavilion, cheering and dancing, to greet us upon our return. Then in April, we visited the White House with the UNLV team, the men's NCAA champions. We listened to President Bush congratulate us in the Rose Garden, then an aide tapped me on the shoulder.

"The President would like to see you," he said. Jerry Tarkanian and I were ushered into the Oval Office, where we chatted with President Bush for about 15 minutes. I can't remember a thing we talked about. I was too busy trying to figure it all out. Basketball, the sport that had once seemed such a dead end for my ambitions, had landed me in the Oval Office with the President of the United States. I told reporters later it was a once-in-a-lifetime experience. Not that I didn't expect to have other triumphs in my life, maybe even another national championship and another trip to the White House. Our Stanford team, with our strong recruiting classes, would be in the hunt for at least the next several years. But there would never be another moment like walking into the Oval Office that day. It suddenly struck me that I was talking to the President because I had coached the winning team in a sport that, not too many years earlier, I hadn't been allowed to play.

As we walked out the door and down the hallway, Jerry draped his arm around my shoulders.

"This," he said, "is the big time."

I knew I had crossed a threshold and could close the door on all those years of standing on the sidelines, wearing the mascot bear head, scraping food from cafeteria dishes, hearing the thin cheers of a few dozen spectators in the stands.

It was one of those moments that was larger than itself. As intent as I am on my own job, I know that what I do—what any woman in sports does—has meaning beyond the personal. With every accomplishment, we effect some small change. We pull the wagon a little farther down the road, taking up the ropes laid there for us by Babe Didrikson, Althea Gibson, Billie Jean King, and basketball's own pioneer, Carol Eckman.

That's what the 1996 U.S. national team was doing.

If we didn't know it the first few weeks of training camp, we did soon afterward during our months on the road. In towns that considered the college game the best in women's basketball, we were like traveling saleswomen introducing washing machines to washboard owners. They had no idea that a machine like this existed.

Perhaps no tour stop illustrated the wide gap between the national team and the college teams better than our visit to the University of Connecticut. UConn was coming off a 35–0 season and a national championship. Local reporters and fans wondered how the U.S. team would measure up, since UConn was considered one of the best, if not the best, team in women's basketball, even without Rebecca.

A sellout crowd of 8,241 UConn fans packed into Gampel Pavilion on the UConn campus to find out.

7

*"There is only one way to success in anything,
and that is to give everything.
I do, and I demand that my players do."*
—*Vince Lombardi*

UConn had the feel of enemy territory. Everywhere on the tour, people cheered for us along with their own players, but not here. The UConn fans are so passionate about their team that they are blind to all others, including the one that would represent their country at the Olympics. Still, I was a little taken aback when I was booed during introductions. I don't think I had ever been booed, not even at the University of Washington, our Pac-10 rivals.

I knew why they were booing. During a telephone press conference a few days earlier, I had told the local reporters that Rebecca would not be in the starting lineup. The reporters seemed to be under the impression that she was the focal point of the U.S. team, as she had been at UConn. I was honest. I told them Rebecca was a role player. She was a rookie. She hadn't shown up to camp in great shape. I said she was like a high school kid moving up to the next level, or a college kid going pro. She had a lot to learn.

My comments caused a bit of a stir in the local papers. I got letters from UConn fans afterward saying that I was picking on Rebecca because UConn had beaten Stanford in the NCAA tournament the previous spring. It's mind-boggling to me that people could actually believe this. I was out to win the gold medal, not settle old scores or play little political games. Winning the gold was exactly why I didn't start Rebecca for her homecoming at UConn. It's why I didn't start Katy Steding for her homecoming at Stanford. I started who deserved to start. This wasn't a traveling circus. It wasn't a dribbling and shooting exhibition. We needed to use each game to get us closer to the gold, so we constructed a starting lineup with that in mind and nothing else.

The fans might have been upset about Rebecca not starting, but Rebecca never showed any anger. I learned a lot from Rebecca, just in witnessing how mature she was. She knew I got frustrated with her at times, though I always understood she was doing her best. She simply didn't have the experience to play as effectively as most of her teammates. My frustrations at practice were born not so much of Rebecca's shortcomings, or any other player's shortcomings, but of a general fear that we didn't have enough big bodies. Only Lisa and Katrina could play reliably down low—close to the basket—and neither one had the bulk I felt we needed to bang with the big players internationally. The weakness at the position was glaring. The necessity of having big players is basic: If your opponent has a six-foot-seven-inch player dropping balls in the basket, you better have a six-foot-seven-inch player trying to stop her. Russia dominated international basketball for many years in large part because of their seven-foot-two-inch center, Uljana Semjonova. When she got the ball under the basket, there was nothing anybody could do. In 1988, the United States won the gold medal with Anne Donovan, who was six feet, ten inches tall. When a team is significantly larger than its opponents, it's like adults versus children.

Throughout our tour, college and international coaches would come up to me and ask, "Where's your center?"

"Good question," I'd say, "where is she?"

My fears were deepened in an exhibition against Athletes in Action in Cincinnati before we began the college tour. The team's center, Heidi Gillingham, rose up to block several of our shots. If she could block us, how much worse would it be against Russia and China and Brazil? My obsession about having no wide-bodied post player came to be known among our staff as the Horse, as in beating a dead one. I couldn't let it alone. And in the back of my mind, I couldn't help wondering if we'd be better off replacing a few of our players with ones who could give us more effective post play. I was getting attached to all the players, and it was clear they were attached to one another. But this wasn't a sorority. We couldn't make decisions based on our feelings. There could be only one criterion for staying on the team: Can you help us win the gold?

At UConn's basketball arena, the USA players cheered along with the fans as Rebecca stood next to her former teammates before the game. The school presented the players with their NCAA championship rings and unfurled the championship banner from the rafters. UConn's place atop college basketball was reinforced by the attention the game attracted. ESPN was broadcasting the "showdown" on live television. *Sports Illustrated* was there, the *New York Times,* NCAA administrators, NBA executives. I had the sense that many, if not most, of the people in the arena thought UConn had a good chance to win.

The Huskies jumped to a 4–0 lead and led 14–9 after the first five minutes, scoring five or six backdoor layups right off the bat. The crowd got even louder, and UConn's confidence grew. Rebecca went into the game midway through the first half and scored the layup that tied the score at 14–14. The court announcer—presumably the same person who had called Rebecca's name a thousand times over four years—inexplicably gave the basket to Katy Steding. Nice welcome.

I was impressed with UConn's offense. We, on the other hand, couldn't shoot worth a lick. Part of the problem was switching to the smaller ball the college teams use. We play with a regulation-size ball internationally, so we had been debating which to use in practice. Since we had scrimmaged the Ukraine in Colorado, we had been using the larger ball. Now the players struggled to adjust, a problem that would follow us through the tour as we switched back and forth from international opponents to college opponents. Still, we took a 45–29 lead into halftime and dominated the second half, winning easily, 83–47. Connecticut turned the ball over 35 times.

One of the first questions in the press conference afterward was whether I was surprised by our margin of victory. People didn't understand yet. They didn't know how much better the women get when they leave college. I had to remind myself that women's professional basketball was new to America and that this tour was like a mobile classroom.

"We *should* be doing this to college teams," I said. "Look at the people we have. Would anyone be surprised if an NBA All-Star team blew out the best college teams in the country?"

Lisa fielded the same question.

"People are surprised by how intense it is," she said. "Fans watch their college team and watch us sweep up in all aspects of the game. They're really shocked. They didn't know there was that much of a difference. They didn't realize how much faster we are and the fact that we are so much stronger than the other girls. Some of them go, 'Wow, you guys have muscles. You look like women,' I say, 'Well, we are.' "

The next day, we flew on a commuter plane to the University of Virginia, Dawn Staley's alma mater. We got in late, and on the bus to the hotel the players sang a gospel song called "Work It Out." The next day at practice, I announced that for every uncontested layup the team gave up in a game, they had to run a sprint. We had given up six against UConn.

"All right now," I said, "we're going to work it out. We're going to run."

Work it out. I had used the same words as the song. But it registered with the players. We were having an open practice that day at Virginia, and there they were, some of the best basketball players in the world, running sprints in front of people who had come to see crossover dribbles and reverse layups. The players were not pleased. For the rest of the year, even when the coaches requested it, they never sang "Work It Out" again. It reminded them of the sprints.

Dawn was excited to be back at Virginia, where she had led her teams to three Final Four appearances. A few hundred family members and friends drove down from Philadelphia for the game, all wearing T-shirts with Dawn's name and number on the backs and all waving sticks with a life-size cut-out photo of Dawn's face on each one. I was worried about Dawn. In our first practice on the road, she had been running a little cutting drill and felt something in her left knee tweak, leaving it sore and fragile. Her other knee wasn't much better. Both had been operated on several times over the years. She rested in our opener against Georgia, but started against UConn. She hit just one of four shots from the field.

Starting against her old team, she drew two quick fouls. My rule was that if you drew two fouls in the first half and our team was ahead, you left the game. But Dawn's family had just arrived when she drew the second foul, so I broke my own rule and let her stay in the game so they could watch her. ("Tell Tara thanks," Dawn told Renee after the game.) Dawn dished out 12 assists and had only one turnover in 26 minutes of play, helping us to a 96–68 victory. But she missed her first seven shots before scoring her one basket of the night. Two baskets in two games. Dawn clearly wasn't herself.

We talked with the USA Basketball trainer and with Dawn's doctor in Virginia. They recommended arthroscopic surgery to clean out loose debris in the left knee. They assured us and Dawn that she would be back playing within weeks, but as with any surgery there were no guarantees. The thought of going through the year without Dawn really scared me. She was such a spark. She poked at everybody. She would do silly things like try to unsnap my bracelet while I was talking in the huddle. If someone was frustrated about something on the court, Dawn would needle them until they were laughing about it.

Dawn was the consummate team player, and she was especially close to Lisa, though at first glance they seemed so different. Lisa is six feet, five inches tall, Dawn, five feet, six inches. Lisa is elegance personified. She walks with a grace and a proud posture that seems born of royalty. She loves to dress up and dazzle, earning the nickname "Hollywood" from her teammates. Even as she rose through the basketball ranks to become one of the best players in the world, she dreamed of leaving her Nikes behind for the heels of the fashion runway.

Dawn, I think, couldn't imagine a life without basketball. She is pure Philly, tough, smart, and quick. She wears a rubber band around her wrist when she plays and snaps it as punishment when she makes a mistake. She and Lisa have played on so many national teams together, Dawn dishing the ball to Lisa, that they had developed a sixth sense about each other on the court. They played as if wired to the same circuit panel.

Our team would be different without Dawn. I had counted on her to be our point guard, who is like the coach on the floor, directing traffic, making things happen. With Dawn gone, I had to decide who would take her place: Jennifer or Teresa. Jennifer had been the starting point guard at the World Championships in Australia, but

I felt the point wasn't her strongest position. Teresa had played the "two" guard a lot, which is the shooting guard, but Ruthie had that job locked up. Ruthie was so strong on both sides of the ball: She was quick enough on defense to guard the opposing point guard and she could shoot the ball like a machine. So in the beginning, Teresa didn't have a spot in the starting lineup. But now with Dawn hurt, we decided to try Teresa at the point and use Jennifer off the bench or as a third guard in the starting lineup.

When we began in October, Teresa was only a distant option at point guard. I was counting on Dawn completely. Jennifer was, ostensibly, the backup point guard, but she really didn't have the feel for the position. She did a great job in transition—running the ball up the court on fast-breaks—but wasn't as strong when we ran a half-court offense (moving the ball around to create an open shot). I had always thought point guard should have been Teresa's position, but she always preferred off-guard. On this team, however, Ruthie was the off-guard, or "two" guard. Sheryl or Nikki was going to play small forward, or what we call the "three." So the only chance Teresa had at playing was to learn the point guard position, especially once Dawn got hurt.

The advantage of Teresa at point guard was that she was significantly taller than Dawn. Teresa was five feet, 11 inches, Dawn was five feet, six inches. On defense, Dawn could match up only with the opponent's point guard; she's too small to guard anyone else. But Teresa could match up with the off-guard or small forward, freeing up Ruthie—our best defender—to guard the point guard. Ruthie frustrated the point guards, causing them to lose control of the ball or make poor passes. So though Dawn was clearly our best point guard offensively, we didn't have quite as much of a defensive edge when she was in the game.

I knew if Dawn was out, Teresa was our best hope. She had the court sense, the smarts, and the passion. But could she learn the nuances of the position well enough to lead this team to Olympic gold? At an airport restaurant in Virginia the morning after the game, Teresa sat down with Renee and me for breakfast. She talked about her family, how she was the oldest—and only girl—of five children of a single mother in Cairo, Georgia. Her father lived down the street. She said she didn't so much choose basketball as it chose her. It was the only game in which she could go up against the boys and beat them. And it became her ticket out of the hardscrabble life her parents lived. Teresa worked one summer with her mother in a local factory and couldn't believe her mother endured this work day after day.

"I knew I was getting my degree because there was no way I was going to work that way," she told us.

With her first big paycheck from the Italian pro team she signed with after college, Teresa bought her mother a house.

We couldn't know it at the time, but Teresa's journey toward becoming our starting point guard began at that table. Something seemed to shift in our relationship, as if we knew we needed to get to know each other better. Coaching a team is sometimes like trying to hold a cloud in your hands. It is constantly changing shape. Bits and pieces escape. And you have to change along with it, adjusting to each new form. Dawn, so crucial to us in October, would never get her starting job back.

The day we left Virginia, November 8, I got lost on my morning run and arrived at the team bus 15 minutes late, drawing a fine. That was one bus I didn't want to miss: It was headed to the plane that would carry me home, back to Northern California, where we were going to play Stanford. We arrived midafternoon and went directly to the Stanford weight room. I don't think the players were thrilled, but I wanted the Stanford strength coach to work with us on abdominal muscles. Everywhere we went, we tapped into the expertise of the trainers and coaches, picking up tips on health and conditioning.

When I arrived on campus, good news was waiting: That morning, Stanford had signed the three guards we had so vigorously recruited. I was in a great mood. I was home. I could sleep in my own bed, eat at my favorite Mexican restaurant, get my hair cut, see my friends.

"We should play in California all the time," one of the players cracked. "Tara's so happy."

I was especially happy to see my Stanford players. As the outsider, I could be more the grandmother than the mother. I could be completely encouraging and supportive, while interim head coach Amy Tucker and co-head coach Marianne Stanley had to be the critics and disciplinarians. It was great seeing Marianne coaching again. She had just spent two years in exile over a salary dispute with the University of Southern California, shut out of every coaching job after 16 years as a head coach. Her plight is a pointed reminder to any woman who thinks the equality battles have been fought and won. The battles persist— and claim victims—some 20 years after Title IX.

In the summer of 1993, when all hell broke loose in Marianne's career, I was with her in Brazil coaching the World Championship Qualifying team. She was in the midst of negotiating a new contract with USC after four years on the job. She was one of the most respected coaches in the country: She had coached three national championship teams at Old Dominion before going to Penn and then to USC in 1989. Two years after her arrival, she led USC to the NCAA Final Eight.

When the school offered her substantially less than what the men's coach was making, Marianne argued that the jobs were comparable so the compensation should be, too. This concept seems so basic that I am constantly startled by the resistance to it. People think it is somehow OK to pay a woman less because she's a woman, as if we don't need money as much as a man does. Do they think that when we go to buy a house, people say, "OK, you're a woman, you get the house for half-price"?

In Brazil, Marianne was on the phone with USC and with her lawyers, trying to decide what to do before the season began in the fall. As deeply as I believed in her stance, I discouraged her from suing. I was afraid for her. I have always favored working within the system, doing anything you can to solve your problems without creating new ones. I had gone through my own salary negotiations with Stanford a year earlier. I had read in the paper I was making $100,000 less than the men's coach and brought this to the attention of athletic director Ted Leland. He clarified that the figure was $60,000, not $100,000, but he immediately agreed the gap should be closed. Within a month, he returned with a plan to increase my salary— and my assistant coaches' salaries—in increments over a year until we had come into line with the men's program. Some people said I should have sued for back salary, but I never considered it. When I asked for the raise, Stanford promptly responded. I was not out to cause trouble or make some huge statement. I just wanted what was fair, as did Stanford.

USC took a different path, and so did Marianne. She decided to sue. Because she refused to sign her contract, she was out of a job. And because the breakdown in negotiations happened so close to the start of the season, she couldn't line up other work. When the case went to court, she lost and appealed. As of last spring, the 9th Circuit Court of Appeals had yet to render a decision.

In the meantime, as she tried to get work, she found nothing but closed doors. She applied for dozens of jobs and was called in for just one interview. Basically, she was blackballed. Most female coaches who leave their jobs never resurface. They go into other lines of work or go to graduate school to join the academic life. Men tend to move more easily from coaching job to coaching job. One reason is that they have many more opportunities. Men can coach college men, college women, and NBA men and now pro women. Women can coach college women. And men seem to take care of one another better than women do. Perhaps it's because they have more clout with the administrators in recommending one another for jobs. Or perhaps they're not as busy keeping their own programs afloat, as many women are, and so have more time and energy to give to one another.

This isn't to say women coaches are not supportive of one another. I think we are. For instance, when I get a salary increase, one of the first people I call is Pat Summitt at Tennessee. "The bar has been raised," I'll say.

I strongly recommended that we hire Marianne at Stanford. Ignoring the suit still pending against USC, Stanford brought her in to be promotions director for women's basketball on a temporary basis. The job ended in October 1994, but when I accepted the Olympics post five months later, we hired her back as co-head coach. She had the head coaching experience that Amy lacked, so I thought they would be a dynamic combination.

Naming Amy as interim head coach didn't sit well with my other two Stanford assistants, who felt they had been unfairly passed over. They left the program, leaving me scrambling to hire two new assistants for Stanford as I was also hiring assistants for the national team and assistants for the Olympic team.

Marianne knew her coaching job at Stanford was just for the year I was gone, but she hoped, and we all hoped, that the visibility of coaching the 1995–96 season at Stanford would help get her back into consideration at other schools. It did: At the end of the season, she would be hired by the University of California at Berkeley to take over the job vacated by Gooch Foster.

Our first night at Stanford, we were supposed to scrimmage against a men's team. But I canceled it because we were too tired. The traveling was starting to catch up with us. It didn't help that we were hauling around 65 pieces of luggage, a dozen basketballs and a cart, two sets of practice uniforms, two sets of game uniforms, workout sweats, a portable video machine, two cases of tapes, and a trainer's table. Katy began collecting a couple of dollars from everybody to pay the porters at the airports to unload the bags. But even then we had to help out and make sure that every bag was accounted for. Teresa and Katrina always seemed to be the ones staying behind as others headed for the phones or something to eat. Time and again, it was the three-time Olympian and the two-time Olympian with their heads inside the bowels of the bus pulling luggage out. Anyone who wonders if Sheryl was a prima donna should have seen her in the hotel late one night during a stop in Columbus, Ohio. Everyone was exhausted and just wanted to crash in her room. Tennessee was playing Stanford that night on TV and I was rushing through the lobby to my room to catch the end of it. There were Sheryl and her husband, Eric, stacking the bags onto luggage carts, making sure everyone was taken care of before they took care of themselves.

People not sticking around to help with the luggage was one of those little things that I felt could grow into something big. A similar situation had arisen in Italy the previous spring. Jennifer, Katy, and Rebecca—the three white players—had gone to the beach together every day, giving the appearance of forming a clique, though that was never their intention. Renee sat all the players down and asked them what kind of team they wanted, one where the white players stuck with the white players and the black players stuck with the black players? That was the first and only time a race issue came up, and it really wasn't a race issue but simply the appearance of one. Some of the players called Jennifer "White Bread" because she was so suburban and wholesome, but the nickname was used with affection. At one point during the tour, Teresa said to

Jennifer, "You're not white anymore." She meant that Jennifer no longer had any color. She was just Jennifer. (Later, when one of the players cornrowed Jennifer's hair, they called her Cornbread.)

This is the intangible you hope to see emerge among your players: a deep respect and caring for one another. Players are supposed to think about their teammates as much as they think about themselves, a point Carol mentioned when she talked to the women about doing their fair share with the luggage. It was never a problem thereafter. I remember once when there were no carts or bellmen at a hotel to help transport the bags up to our floor. It was freezing outside. The bus pulled up alongside a side door and we created a line up the stairs and down the hall, passing the bags from hand to hand like an old-fashioned fire line.

Sometimes I wish we had a video of the whole year, all the bits of selflessness and thoughtfulness that made this team special. When fans complain about the dearth of role models in sports, we could roll the video and say, "Look. They're right here." As we set out on our tour, Alonzo Mourning had just turned down $11 million from the Charlotte Hornets and signed with Miami instead. Cleveland Browns owner Art Modell had turned his back on the hometown fans because $38 million in guaranteed TV money, plus huge crowds at every home game, weren't enough, and he moved his team to Baltimore. Baseball owners and players, unable to agree how to split their billions, still didn't have a labor agreement, and a possible lockout loomed for spring training.

Onto this sports landscape walked 11 women who saw a world beyond their own checkbooks.

"Sometimes you can't look at money," Katrina told the *Washington Post* when asked why she declined a $300,000 salary overseas to play for $50,000 at home. She had just turned 30. She knew her career had only a few $300,000 seasons left.

"Sometimes it's better to look at what's good for everybody," she said. ". . . [The] future of women's basketball rests on this national team. If a [pro] league is ever going to succeed, it has to be now. . . . It has to grow out of this team."

The women showed their character, too, in the time they spent at hospitals and schools and recreation centers. Our second day at Stanford, the players visited the Onetta Harris Community Center in East Palo Alto, a low-income, predominantly black city a few miles from Stanford. They spoke with kids about academics and confidence and showed them a bit of basketball, too. They shared their own stories of growing up poor or of being shunned by the boys or of struggling with the self-doubts that come with loving basketball long after one's friends have moved on to more "feminine" interests.

Earlier in the week in Virginia, the team visited a children's hospital. The players sat and talked with the kids, got to know them a little, met some of their parents. They knew a cheerful visit could make a difference for a child, even if just for a day. At the Virginia hospital, Jennifer had met a little boy with leukemia. She promised to write to him, and she did. Later on, her letter was returned. The boy had died.

The day of the Stanford game, I felt strange being in the visiting locker room and giving a scouting report on my own Stanford players. The words caught in my throat as I began down the list, starting with point guard Jamila Wideman. I felt as if revealing my players' weaknesses was a bit of a betrayal. But of course it wasn't.

"She's very left-handed," I said to the team. "Make her go right."

Amy had watched us on TV, so she knew what she was in for. I had given her some advice. After we had annihilated Georgia, I didn't want that to happen to Stanford.

"Look," I said, "just take care of the ball. Don't turn it over. Don't let us get into a running game."

I wanted Stanford to do well, but at the same time, it wouldn't be fair to the USA team if I approached the Stanford game differently from any other game. I wasn't going to hold the USA team back just to make Stanford look good. My priority was the USA team. We would do whatever we needed to improve. If that meant running over Stanford like a steamroller, so be it.

When I walked onto the court for introductions, the sellout crowd of 7,300 fans stood and cheered, as they did for Jennifer and Katy. Even the players on the Stanford bench joined in the ovation. I didn't expect such a response, which made it all the more touching. The school presented Jennifer and Katy with clocks before the game, and they gave me a beautiful black chair for my office.

I watched both teams as the game began, almost as if I were a spectator instead of a participant. We and Stanford were running the same offense, which we were developing simultaneously. But they were executing it better than we were, primarily because they practiced more than we did. When I yelled instructions to the USA team, I noticed the Stanford players instinctively turning their heads toward me. They were still tuned in to my voice as their coach. When they scored, I'd find myself hollering, "Good shot!"

Stanford played great early on. Their post players got inside for some close-in baskets. They gave up few turnovers, and they defended us well. They had us down by nine points early on, and we took just a six-point lead into the locker room at halftime.

My competitive juices were flowing at full capacity by then. Stanford or not, I wanted our team to play at top form. I wasn't happy with what I was seeing.

"Look, if you want to lose to a college team, that's fine with me," I said at halftime. "If you're trying to show that professional basketball is at a whole different level from college ball, then you've got to show it. You can't talk about it. You've got to go out and do it."

As I passed the Stanford bench for the start of the second half, I told the coaches: "Get ready. The hammer's comin' down."

"What does she mean by that?" one of the new assistants asked Amy. Amy smiled grimly.

"Watch," she said.

The second half was total destruction. We went on a 23–4 tear with Ruthie making shots from all over, including some that were such long shots that the players on the bench were incredulous. We won by 37 points, 100–63. Katrina had a double-double—12 points and ten rebounds. "Her rebounding is no joke," Stanford forward Olympia Scott said afterward. "She'd go up and then she'd go farther up." Seven players scored in double figures. Teresa had ten assists in her first start at point guard. (The players had not forgotten Dawn, however. On the bench, they placed a tiny red doll's jacket with her number on it as a reminder and an affectionate joke—everyone always kidded Dawn about her size. The jacket would appear on the bench at every game Dawn missed.)

I liked what I was seeing in Teresa at point guard. I liked her vision, and she was a great passer. Early on, she still tried to do too much sometimes, make plays that weren't there. But over the course of the year she would cut down on her mistakes, and she improved immensely on defense. Renee helped me a lot in communicating with Teresa. Teresa felt, as I do, that the point guard—more than any player on the floor—needs to be on the same page as the coach. I think Teresa felt if she knew me better off the court, maybe we'd be more in tune on the court as well. I felt I talked pretty easily with Teresa, but I wasn't going to pry into people's lives. It's a fine line between getting to know your players as people and getting too friendly, which complicates the coach-player relationship.

"Tara's all about basketball," Teresa would tell my sister Heidi, then the coach at Eastern Washington. Heidi became friends with Teresa when she worked at various national team training camps with me.

She was right about me being all about basketball that year. No matter what was happening in my life, I never let it bleed into basketball. My brain was like a desk, with my thoughts about basketball in neat piles on top, always visible. Everything else was shut away in drawers and cabinets. Perhaps such single-mindedness bothered my players at times. Maybe they wanted me to let my hair down a bit, talk about my love of music, playing the flute, the books I read. But I think they also recognized that my intensity helped keep our edge and stave off complacency as we trounced one college team after another.

Keeping that edge is what I talked to Pete Newell about after the Stanford game. There is no one in basketball I admire more than Pete Newell, the former Cal coach and 1960 Olympic men's coach. When I found out he was running the NBA's Big Man Camp at Stanford when I arrived in 1985, I watched from the stands, listening to everything he said. I remember him working with Chris Washburn, a young player who had just been drafted by the Golden State Warriors. He could not make a left-handed layup to save his life. Pete was so patient and positive with him. All the players listened. Pete inspired a respect from them that few coaches in today's self-centered climate of professional sports enjoy.

Pete and I got to talking after a session, and soon we were having lunch at a Chinese restaurant, scribbling plays on the notebook I took with me everywhere. Five hours later, we were still sipping tea and talking. I asked if he would watch some of our games and practices and give me feedback, which he graciously agreed to do. When he was visiting from Los Angeles, he would watch us, then send me pages of notes, which I devoured. The lunches at the Chinese restaurant became an annual event. The owner groaned every time he saw us walk in because we were going to tie up a table all afternoon. Pete's support meant everything to me. He'd tell reporters that I was one of the best coaches in the Pac-10, male or female. He'd tell them I could coach in the NBA if someone gave me a chance. If I ever suffered a lack of confidence, I could always turn to Pete. It's not that I needed people propping me up, but I knew if I ever had a problem I could call on him.

Pete watched our USA team play Stanford, and afterward he gave me some advice. First, keep doing what we were doing. Second, foster a sense of urgency even when there was nothing on the line in the games. And last, find ways every single day to make the players a better team than they were the day before.

We couldn't gauge improvement by our victories, as most teams can. We gave the players goal sheets—both team and individual—to keep them pushing themselves. I first saw Bobby Knight use them when I was a student at Indiana. I began using them a few years later at Ohio State to motivate our team after lopsided losses to two powerhouses, Louisiana Tech and USC, and the players were completely discouraged.

"What's going to keep them motivated the rest of the season?" I asked myself.

They needed goals beyond simple wins and losses. I printed up sheets that listed ten or so elements of a game we could focus on as a team, such as rebounding, turnovers, using the clock well, getting back on defense. It helped the players to think about what they were doing well and what they weren't. And the goal sheets helped establish a postgame routine. We no longer looked just at the final score, but at how we arrived at the final score. What exactly did we do and what didn't we do?

I have used goal sheets with every team since. I felt they would be especially important with the USA team. We were going to be beating college teams by 30 and 40 points every night, so we needed to gauge our progress by measurements beyond the final score. We had team goal sheets and individual goal sheets. After each game, Renee would review the goal sheets with the post players, Nell would take the perimeter players, and I'd take the point guards. The goal sheets gave each game purpose and helped keep the players focused when the scores got out of hand.

After Stanford, we beat San Diego State by 57, Southwest Missouri State by 51, and North Carolina State by 46. Lisa gave me a scare at Southwest Missouri State. She was the only player on the team who dunked, one of the only players in all of women's basketball who dunked. So opposing players weren't accustomed to it. She went up for a dunk in Missouri and her defender undercut her in the air. She crashed to the court, and my heart leaped to my throat. Dawn was already out. I shuddered to think what would happen if we lost Lisa, too. If either she or Katrina was hurt, in my mind the gold medal was gone. Lisa was shaken up, but thank goodness she was fine. That was the end of the dunks. I told her she could do them in warmups but not in the games. They weren't worth the risk. Lisa readily agreed.

We had another scare at North Carolina State. Renee was running the post drills at practice in NC State's old basketball arena. Usually the post players would be trailing the offense and pulling up for three-point shots. But Renee changed the drill and had them shooting closer to the basket. In the middle of the drill, we heard a faint hissing sound but couldn't tell where it was coming from. Suddenly a spotlight—about the size of a peach basket—fell from the ceiling, bouncing first, then shattering on the court. It landed right where the post players would have been had they been running their usual drill. The accident shook us up, but after the custodian swept up the fragments we continued to practice.

After we beat NC State 98–52, their players were shaking their heads.

"I thought I was out there with a bunch of men," one

135

SHOOTING
FROM THE
OUTSIDE

of them told reporters. "They were really quick. I couldn't get a rebound or a shot. I've never seen any women play like that."

While we were at NC State, I talked a lot with their coach, Kay Yow, who had been the 1988 Olympic coach and had headed up the committee that chose me as the coach for 1996. When I found myself venting about our lack of post players—the Horse—she was blunt: Don't count on USA Basketball to replace any of these players. The team we had now would almost certainly be the team we'd take to the Olympics, though we would add a 12th player. It wasn't what I wanted to hear. I wanted options. I wanted the best possible team, and I wasn't convinced we had it. Kay told me to let go of what I couldn't control and focus on what I could.

"You should concentrate on who you want in the 12th spot," she told me.

The 12th player would not be my choice, but I expected to have greater input than I had had with the other 11. By the time we added the player next spring, who would know the team better than I? I imagined the committee would defer to my observations.

That's when I began thinking about Venus Lacey.

Venus had not been invited to the tryouts. She had been cut in the previous tryouts and had been playing overseas ever since. But I knew Venus was a force to be reckoned with from her college days at Louisiana Tech, where she led the team to the 1988 national championship. She's big—a bulky six feet, four inches tall—and she knows how to use her size to clear out space under the basket and overpower her opponents. Venus doesn't take anything from anybody. She'd flatten you for looking at her funny.

I think this fierceness grew out of a difficult childhood. She wore heavy wooden braces on her legs from age two to age eight. When her brother would carry her home from school on his back, the other children taunted her. As the eighth child in a family of ten in Chattanooga, Tennessee, she had little money for physical therapy. So her grandfather stretched and strengthened her legs in the hope that she might one day walk like other children. When the braces finally came off in the fourth grade, she was determined to be an athlete. Only when she was cut from her junior high volleyball team did she turn to basketball.

I didn't know if she would be interested in trying out for the 12th spot or what her contractual obligations were with her pro team in Greece. And Val Whiting, the former Stanford player, was still a possibility. She wouldn't be starting medical school for another year at least.

But whenever I thought of the final player to add to the team, I found myself thinking more and more of Venus.

By the time we played Tennessee on November 22, we had been on the road for 28 days. It was our last stop before the Thanksgiving break. I spent the afternoon in the Knoxville Holiday Inn laundry room, sketching out-of-bounds play while my third load dried. Keeping clothes clean was one of the great challenges of the trip. Hotels could have 24-hour room service, marble lobbies, crystal chandeliers. But our favorite hotels were the ones with coin-operated washers and dryers.

A few days before we arrived, Tennessee coach Pat Summitt told me that Nikki McCray's boyfriend wanted to surprise her by proposing on the court after the game. Nikki had been Southeastern Conference player of the year at Tennessee in both 1994 and 1995. She was Miss Personality, who never met a camera she didn't like—she and Ruthie both. Renee would tell me that she'd take a roll of 36 pictures, and when she got them developed, 24 would be of Nikki and Ruthie.

Nikki had come a long way in a short time. Two years earlier, when she was about to begin her junior year at Tennessee, she was one of 18 players who came to Stanford to try out for the 1993 World Championship Qualifying team that I was coaching. I was down on the floor as the players scrimmaged, and Amy, my Stanford assistant, was watching from the stands. The first time Nikki touched the ball, she went up for a layup and hit the shot clock! She had a reputation of being erratic on offense and confirmed the label right away. And she had no experience in international ball on any level. When I mentioned Nikki among the players I was planning to cut, Amy shook her head.

"I would not go out of the country without Nikki McCray," she said.

"What do you mean?" I trusted Amy's judgment about players more than I trusted my own. She has a great eye for talent. She had spotted Jennifer Azzi when few other colleges recruited her. She had pushed for Sonja Henning when others said she wasn't quick enough, and for Val Whiting when others thought her clumsy. And once, when I was eager to sign a very tall high school senior, Amy said I would do it only over her dead body. Sure enough, the girl went to another college and never amounted to anything.

"Nikki McCray is your best defender," Amy said.

"Yeah, but . . ."

"It doesn't matter if she's wild," Amy said. "You're going to need her."

The tournament was in Brazil, where the home team was favored to win. In a preliminary round of the round-robin competition, we lost to Brazil by seven points. Hortencia Marcari Oliva, Brazil's star player, lit us up, scoring 37 points. If we were going to beat them in the championship game, we'd have to shut down Hortencia. Nikki was young and inexperienced, but I decided she would guard Hortencia. The day before the game, I sat with Nikki and we watched films of the great Brazilian heroine.

"Nikki," I told her, pointing to a freeze frame of Hortencia driving to the basket, "you need to stop this girl right here." I went over everything I had observed about Hortencia's tendencies, strengths, and weaknesses. Nikki studied her, memorizing the moves she liked to make in different situations.

The next day when we arrived at the arena, 15,000 fans were screaming for Hortencia and Brazil. Soldiers with machine guns stood at courtside. I don't know if that was usual for basketball games, but I could see why they might be necessary. The place seemed on the edge of chaos. People were kicking beach balls in the stands, singing, shouting, drinking, throwing trash. The din was so loud I couldn't hear my players if they were farther than five feet away.

The atmosphere didn't intimidate Nikki. When the game began, Nikki became Hortencia's worst nightmare. Hortencia was so frustrated that she was pushing and punching Nikki. Nikki just took her out. Hortencia had been averaging about 30 points a game on her home court, but she scored just 15 that day—and only two while Nikki was in the game. On a jump ball, a Brazilian player elbowed Lisa in the neck but drew no foul. Another suckerpunched Ruthie in the back. The refs were calling Dawn for traveling when she wasn't. She was getting angry.

"Dawn, you grew up on the streets of Philadelphia," I told her during a time-out. "Go out and bury 'em."

We beat Brazil 106–92, a victory that incited the crowd to pelt the court with cups and paper. We needed armed security to escort us to the team bus. While the bus tried to inch through the crowded parking lot, fans surrounded us and began rocking the bus. Security guards ordered us to duck low in our seats, away from the windows, in case the fans hurled rocks. It took ten motorcycle police officers to free the bus from the crowd and guide us to the airport. It was one of the most satisfying victories of my career. We had lost to them two days earlier, and to come back and win in that atmosphere with players who weren't considered marquee players at the time—there was no better feeling.

Now Nikki was on the Olympic team, again primarily

for her defense. Everybody loved Nikki. Her mother in Collierville, Tennessee, would bake cakes for the team and ship them to wherever we were. Nikki would cut them and put them in little Baggies to keep them fresh. The team went crazy over those cakes, especially when we traveled overseas and craved American food. We had few clashes on this team, but the special caramel cake Nikki's mother made always carried the potential for physical confrontation.

When Pat asked about her boyfriend Thomas's surprise proposal, I said it was OK with me if it was OK with Nikki. I didn't want her to be embarrassed if this wasn't what she wanted. Can you imagine? What a disaster. I had Renee poke around to make sure Nikki would say yes.

"Trust me," Renee said after her reconnaissance mission, "this is what she wants."

None of the players knew what was happening when Nikki was summoned to a chair at midcourt. Then Thomas walked out and handed her a bouquet of roses and dropped to one knee. With a microphone in one hand and a jeweler's box in the other, and with 6,000 people listening in, he asked Nikki to marry him. Our players fell off the bench, laughing and howling and slapping the floor. Nikki screamed when she saw the ring, stomping her feet like a kid at Christmas. It was a great way for the team to end the trip and head home for Thanksgiving.

I wasn't going home, however. I was off to Massachusetts to share Thanksgiving dinner with the Stanford players and watch them play their season opener. I flew in Thanksgiving Day and went directly to their practice, which was winding down. It felt strange, different from when I saw the team at Stanford. There, I had been with the USA team. I had a role. Now I was—what? An outsider. An observer. No longer a part of the action. On a team, you're either in or you're out. There is no in-between. I was out. Here was the team I had been coaching for ten years and now I was watching like any other fan off the street. Sports teams are very closed communities. Even when a player is injured, there is a subtle distance that springs up between her and the team. You're not in unless you're on the court working, contributing your sweat to the cause. I knew all this, and I knew that's what makes teams strong. But still I was surprised at how quickly the team filled the hole I left behind. As much as I was focused on the USA team—I wore no Stanford clothing the whole year, only red, white, and blue outfits—I found myself wistful for Stanford. When something is taken away from you, I think you appreciate it even more.

The parents of Stanford point guard Jamila Wideman hosted us for a wonderful Thanksgiving dinner at their home in Amherst. Jamila's father is John Wideman, the writer of *Brothers and Keepers* and ten other books. He teaches at the University of Massachusetts, which was Stanford's opponent the next day. The game was put on the schedule especially for Jamila, who is a local legend in Amherst. She helped lead the Amherst Lady Hurricanes to the state high school championship in 1993, a season chronicled in the great book *In These Girls Hope Is a Muscle* by Pulitzer Prize-winner Madeline Blais.

Jamila's return to Amherst helped sell out the arena. More than 7,000 fans packed the stands, and I'm willing to bet none was as nervous as I was. Stanford got me a seat on press row, which was down on the court between the two teams' benches. My cousins who live in Massachusetts came to the game. I hadn't seen them in ten years, but I couldn't visit during the game. I told them I'd see them afterward.

Right from the opening tip-off, I was screaming. Not just cheering, screaming. I was yelling instructions, offering encouragement, making a total fool of myself. I didn't notice the reporters staring at me. Apparently, you're not supposed to cheer on press row.

"Coach VanDerveer," someone from UMass finally said

to me, "you have to stop cheering or find another place to sit."

"Then I gotta move," I said. There was no way I could watch without yelling. I was in full coaching mode. I moved into a seat in the stands farther from the Stanford bench, but I was loud. Amy and Marianne were so wrapped up in their own coaching, either they didn't hear me or they just ignored me.

I don't know how fans do it. It's hard to be a fan! It's much easier coaching or playing. When you're a fan, you just sit there and can't do anything.

A reporter wrote something pretty negative about me in the paper the next day, about how this wasn't the way for the Olympic coach to act. But I don't know any other way. Those were still my players out there and I wanted more than anything for them to play well, and they weren't. I wanted them to win for themselves but also for Amy. She was in a tough spot, taking on the responsibility of being a head coach for the first time while working with three new coaches on the staff. (Amy was the only coach left from the previous season.) I've been coaching for 18 years and still struggle to get things done the way I want them, so I couldn't imagine how difficult it must have been for Amy. She was amazing in how she dealt with everything from the press to the boosters. I'm still finding out stuff that happened during the year that she never told me, things she thought might be upsetting to me. In her mind, I had enough on my plate without worrying about Stanford, too.

Stanford lost to UMass, a significant upset, and an awful way to start the season. Since Amy and I had arrived at Stanford, the team had never lost its season opener. I didn't go to the locker room. I just got on the bus and waited for the team to board. Amy said little when she sat down, as if shell-shocked. The players filed on silently. I don't think anyone said a word on the drive to the hotel. I talked with the coaches later and assured them this was just a bump in the road and maybe in the long run would serve them well. A loss early on has a way of getting the players' attention. Having seen many of the top college teams on our tour, I said Stanford could hold its own with any of them. I told the players I'd come down to one of their rooms to talk around 9 that night. Anyone who wanted to stop by was welcome, but it wasn't mandatory. They all showed up. I had been reading a book on peak performance and shared some of what I was learning with them.

"I'm not going to talk about today's game," I said. "I'm not here to be a coach. Listen to me. Don't feel that there's no hope. It's one loss. Big deal. Move on. Your team can still go to the Final Four.

"What you have to think about right now is, how are you going to change around what happened? You have to stay together as a team."

People were crying. It was pretty intense.

"It's been really difficult for me to be away from this team," I said. "But sometimes you have to go through painful things to get something better. I think that's what we're both doing."

I said things to them I probably wouldn't have said if I were their coach. A coach obsesses: "Oh my God, we just lost to UMass." When a team loses, the thought flashes through a coach's mind that her team will never win again. But I was able to step back and see the larger picture. Basically, I was there to build their confidence, soothe their fears, convince them that everything would be OK.

I was wishing somebody would do the same for me with the Olympic team.

8

Without dreams, there is no need to work.
Without work, there is no need to dream.

The players were getting cranky. As if the demands of travel weren't enough, they were living two to a room on the road. These were adult women. Two of them were married. Two were engaged. All needed privacy, if for no other reasons than to talk on the phone and enjoy solitary time away from basketball. Sheryl, who was a newlywed, paid for a single room whenever her husband joined us on the tour and it wasn't her turn in the team rotation to get a single room. Katrina paid for a single room right from the start. Sharing rooms became a big issue with the players, and we feared it could change respectful, solid relationships into prickly, defensive ones.

In early December, Carol asked USA Basketball to approve single rooms for everyone. It was a major financial commitment, but they agreed to it. Only Dawn didn't want a single room. She loved being around her teammates. She had returned to the team after the Thanksgiving break, though she couldn't play or practice yet. She told a reporter that she never got homesick while with the team on the road, but she had been "teamsick" during her three weeks at home rehabilitating her knee. Still, returning to the team was difficult. Teresa had moved into her position. And our relationship was no longer as close. We didn't seem to communicate as well. Dawn is such a fighter, and I could see how fiercely she wanted to play. I could see, too, that she was feeling a bit like an outsider, the way I felt with the Stanford team after being away. I wanted her as my starter, but I had to have a backup plan. I was spending more time working with Teresa because if Dawn wasn't going to be 100 percent healthy, Teresa would be the woman leading us on the floor at the Olympics.

With each game, Teresa gave me more reasons to believe in her. In the game with Vanderbilt on December 3, for example, one of the Vanderbilt players had a breakaway layup. She was streaking down the court, all alone, with a clear path to the basket. There was no way Teresa could do anything. She was way out of the play. Anyone else would have conceded the layup. But Teresa flew down the court, leaped up, and basically pinned the ball against the backboard. When she descended, she had the ball. You needed to see only that one play to understand how competitive Teresa is. It was a great lesson for the young players, not to mention for me.

We had been totally dependent on Dawn in October. I had never seen her play better than she was playing then, so I couldn't imagine competing in the Olympics without her. But she wasn't the same player when she returned. She wasn't as quick, and she had lost some of her timing. And others, namely Teresa, had improved. Yet I felt my history with Dawn allowed me to kid with her, even in such an uncertain time for her.

"Dawn, you've got to be healthy or I've got to get somebody else," I cracked during a pregame meal one day. Renee told me later the remark really hurt Dawn, something I never intended.

In addition to the strain of sharing rooms, I was also

getting impatient with the maddening game of musical trainers. The United States Olympic Committee, which provided our trainers, had set up a rotation of five different trainers who would catch up with us at various stops during the tour. After the third one, we'd had it. The new trainers would arrive without knowing the players' preferences in taping their ankles and legs, or how each responded to physical therapy treatments, what routines the players liked to follow. They didn't know injury histories or levels of pain tolerance, all important information to help the players feel safe and help me feel that we were doing everything possible to prevent injuries. Trainers are like doctors. How would you like to have five different doctors in a year?

When I was told we were to get yet another new trainer once the Olympics began, I protested to USA Basketball.

"Being on the road for a year is tough enough on the players," I said. "Please don't make them adjust to any more new situations than they have to."

Again, USA Basketball came through. It got the USOC to assign us two trainers who shared the job the rest of the year.

It was easy to get immersed in the tight little world we had created for ourselves. Despite our games and public appearances, we often lost sight of what the team meant to others, where it fit in the evolution of women's sports, how it might be connected to other women in other professions. Three days after playing Vanderbilt, we found ourselves in Washington, D.C., with a couple of free days before we played Old Dominion in Norfolk, Virginia. Those two days were like spiritual feasts, filling us with a sense of history and purpose. If we hadn't grasped the cultural significance of this team, it was illustrated to us in Washington, D.C.

The women of Washington welcomed us as if we were old friends. We had lunch with several U.S. representatives, among them veteran representative Patsy Mink of

Hawaii. I had never heard of Patsy Mink, but I soon discovered that she had been instrumental in my career and the careers of every one of the players. She was one of the two authors of the Title IX legislation.

"When you play," she told us at lunch, "when you win the gold medal, you aren't just playing for yourselves. You aren't just winning the medal for yourselves. You're winning it for thousands of little girls across the country who want to do what you're doing.

"It's rare as a legislator that you fight for legislation you believe in, and then stay around or live long enough to see it come to fruition. This is very gratifying for me."

Some of the players, amazingly, were only vaguely familiar with Title IX. It's like today's tennis players having no idea who Billie Jean King is and what she did for their careers.

"What do you mean there were no scholarships?" one asked me when I described life before Title IX. It's the same with their shoe contracts. Like kids finding out there was once a time without television, the youngest players can't believe players didn't have shoe contracts.

From Capitol Hill, we went to the Supreme Court building. We were led to a small room where a TV crew was waiting. I had been told the justices didn't want cameras at the meeting, but when Sandra Day O'Connor and Ruth Bader Ginsburg arrived, they just looked at the cameras without complaint.

"We're the best on our court," I said in thanking them for seeing us, "and you're the best in yours."

Justice O'Connor spoke briefly, then turned to the TV photographer.

"Are you finished?" she asked firmly.

"We are now."

She was not a woman one questioned.

Then her demeanor lightened. "I can't wait to show you this special room in the justice building," she said. "It's a surprise."

First they showed us the chambers where they hear cases. "I wanted to meet you because what you're doing is important," Justice O'Connor said to the team. Then, looking over at Justice Ginsburg, she said, "I can't tell you how happy I was when she got to the court. It makes a night-and-day difference to have women on the bench."

We were in awe, sitting in that historic room with the first two female Supreme Court justices. We were looking at excellence. We could see it and feel it and understand it.

"OK, now for the surprise," Justice O'Connor said.

The justices led us upstairs to the third floor, past the library where young clerks were darting around like mice. Justice O'Connor opened the door near the end of the hall, and there was a basketball court.

"This is the highest court in the nation," she said.

The two justices were so delighted with that court, even though the ceiling was so low you would have to bank the ball off of it to make a basket from the corners. Our players dribbled and shot the ball, and so did Justice O'Connor. She hit a short jumper, then high-fived the team.

Back on the bus, Val Ackerman of NBA marketing, who had gone with us, delivered the Supreme Court scouting report. "O'Connor had the nice little hook shot," she deadpanned as we laughed. "But she didn't go well to her left. Good backspin on the ball, though. Ginsburg needed a little help. Not a shooter. More of a role player."

We walked over to Capitol Hill, where all eight female U.S. senators were waiting for us. Kay Bailey Hutchinson invited Nell and Sheryl, the Texas folks, to her office. Dianne Feinstein took Jennifer, Katy, and Lisa, the players with the California connections. The rest of us hooked up with the other senators for a chat and a tour of the Senate. I trailed the pack, trying to keep tabs on where everybody was. As I walked and listened, I let the day sink in. I was struck by the clear and immediate connection between the team and the women we had met. We were just athletes and coaches, and they were powerful politicians and judges, people whose actions affected American lives. But maybe our actions affected lives, too, in a subtler way. When Teresa bounced a no-look pass to Katrina, or when Ruthie stripped the ball from her opponent and glided down the court for a seamless layup, maybe a woman watching at home felt her limitations give way just a little. I'm not sure I believe that the accomplishments of one woman lifts all women, but women who lead the way—as these remarkable women in Washington have—make our own journeys easier. We ride in their wake, protected and pulled along.

That night, we stayed out until midnight at the Washington Bullets game, where Ruthie and Nikki sang the national anthem. We didn't find out until we returned to the hotel that the President had agreed to jog with us in the morning—6 A.M. It was supposed to be a day off for the players, and several had made plans to fly to New York for a Nike appearance—something I wasn't crazy about. I wanted them to use their days off to rest. (We solved the problem by not including days off on the schedule, making them more of a surprise instead.)

We waited in the White House, drinking orange juice, because President Clinton was still sleeping. When he arrived, Teresa gave him a USA Basketball sweatshirt that was clearly too small, but good sport that he was, he wore it anyway. Our van followed his limousine to the park, where we found him fiddling with his watch. The Secret Service had warned us not to go near the President, but Nell went right up to him.

"What kind of watch is that?"

Clinton gave her a quizzical look. "An Iron Man," he said.

"Oh, I know how to work that," Nell replied.

She moved in closer. "Jeez, Nell," I was thinking, "don't touch him!"

Playing at Indiana in 1975—shooting with my right hand off the left side!

Courtesy of the author.

Amy Tucker and me at the Kodak All-American Banquet.

Courtesy of Amy Tucker © 1996.

he Stanford Connection— nnifer Azzi, Katy Steding, d me.

urtesy of Nancy Darsch © 1996.

Ohio State 1985 Big Ten Champions pose for reunion during the USA National Tour stop in Columbus. *Courtesy of Nancy Darsch © 1996.*

Lisa Leslie, Nikki McCray, Ruthie Bolton, Renee Brown, me, Tracey Williams of the ABL, and Dawn Staley posing after the Naismith Awards Banquet. *Courtesy of Renee Brown © 1996.*

Renee Brown and me in Siberia—one foot in Europe and one in Asia!

Courtesy of Renee Brown © 1996.

Nell Fortner in Siberia— party on!

Courtesy of Renee Brown © 1996.

Nick and me skiing at Vail.

The USA team at Disney World.

Courtesy of Nancy Darsch © 1996.

Carol Callan and me enjoying
a day at Disney World.

Courtesy of Carol Callan © 1996.

The team before the opening ceremonies at the Olympics.

Courtesy of Beth VanDerveer © 1996.

Meeting President Clinton in the Georgia Dome locker room at the Games.

Courtesy of USA Basketball © 1996.

My mother Rita, brother Nick, and sister Beth at the Olympics.

Beth VanDerveer, Amy Tucker, Heidi VanDerveer, and Karen Middleton at the Olympics.

1984 Olympic coach Pat Head Summitt and 1976 Olympic coach Billie Moore post–Gold Medal Game looking for a towel for me after a wet congratulations. *Courtesy of Renee Brown © 1996.*

Olympic staff (Ceal Barry, Nancy Darsch, me, and Marian Washington) all smiles after our victory in the Gold Medal Game.

Courtesy of Nancy Darsch © 1996.

But she just reached out, turned a button or two, and, sure enough, fixed his watch.

Nell kept chatting as we began to run. Then Ruthie moved up to the front and started to sing a military drill song. There was a boat in the water, a helicopter overhead, and security people everywhere, but no one else in the park but us and the President. We stopped when we reached the river, and the President stood and talked with us as if we were old friends. I asked what he liked best about his job. He said making a positive impact on people's lives, such as introducing the Family Leave Act and a new student loan program.

"I also like that when I go out in the world, I represent America," he said. "As Americans, we represent hope."

I could sense his words sinking in for every one of us. We were wearing our red, white, and blue sweats with USA printed across the fronts. I had worn nothing but red, white, and blue all year: every jacket and pair of slacks; every sweater, sock, bra, and T-shirt. For the entire year, and especially at the Olympics, we represented America, and the weight of that responsibility began to mount.

There were moments during the year when I felt I was living inside a movie, and this was one of them. We were standing by the Potomac River, in the shadow of the Washington Monument, talking to the President of the United States. I half-expected to hear music rising in the distance, maybe a soft gospel rendition of "America the Beautiful." We were like characters moving toward the story's climax, and we had only one ending in mind.

By then my vision of that ending had changed slightly. I didn't just want us to win. I wanted us to dominate. And we left Washington for Norfolk, Virginia, and Old Dominion believing we could.

We arrived in Norfolk with a 13–0 record. We were winning by an average of 44 points. We had traveled more than 15,000 miles, passed through 20 airports, and rented 25 cars, buses, and minivans. We'd step off elevators and forget which room we were in. Was it 236, or was that the room in Nashville? We'd wake up in the morning and check the hotel stationery to remind ourselves where we were.

Yet the rooming situation had been resolved. The problem with the trainers had been settled. My mind was easing a bit. We were riding a high from our adventures in Washington.

Then we played Old Dominion.

I was angrier after that game than after any other game all year. We were awful. We turned the ball over 24 times, Lisa got into foul trouble, Ruthie had a few knucklehead plays, Rebecca played 27 minutes without a point. Old Dominion's post players exposed us for what we were: a great team with a weakness at the post.

The Horse.

It might seem stupid that I was so upset when we won by 57 points, but I was. The final score in any of the college games was irrelevant to me. We had set a dozen goals for the game, and I doubt we hit more than one or two.

I laid into the players in the locker room afterward in a way I had not done to that point.

"If you want to make the final Olympic team, you need to be effective," I said. "We're not getting the job done, and we need to get people in here who will. We need people who are going to be aggressive inside and rebound, who are going to get on the low block and score.

"Maybe we need to make some personnel changes."

I didn't stick around to see their reaction because I had to go to the postgame press conference. The Old Dominion players were still talking when I arrived in the press room, and they didn't notice me walk in. Someone asked about our post players.

"To be honest with you," the Old Dominion player said, "it was tougher last week when we played Stanford."

It was like throwing gasoline on the fire. That was all I

needed to hear. My mind was racing. We needed people who didn't just do the showboat stuff, the interviews and public appearances, but who could really deliver on the court. I was beginning to feel physically sick about all the time and money being sunk into this program and wondering how in heaven's name we were going to win. Old Dominion's post players had just outplayed us. What would China, Russia, Australia, and Brazil do against us?

Every month I had a telephone conference with the player selection committee. I'd fill them in on our progress and bring up problems. In every conference, I talked about our weakness at the post position—we had four forwards and one center. But I sensed they saw me as the boy who cried wolf. We were winning, weren't we? And by huge margins. The more we won, the more difficult it became to convince them there needed to be changes.

I know a coach always sees her team differently than anyone else sees it. A coach sees the glass half-empty because you concentrate on your weaknesses. Whatever you're not doing well, that's what you're trying to fix because that's what your opponent will try to exploit. I watched the team in practice every day, so I saw the nuances no one outside the team did. I worried that we might not have enough ammunition to win the gold medal. And what if there were injuries?

I felt caught in the middle of competing interests. The team looked great on paper, just as the 1994 World Championships team did. And the NBA was doing a wonderful job marketing it. Every player on the team was terrific with the public. But wasn't my purpose to win a gold medal? I wasn't interested in keeping players for any reason other than to help us win.

When I voiced my concerns, USA Basketball would say, "OK, thank you." And that was the end of it. Despite Kay Yow's advice to accept what I had, I simply couldn't yet, even though I knew my complaints didn't sit well with some people. One member of the selection committee pulled me aside during one of our college stops and said he didn't like what I had been saying about the makeup of the team.

"You're going about this the wrong way," he said.

"I don't know any other way to deal with it," I said. "I don't know how else to get people to understand that we need help."

It puzzled me that women's basketball was working so hard to become big business, yet it clung to the quaint notion that we had to tiptoe around people's feelings. If some players on the team weren't up to the task, then I felt we ought to replace them with new players. Do you think an NBA general manager waffles about cutting a nonproductive player from training camp because the player and his teammates would feel bad about it, or because the marketing department might object? Of course not. If we were professionals, then I felt we should make decisions like professionals.

It was at times like this that I'd get a nervous queasiness about how much money was riding on our success. Sponsors such as Topps, Sears, Kraft, Champion, State Farm, Lifetime television, and Tambrands had spent hundreds of thousands of dollars to help us produce a winner. The financial futures of the players would rise or fall on how we played in the tour and at the Olympics. Already the players were getting a taste of what awaited them if we came through with the gold medal. Teresa had landed several major endorsement contracts, including ones for Georgia Power company, AT&T, and Nike. Nike, a marketing partner with USA Basketball, was running a great commercial featuring Sheryl, Dawn, and Lisa playing playground hoops against guys. Sears was shooting a commercial featuring the team. Nike painted a gigantic mural of Dawn on the side of a building near her neighborhood in Philadelphia. Topps was marketing a set of USA Basketball trading cards, the first collectible inspired by a women's team.

Corporate America was climbing on the bandwagon in a way it had never done with women's team sports. Companies had always been reluctant to support women's sports because they believed women themselves didn't support them. I think women are very supportive of women's sports, but they don't always have the time to come to the games or watch an entire telecast. The typical 18- to 35-year-old woman's plate is full with just surviving the day. Most of them have jobs. Many have children. And most still do 70 to 90 percent of the cleaning, cooking, shopping, and child care. But just because they can't park themselves in the bleachers or in front of the TV for every game, it doesn't mean they aren't aware of companies that advertise and help fund women's teams. They bring this awareness into the marketplace, where they are the primary consumers, buying more groceries, clothes, cars, and appliances than men. I'm not a big shopper myself, but I know who supported our team, and those are the companies I am going to patronize. I believe our fans feel the same way, and corporate America finally did, too.

Obviously we weren't playing to sell shoes and American cheese. Winning the gold was the top priority, but riding on that success, just below the surface, was the future of women's basketball itself. Maybe that sounds like hyperbole, but it's not. Our success would shape the fate of a women's pro league. If people responded well to us, and if we produced great basketball, advertisers and television networks would embrace the viability of a pro league.

Having a pro league would affect every layer of women's basketball. It would boost interest in the college game because fans would want to see the next generation of stars before they're stars, just as they do in the men's game. As a result, more college games would get on the air and into the newspapers. And as college players became famous, the way male college players are now, girls in junior high and high school would have more role models and more incentive to pursue sports, widening the pool of talent, improving the level of play, and creating whole generations of female fans who—unlike our mothers and many of us—enjoy the game because they know what it's like to be down there on the court.

As we began our year of training, one league had already been born: the American Basketball League, founded by a group of business executives and athletic administrators from California and Georgia and based in Palo Alto. Undeterred by the failures of previous pro women's leagues, the ABL founders had come to their decision based on sound numbers. Basketball had become the top participation sport among girls in America, according to the National Federation of High School Sports. Attendance at NCAA Division I women's games had tripled in the last ten years, rising to 3.9 million for the 1994–95 season. As a result, gate receipts, media coverage, and TV ratings had also increased.

Nine of the 11 national team players signed with the league, and eight had attended the San Jose press conference announcing the league in September. Sheryl spoke to the press by video because she was in Chicago for a Nike promotion. The founders raised about $4 million in capital for the eight-team league, which would begin play almost immediately after the Olympic Games. The players would be paid between $40,000 and $125,000 a year, less than most had earned playing in foreign leagues.

"I might have made more overseas, but I spent more, too," Dawn cracked during the press conference. "I'm probably in debt a little to everybody on this panel here."

"I'm not in debt to them," said Carla, who had played five seasons in Europe, "but to every credit-card company—and AT&T."

Back in New York, the NBA was quietly piecing together the components for its own eight-team women's league. Former basketball great Carol Blazejowski, who worked for the NBA, had attended the national team tryouts and dropped hints about the NBA's interest. Carol had played for the New Jersey Gems of the Women's Basketball League that lasted from 1979 to 1981, so she had a better sense than most about what was necessary to make a new league work.

"Exposure, exposure, exposure—that's the key," Carol said to anyone who asked during the trials. "The difference now is that women's basketball has momentum after another great college season. And there is an acceptance by the public that women can be athletes. That's why you see participation in women's sports at an all-time high."

The NBA also understood the economics at work. Most families in America can't afford tickets to an NBA game, which run from $30 to hundreds of dollars a seat. So these families might turn to women's pro basketball as an alternative.

With rumors of an NBA-sponsored league surfacing, TV negotiations for the ABL stalled as networks waited to see what the NBA would do. The NBA would not officially announce the birth of its league until April, six months after the ABL, but it clearly was going to happen. A few players on our team who had already endorsed the ABL began to question their decision. An NBA league promised better marketing, more TV exposure, instant credibility.

But other players, particularly Dawn, Jennifer, and Teresa, were unwavering in their commitment to the ABL. They saw the WNBA as the weak stepsister to the NBA. Already existing NBA franchises would run the women's team in their cities. The women would play a 28-game schedule during the summer, the NBA's off-season, thus using the basketball arenas that would be empty otherwise. To the ABL proponents, this smacked of second-class status. They liked the grassroots feel of the ABL, the smaller markets, the involvement in the communities in which they would be playing, the fact the league was created from whole cloth solely for women.

"I've taken pride that women's' sports have always seemed a little deeper than money," Jennifer liked to say in defending the ABL. "It would be sad to see it get so that money is more important than anything else. I believe in this league and what it stands for. It's growing from the bottom up. It's part of the community because players are from the areas where they're playing. If you go somewhere and just play for a few weeks in the summer, it's hard to have any kind of feeling for the town."

But when I looked at both leagues taking shape, I saw that the WNBA had the money and the know-how. Throughout the year, the players kept abreast of each league's progress. The WNBA continued to strengthen its position in the market, even though it would not sign a single player until after the Olympics. As Carol Blazejowski said, the key to any league's survival is exposure, and in the 1990s that means television. With the muscle of the NBA behind it, the WNBA landed the best TV deal of any new league in the history of sports. It signed a five-year contract with three networks: NBC, which carries NBA broadcasts; ESPN, which would like to carry NBA broadcasts; and Lifetime, which caters to a female audience. ESPN and Lifetime agreed to televise one prime-time game per week, with NBC carrying games every Saturday afternoon and televising the championship game on August 30.

"This is the first time in history a women's team sports league of any kind secured a national broadcast contract," NBC Sports president Dick Ebersol told reporters when the partnership was announced. "Women's basketball and NASCAR racing over the last three years are the best of the growing sports on the horizon.

"By starting the WNBA a few days after the end of the NBA playoffs, with the promotion and attention of prime time, you can't do better in launching a new league."

The ABL had hoped to sign with ESPN but instead

signed a two-year deal with SportsChannel Regional Network, an emerging cable network that reaches about 16 million homes, no match for NBC and ESPN. By contrast, Lifetime alone reaches 64.7 million homes.

The interest in women's basketball, as evidenced by the battle being pitched by the two leagues and the sponsors eager to tie their products to us, seemed to outsiders like a sudden explosion with no context, like Pet Rocks or Tickle Me Elmo dolls, a fad that would fade as soon as the Olympics was over. It seemed as if we had burst through the arena floor full-grown with agents and cross-over dribbles and Nike commercials. But as those of us on the inside knew, nothing could have been further from the truth. I liked what Donna Lopiano, the executive director of the Women's Sports Foundation and former women's athletic director at the University of Texas, had to say.

"It's not an explosion but the tide coming in," she said. "It's been building over time. You add all of the things up—Title IX, gender equity, television and corporate interest—and you've reached critical mass. This is not an accident in history. This is a major cultural change that I don't see going back."

And we, the USA basketball team, were riding the front edge of the change.

I worried that the pro league debate could cause division among the players. The only time it became an issue was one night during our tour through Australia in May. The NBA in Australia invited the team out to dinner. This caused some consternation among players loyal to the ABL and those on the fence. The dinner seemed to become a symbol of choosing one league over the other. I called a team meeting.

"This is one of those things that can divide a team if we let it," I told them. "So I'm going to put it to you this way: This is a free dinner. If you want to go, fine. If you don't want to go, fine. It's not a statement that you're for one league or another."

Most went to the dinner.

The expectations of the sponsors, the players, the new pro leagues, the public—they all coalesced into the frustration and heightened sense of urgency that came pouring out after the Old Dominion game.

There's an old wives' tale that bad things come in threes. If the Old Dominion game was the first, the plane trip to Arkansas the following day, December 10, was the second. It was the trip from hell. USA Basketball had an arrangement for tickets on United Airlines, so we were at the airline's mercy as far as routing. We flew north to Chicago. Changed planes. Then west to Denver. Changed planes. Then back east to Tulsa, Oklahoma. Then we rode a bus two hours across the border to Fayetteville. We got to bed at about 1 A.M. I woke up so sick with the flu that Renee had to coach the game against Arkansas two days later as I sat on the bench as her assistant. In the pregame talk, she stood up in the locker room as the players waited to hear her final instructions and pearls of inspiration.

"OK, you guys, let's play defense!" she said. "Let's go!"

The players cracked up. "That's it?" they asked.

Renee did a great job during the game, which we won 101–53.

The players were in a good mood, looking forward to the Christmas break. After Purdue and Ohio State, we'd have 11 days off for the holidays. We were happy, too, because Dawn was given clearance to practice with us for the first time since her surgery.

This was the final bad event in our set of three, and it was the worst.

In Dawn's first practice, we were scrimmaging a team of men, as we usually did. Somehow Dawn fell. She put out her hand to break the fall, and it smacked against the floor at an awkward angle. Just from the way she held it when she stood up, I thought she had broken it. She didn't have it X-rayed, though. Instead she had the trainer wrap her hand in bandages, hoping it was just a severe bruise. By the time we reached Columbus a few days later, the pain had become intense. Dawn flew back to her doctor in Virginia for an examination. Sure enough, the hand was broken. Dawn was going to be out another four weeks.

The news hit us hard. We had been so excited to have Dawn back. The team loved her. But maybe there was a silver lining. The broken hand would give her knees more time to heal. The little red doll's coat returned to our bench.

We beat Purdue 90–50, then bused into Columbus late the same night. Stanford had played top-ranked Tennessee that day, a huge game for Stanford, and I bolted to my room to find out the outcome. I turned on CNN Headline News and waited for the score to appear on the ticker tape that scrolls across the bottom of the screen.

"Stanford 90, Tennessee 72."

I wasn't sure I saw it right. Eighteen points?

The score scrolled by again. It was right. Stanford had blown them out. I called Renee right away and then Nell. "Did you see the Stanford-Tennessee score?"

Then I called Stanford and caught the team while it was still in the locker room. Everyone was so excited. I wanted to be there with them. I missed watching them and talking with them. I was so happy for the players and for Amy I could hardly sleep that night.

Returning to Ohio State was like returning home. I still had so many great friends there, including Nancy Darsch, who would be one of my Olympic assistants. The 8,600 fans who came to the game gave me a warm reception. At halftime, the school honored the 1985 OSU squad, the last of four Big Ten champions I coached there. So I got to see many of my former players, and Amy, who was my assistant on that team, flew in for the tribute. It meant a lot to me. There aren't many monuments erected for women. We don't celebrate women's successes very often. So it was great to hear the ovation for a group of women who hadn't been on the court in ten years, yet were still appreciated.

We won 118–49, hitting 13 of 19 three-point attempts.

After the game, the players gave me, Renee, and Nell all the collector's trading cards of the players and coaches in a frame. I think Teresa had been in charge of the gifts, and she put Ruthie's card next to mine in the frame, knowing the special respect I had for Ruthie.

We had been together as a team for three months. We had won 16 straight games. We had faced problems and worked them out. We had worked harder than any of us had ever worked. The team was growing very close.

"This is one of the best teams I've ever been on as far as relationships go, and that's off the court," Lisa told a reporter. "Not only do we have the best players in the world, but we have really good people. And I'm not just saying that. I love all my teammates. I think we have a closeness that carries over to the court. We're looking out for each other. You can't mess with one without messing with the other. That helps us, especially on defense."

By Christmas, I was feeling that closeness included the coaches on some level. When you're a coach, you're never one of the gang. You're in charge of the gang. You have different people in different orbits around you. Some are closer and some are farther away, but they all have to be in the constellation somewhere. The players' Christmas presents somehow seemed to pull us coaches into their tightening circle—if not all the way in, then at least to a comfortable inner sphere.

I flew to Florida, where my family was spending the holidays. Mostly I slept. I didn't realize how exhausted I was until I allowed myself to rest. But the day after Christmas, having spent four days in Florida, I was on another plane to another hotel to meet the Stanford team in Lubbock, Texas. In the airport, I picked up a newspaper and read a list of the top 95 sports stories of the year. Rebecca was listed as number 11.

I enjoyed working with her and with Carla, too, but I still wasn't convinced they gave us the firepower we needed inside. We needed a larger, fiercer presence at the post position. I felt very conflicted. On the one hand, I was investing myself psychologically and emotionally in the players on the team. Yet in the back of my mind, I knew they might not make the final cut—and, in fact, I was the one who was pushing to make the changes. I was scheduled to talk with the USA Basketball selection committee after the first of the year, and I planned to beat the Horse yet again. I hoped the committee would listen. I felt we'd be stronger with different players, Val Whiting maybe, or Venus Lacey or Kara Wolters or Shanda Berry. I hoped to get a sense at the meeting who the committee had in mind as the 12th player.

I vented my frustrations to my close friends in basketball—Amy, Ceal Barry, Renee, Nell, Nancy Darsch—and to Carol Callan, but I said nothing to the press. At least not then. My mouth would eventually get the better of me, as it has been known to do. I worked hard all year to protect the team from distractions and divisiveness, and then I went and caused the biggest controversy of all. But that wouldn't happen for another few months.

I caught up with Stanford in Lubbock on December 26 and watched it lose to Texas Tech. I was beginning to think I was bad luck.

I spent the next few days back home in California before joining the national team in Alabama on January 2 to play Auburn, Ruthie's alma mater. More than 150 of Ruthie's family and friends, including most of her 19 siblings and 67 nieces and nephews, rode in four buses from McClain, Mississippi, for the game. Her brother James and sister

Mae Ola sang the national anthem, but Ruthie was too nervous to join in. Ruthie's family sang and chanted the whole game.

"Ruthie Bolton's in the house," they'd say in a sing-song chant. Then: "Lisa Leslie's in the house." And so on with every player. Their voices were so beautiful and energetic, I found myself listening to the chants and songs. We won 98–46, building our record to 18–0. Afterward, I went into the stands to meet Ruthie's family and tell them what a great representative she was of their family and of her country.

We had another three days off, which I spent skiing. I kept thinking as I glided down the slopes of the Rockies with my brother that if I ever won the lottery I'd leave coaching and ski the rest of my life. One of the great perks of the USA coaching job was time to ski. During the college season I rarely had a day to escape to the mountains. I made use of every minute, though I actually had no choice. My brother Nicky skis this way: He's the first one on the lift at 8:30 in the morning and the last one off at night. He doesn't take his boots off for lunch.

"Nicky," I'd tell him, "I'm 42 years old. Take your hat off. Please relax and sit for 30 minutes because I can't go anymore."

We just killed ourselves on those hills. It was the perfect break from basketball, except I had another conference call with the USA Basketball committee. Again I went on record with my concerns about the post position, and again I got no response.

We beat the University of Colorado, 107–24. Everybody got a lot of playing time, which was good. We were about to start facing international opponents, and against them, I would be less democratic about playing time. The best players would play. I wanted to see what, exactly, we had in our starters and top reserves. And I wanted our opponents to see a solid U.S. team. It was a fine line we walked against potential Olympic opponents. We didn't want to show everything we had and give them time to prepare. But we wanted to show them enough to be intimidating, to keep them from gaining too much confidence.

All of us who committed to the USA team knew we were in for challenges and sacrifices: separation from families, grueling workouts, exhausting travel. But even the most dedicated among us couldn't have expected what awaited us on the tour schedule:

Eleven days in Siberia and the Ukraine.

In January.

9

*The price you are willing to pay
will determine the prize you receive.*

We felt as if we had flown to the end of the earth. We left Colorado at 4 in the afternoon of January 13 and arrived in Ekaterinburg at 10:30 the night of the 14th. The plane descended onto a dusky landing strip, pulling up beside a terminal that seemed to be nothing more than four sheets of corrugated tin and a roof. We made our way through the snow and into the dingy building to collect our luggage. Czar Nicholas and Alexandra met their deaths in Ekaterinburg. The place looked well-suited for the deed.

From the gloom of the airport emerged a woman in a floor-length fur coat and fur hat. With a Russian accent right out of the movies, she introduced herself as Natasha—what else? She called everybody "dahling."

As we left the airport for the hotel, I asked the temperature.

"Oh, 25 or 30, dahling," she replied.

I calculated Celsius to Fahrenheit and knew she couldn't be right. "Wouldn't that be over 80 degrees?"

"No, 25 or 30 *below*," she said, smiling.

I didn't want to calculate what that was in Fahrenheit.

Nearly everyone on the team had traveled extensively and knew to bring toilet paper and food. Everyone had her own stash, and USA Basketball also brought food for the team that our manager, Lori Phelps, rationed out: 72 packs of gum, 37 bags of assorted sweets, 20 boxes of crackers, 20 rolls of toilet paper, 19 jars of peanut butter, 15 different boxes of cookies, ten boxes each of graham crackers and breakfast foods, nine boxes of toaster pastries, seven packages of chips and canned cheese, six jars of jelly, five air fresheners, four containers of laundry detergent, and one box of powdered milk.

I carried my own supply of powdered milk, which doesn't sound very exciting, but everybody was pounding on my door for milk for their cereal in the mornings and for their macaroni and cheese in the evenings.

The hotel stood across the street from the Uralmash heavy-machinery company, which sponsored Club Uralmash, the team we would play three times during our stay in Siberia. We had been told by the American embassy that crime was on the rise, but we still were taken aback when a guard padlocked the gate in front of the hotel after we entered. I wondered how we would get out in an emergency. Jump out our windows, I supposed, but when I got to the room, I saw iron grids over all the windows. If there was a fire, we were dead.

The night after our arrival, we played our first game against Club Uralmash. Several of the Uralmash players were also on the Russian Olympic team, so it was helpful to see them. The game was in a freezing gym on a floor that had been laid over an ice rink. It was so cold that our players wore gloves and jackets when they weren't in the game. Uralmash went into a zone to shut down our inside game. They clogged up the lane under the basket, thwarting our attempts to pass the ball inside to Lisa or Katrina. So Katy did what she was on the team to do: She hit threes. With so many of their players defending the basket, Katy could spring free for open shots from the outside. I had been thinking that Katy might be on the bubble, a player the committee might choose to replace, if it replaced anybody. But she would be so valuable if we faced the Russians, who play a lot of zone defense. When her shot is on, nobody is better from the three-point line. We won handily, despite monstrous jet lag.

We were supposed to scrimmage the next day against a team of men and then play Uralmash again that night. But when we arrived at the gym where we would be playing, I saw that it had a tartan floor, which has a rubbery surface. I had seen tartan floors tear up players' knees, and I wasn't about to put our team at risk, no matter how much money we had spent to travel here. I told Carol we couldn't play. By late afternoon, Club Uralmash had found another small gym with a wooden floor, where we played our two remaining games against them.

After every game, I talked with Russian reporters who kept asking the same two questions: Where is your center? Where are the men?

I understood the first question better than anyone. We had no one the size of Russia's six-foot-eight-inch Marina Bourmistrova or the Ukraine's six-foot-seven-inch Elena Mateeva.

But the second question stumped me.

"What do you mean, men? This is a women's basketball team," I said.

"How can a team travel all this way without men?" they asked. "How can a team be coached without men?"

I took the questions in stride, chalking them up to cultural differences, but eventually the questions got old. They went on and on, everywhere we went in the former Soviet Union. It was surprising to me. Their women athletes are among the most accomplished in the world, yet they apparently believed the women weren't capable of running the show. The reporters' questions, though, served to heighten my enjoyment of a clinic we gave one afternoon to the coaches in the area, nearly all men. It was still fairly new for them to see women as coaches, so I felt Nell, Renee, and I gave them something to think about. And maybe we gave women players in the country a bit of inspiration: If American women can coach, so can we.

The most exhausting part of the trip was not the playing but the partying. These people toasted everything: our arrival, the first game, the second game, the third game, our departure. So Carol and I made a pact. I would talk and she would drink. We had Carol sit at the head table with the dignitaries because she'd eat just about anything. Ruthie would, too, for the most part. The rest of us spent every banquet moving caviar and brown meat around our plates so we appeared to have eaten some, then filled ourselves with oranges and apples from a bowl at the center of the table. After one dinner, our hosts and the Uralmash team wanted to learn the latest American dances, so our players sang and danced and fended off the advances of old Russian men. Nell was especially popular. She was blond, trim, and outgoing. The men wouldn't leave her alone, pulling her back onto the dance floor every time she tried to sit down. The players were merciless in their teasing. On the plane back to the States a week later, Jennifer told the flight attendant that Nell had become engaged in Russia. The flight attendant happily announced the news to the entire plane, which came as quite a surprise to Nell. Her pique at Jennifer diminished considerably, though, when the attendant brought her a bottle of champagne to celebrate the upcoming nuptials.

I had worried all year about complacency as we blew out one college team after another. Traveling to Siberia, as inconvenient as it was, turned out to be just the antidote. Our third and last game in Siberia presented us with our first test. As I watched the game unfold, I knew that how we responded would go a long way toward revealing who we were as a team.

We were down 12 or 13 points in the second half, the first time we had trailed any team that late in the game. The officiating was atrocious, full of blatant hometown calls. We got called for seven three-second violations in the second half alone. (A three-second violation is called when a player on offense stands in the lane—the area from the free-throw line to the baseline—for three seconds or more.) Nell and Renee were getting more and more irritated, and I saw the players showing signs of frustration.

I called a time-out.

"Are you going to let them steal this from you?" I asked the players in the sideline huddle. "OK, get out of the lane. No one in the lane. We need to get our defense going so we can force turnovers and make things happen off the defensive end of the floor."

Here we were, having traveled halfway around the world; we were tired, we'd been eating macaroni and cheese every night, and the game really didn't mean anything, except to prolong or break our winning streak. Jennifer had contracted food poisoning over there and had spent an afternoon hooked up to an intravenous tube. Katrina was bothered by a hip problem. Rebecca had not traveled much and was taken aback by the conditions.

"This is what it would be like to play over here professionally?" she asked on the bus one day.

"If you play your cards right," Katy replied, "you'll never have to."

In the second half against Uralmash, the team plugged on in workmanlike fashion, chipping away at the Russians' lead, swallowing the indignation that rose with every awful call. When we won the game by 12 points, we felt something we had not felt after any previous game: true satisfaction. We expected to win the college games and were disappointed if we didn't win by at least 30 points. This was a game we had to fight for, emotionally and mentally. Nobody gave in to the crybaby stuff. We knew it wouldn't do us any good. The players had shown one another, if they hadn't known already, that they couldn't be rattled.

And I knew, too, that we might see these same officials in the Olympics. You never knew who you were going to get. There was no sense in us going crazy about the officiating and making enemies.

Lisa struggled the entire trip. In one game, she had been called for a foul and simply stopped playing. She couldn't seem to find a way to play through her frustrations. I had seen Lisa do this in college. When Stanford played USC in the regional championship game of the NCAA tournament in 1992, Lisa fouled out in 13 minutes and we won by 20 points. Lisa didn't have a history of carrying a team on her back, the way great players do. So I pulled her out and in subsequent games on the trip, I started Carla, then Rebecca, hoping Lisa would get the message that I needed to see I could count on her.

We flew on a Russian airline to Moscow, where we spent the afternoon and ate at McDonald's, a treat for the team after nearly a week of Siberian food. Then we flew a different Russian airline to Kiev that night. I prayed a lot on those flights. I kept thinking about the stories I had heard about Russian pilots drinking and about a pilot letting his kid fly the plane and the plane crashing. But we arrived safely in Kiev, where we played Ukraine four times and won each game by an average of 23 points.

We had already scrimmaged with the Ukraine several times in Colorado Springs during training camp. We would play them three more times before the Olympics and scrimmage against them even more. By year's end, the Ukraine players would be like cousins. We would know one another so well that the games would lose their spark. As the Olympics drew closer, I hoped we wouldn't play the Ukraine for the gold medal. We needed a fresh opponent so we wouldn't get complacent. We wanted Brazil or Russia, Brazil because it had beaten us in the World

Championships and Russia because it had won the gold medal in 1992.

On the way home, we flew through Frankfurt, where our flight was delayed for four hours while we sat on the plane. I was getting hungry and had peanut butter and crackers in my bag, but no knife to spread the peanut butter.

"You want a knife?" the man next to me asked.

"That would be great," I said.

He pulled out a huge switchblade. I hesitated, then took it because I was starving. What if the flight attendant saw me wielding this enormous knife?

"Thank you," I said, returning the knife to my seatmate when I had finished. I kept wondering how he had ever slipped it through the metal detector. And what else had slipped through along with it? That was just what I needed: more things to worry about on the plane.

Carla McGhee had gotten off the plane and returned with an armful of McDonald's food for her teammates. I passed the time playing Scrabble with our team doctor, a tiny woman who had been a basketball player at Virginia. She beat me three games in a row. It was only Scrabble, but I was mad. Losing just makes me more competitive. When we got home, I bought a Scrabble strategy book and learned all the two-letter words. Three months later, she would travel with us to Australia. I'd be ready.

When we got to Chicago, where we each took our separate flights home, I saw on the CNN ticker tape that Stanford was down by 10 to Pac-10 rival Washington on Stanford's home court. I was a wreck on the plane to San Francisco, wondering about the outcome. When Amy picked me up at the airport after midnight, I tentatively asked how it went.

"Oh, we won," she said.

It turned out the score I saw had been for the men's Stanford team.

Stanford had just two losses and had been ranked in the top ten for the whole season.

I recapped our trip to Amy, returning, inevitably, to the Horse.

Lisa had played poorly in Russia, Katrina was hobbled with chronic hip pain, and Rebecca, in her first international games, had shot a team low 33 percent from the field for 3.5 points per game. What were we supposed to do at the post position if we had the same situation at the Olympics? I told Amy I felt I was being sent to the firing squad with the post players I had. Our 25–0 record meant nothing. The college teams and Uralmash and even the Ukraine weren't of the caliber we would be facing in the Olympics. At the time we played, the Ukraine didn't have all its top players, some of whom were spending the winter playing on foreign teams. People didn't understand how good the Olympic teams would be. Brazil was the defending world champion. China was the runner-up at the World Championships. And the Ukraine, Italy, and Russia finished one-two-three at the European Championships.

The American public and press looked at our record and figured we had the gold locked up. There was so much talk about how dominant we were, how we were like the men's Dream Team. I knew otherwise, but I couldn't figure out how to get the committee to see what I saw.

We had only two days at home before gathering again in Louisiana to play Louisiana Tech, where Nell was an assistant coach. She already was wondering if she would be returning to Tech when the Olympics were over. She had made a break by joining our staff and could never go back. She was ready for a head coaching job, and during our travels she got messages on her answering machine from different schools, asking if she'd be interested in interviewing with them. By the spring, she had taken the job at Purdue, inheriting a team in disarray: The coach had been fired and was threatening a lawsuit, and players had transferred to other schools. I knew Nell was up to the challenge. Smart and energetic, she works hard and pushes her players, but manages to have fun. She had learned a lot from Leon Barmore at Louisiana Tech and had gained confidence with the Olympic team. She was ready to move on.

At the hotel before the game, Steve Weiberg of *USA Today* arrived for a scheduled 4 o'clock interview. I was still obsessing about the post players, and I spilled my guts. I guess I was so frustrated I didn't know what else to do. I didn't know how to go about getting what I wanted. It didn't seem like anything was working. So I told Steve everything I had shared with Amy a few nights before, pointing out our weaknesses and mentioning Rebecca and Nikki by name. I didn't mean for the comments to be personal. I was just trying to get across the message that we needed to get the job done and I didn't care who did it. Whatever it took to win the gold, that's what we had to do.

I didn't think about how the comments would look in stark black and white in the newspaper. I didn't think about how it might affect Rebecca or Nikki or anyone else on the team. I was so focused on the goal of winning, I didn't always consider the nuances and layers of the big picture, how we weren't just this isolated team functioning in a vacuum. So I left the interview unconcerned about what the reporter might write or how it might be perceived. I had no clue about the trouble I had just created for myself, trouble that would blow up in my face two weeks later.

Louisiana Tech, a perennial power in women's basketball, was ranked number two in the nation when we arrived to play. They had sold out all 7,692 seats and then sold another 1,000 standing-room tickets the day of the game. Nearly 50 media passes were issued. The town of Ruston was so excited about the game that 2,000 people came out just to watch us practice the night before the game.

No college opponent had come within 24 points of beating us. Yet at halftime, we were tied with Louisiana Tech, 40–40. The crowd was thunderous, anticipating a huge upset. We couldn't rebound, giving Tech second and third chances at the basket. We were shooting absolute bricks and air balls as the players' hands and eyes adjusted to the smaller college ball, one and a half inches smaller in circumference than the international ball.

And Tech was on fire, hustling, playing great defense, hitting the boards. They had a great perimeter game, and they played smart basketball, patiently maneuvering for the open shot. I knew our players were tired from the trip, that they didn't quite have their legs under them. Because we had been delayed in Frankfurt, most of the players had missed their connections out of Chicago on Thursday night and didn't arrive at their own homes until Friday, January 26. They had to leave for Ruston Sunday to be ready for the game on Tuesday.

We were behind most of the second half until we went on an 8–0 run to take a 66–61 lead. We had gone into a zone, and Tech's shooting efficiency in the second half dropped to 29 percent. Lisa saved us, scoring 30 points, ten in the final ten minutes, and pulling down 12 rebounds. We won, 85–74.

For the first time, a team outrebounded us: Tech had 45, we had 44. For the first time against a college team, we trailed in the second half. The game was a great wake-up call, especially with regard to our rebounding and defense.

After the game, I wasn't angry. I understood how tired they all were. I knew Katrina was now nursing a slight ankle injury, Dawn had just returned and was rusty, Sheryl was hurting. So in the locker room I mostly talked about Lisa. I had considered not starting her, but decided against it because sitting her was not in the best interest of the team. But the way she had played in Russia really bothered me. I needed to see Lisa step up and carry the team when it was necessary, the way Katrina could always do, and I hadn't seen much of that.

But she did it against Louisiana Tech. I spent most of my postgame talk complimenting Lisa, telling her in front of the team that it was great that we could depend on her.

We were 27–0 going into our final college game against Texas Tech, Sheryl's alma mater, in Lubbock. We practiced nearby at the gym at Sheryl's old community college, where she had played for two years. I thought it was a closed practice, but when we showed up, 2,000 people were there. My heart sank. We had an open practice in Louisiana, where we couldn't get any work done, and now this. It was loud. You couldn't hear yourself, much less deliver instructions to the players. There were a few times during the tour that I felt I was losing it, and this was one of them. When was I ever going to get any work done with the team?

I think some of my emotion was born of fatigue. And some from being reminded in Russia this wasn't just a tour around America with a really good basketball team, a Harlem Globetrotters–type show. The Olympics wasn't just a fictional goal at the end of some elaborate exercise. It was really going to happen.

My spirits were not buoyed the following night when Texas Tech's six-foot-one-inch post player scored at will against us. We were going to face six-seven, six-eight players in the Olympics, and this six-one player was tearing us up. We still won easily, 98–61, with Sheryl leading us with 19 points and six rebounds.

The players returned home for a week before we would reconvene in Dallas for the NBA's All-Star Weekend, where the NBA marketing folks had booked our players to play in celebrity games, sign autographs, and make appearances. I flew to Colorado Springs instead of home to ski with my brother in Vail. So I was blissfully unaware of the *USA Today* article that hit the stands. I only occasionally read about the team or myself in the paper. It's something else I picked up from *Lincoln on Leadership*. Carol called me in Vail to tell me about it. The article centered on my opinion that we might be better off with players with more international experience than Rebecca and Nikki and that we weren't as good as everyone thought. I sensed from Carol that USA Basketball was not thrilled with my comments.

"OK," I told Carol. "We'll talk about it when I get back."

When I read the article, I knew Steve Weiberg had quoted me accurately. In fact, he could have made it a lot worse. He printed only part of what I actually told him. I thought he wouldn't use names, however. So I was surprised and embarrassed that Rebecca's and Nikki's names appeared. I've always felt strongly that a coach shouldn't communicate to a player through the newspaper, just as I wouldn't want my bosses to send messages to me through the press. The comments were born of frustration and my drive to win.

When I look back on it, I wish I could have been more relaxed about the team, not worried so much about every little detail, not consumed by every possibility of failure. I lived the whole year in constant anxiety. It was a great diet: I couldn't eat and I worked out every day. I was in the best shape of my life. But maybe the fact that I couldn't relax helped the team in the long run. My worries kept me focused, and I think they kept the team on edge just enough to stave off complacency.

USA Basketball called Rebecca and Nikki at home and reassured them of their value to the team. I didn't catch up with them until the All-Star Weekend a few days later. I tried to put myself in their position, and I hoped they could put themselves in mine. I apologized as soon as I saw them.

"I don't think this is fair that you had to read this in

USA Today," I told each player separately. "If I have something to say, I'll tell you directly."

Both players handled the controversy graciously. There was nothing in the paper that they didn't already know, but they would have preferred not to have their shortcomings made public, and I couldn't blame them.

I saw NBA commissioner David Stern at a party at the Six Flags Over Texas amusement park. He made a casual remark in conversation about the article, not condemning but letting me know he was paying attention. Obviously, he wasn't thrilled with the article. The NBA was doing the best job it could to market the team, and here I was second-guessing who was on it.

I suppose there was a naiveté on my part as far as the marketing went. All I thought about was, How can we beat China? How can we beat Russia? What about Brazil and Cuba? I was always thinking about matchups, what players we needed to beat each opponent. I rarely thought about how the public perceived the team, and then only in the context of how our team could boost interest and appreciation of women's basketball overall. Even at that, I still believed the best way to market women's basketball was to put the best possible team on the floor and, of course, win. My job was to make sure we won.

Despite the controversy, I enjoyed the All-Star Weekend because I got to talk with great players and coaches. I chatted for about 30 minutes with the great former Boston Celtics player John Havlicek, whom I grew up watching on television. I had always admired how he hustled and how he was so team-oriented. I talked X's and O's for three hours with Jimmy Cleamons, who was then an assistant with the Chicago Bulls. It was funny listening to him critique players: This one doesn't do this, this one doesn't go there, this one needs to do this. And he was talking about Michael Jordan, Scottie Pippen, and Dennis Rodman!

"Yeah, right, Jim," I said, laughing, though I understood. Coaches focus on the flaws no one else notices.

The day after we returned from the All-Star Game, the Olympic basketball draw was announced. We were in Pool B along with Australia, Cuba, South Korea, the Ukraine, and Zaire. Our first game in the preliminary rounds would be against Cuba on July 21. Then we'd play the Ukraine, Zaire, Australia, and South Korea, in that order.

Brazil was in Pool A. The earliest we could face them, assuming we both won our preliminary games, would be in the quarterfinals.

The thud of Carla's head against the floor stopped everyone in the gym like a gunshot. We were scrimmaging against men in Colorado Springs in mid-February, and Carla was defending one of them on a fast-break. He inadvertently bumped her from behind, and she lost her balance. Carla's head bounced against the court like a bowling ball. It made a sickening thump and then it thumped again. The players rushed to her, and our trainer, Ed Ryan, asked for someone to call 911. Carla was still conscious and clearly terrified. Every day on the court, she had to face down the fear that she would get hit in the face and head, recalling her nightmarish car accident. The paramedics stabilized her head and neck. They feared she had cracked her skull.

At the hospital, she was diagnosed with a concussion, and returned the next day in a neck brace and dark sunglasses to keep out the light. Light aggravated the headache that pounded inside her skull. Doctors said Carla would be fine, though she couldn't join us on the trip to Hawaii and China, which began the following week.

It seemed that somebody was always getting hurt. Dawn had had knee surgery, then injured her hand. Teresa had knee problems early on. Katrina sprained her ankle and was bothered by hip and knee problems. Then came Carla's concussion. And there were plenty more injuries ahead of us. We were completely healthy for only two weeks the entire year. Luckily, they were the two weeks of the Olympic Games.

Des Flood returned to Colorado Springs in late February to help with our shooting before we left for China. Now that we were finished with the college tour, we could practice exclusively with the big ball. I had not wanted to do shooting drills with the small ball, but now we could immerse ourselves in shooting, and there was no one better than Des to lead us. But I'd heard he hadn't been feeling well.

"I know you haven't been in good health, but are you feeling better?" I asked when I called him in California.

"Oh, yeah!" he said.

"We need some tuneups with the big ball. Can you come out?"

"Absolutely, Tara. I'm there."

Everyone was so happy to see him, though he seemed frailer than when we had seen him in October. One day Lisa came up to me in the dining hall.

"I'm worried about Des," she said. "He doesn't look good. I'm not sure he's feeling OK."

There was construction going on at the training center and Des apparently had helped a wheelchair athlete up a makeshift ramp. When I went to the gym to have a look, he seemed to be breathing normally again. When the players had left, I sat down with him.

"Lisa's real worried about you," I told him. "What's going on?"

"I'm OK. I think I just need to rest a little."

Then he shook his head slowly.

"Tara, I feel so bad. I rooted against Lisa Leslie for four years while she was at USC. And she's such a nice girl."

I worried that the cold weather was too much for him, and I questioned whether I should have asked him to come, though the players drew so much from him. After

Lisa expressed her concerns, he sometimes excused himself from shooting sessions to sit down or rest in his room.

He flew with us to Los Angeles, where he lived; we would continue on to Honolulu. I gave him a card on the plane, thanking him for all his help. All the players had signed a card for him, too.

"No, Tara," he said when he read the cards, "you all have given me something really special."

During our four-day stop in Honolulu, Sheryl suddenly grabbed her head in a scramble on the floor during practice. Katrina apparently had hit her leg against Sheryl's head, though Katrina didn't even know she had touched her. The players were totally aghast when Sheryl returned from the hospital in a neck brace and told us she had a concussion. She had suffered a concussion during tryouts for the 1994 World Championship team, which evidently made her more susceptible to another one. Like Carla, she couldn't go on to China. Her teammates descended like vultures, vying for her food stash for China.

We'd have to play eight games in China without Carla or Sheryl. But we had brought former Stanford player Val Whiting with us, so at least we had ten players. The committee was beginning to get serious about choosing the 12th player, and even though Val had been told the China trip was not a tryout, she knew better. How she played in China would either keep her as a candidate or eliminate her. I didn't envy her position. She had only a few days to learn our plays, though she was familiar with some of them from her Stanford days. Val is really smart, so the mental part wasn't difficult for her. But she wasn't in great shape, and she really didn't play the position we needed. She was six feet, three inches tall, not tall enough to be effective against the post players we faced internationally.

The Women's Invitational Basketball Tournament in China included four teams—us, China, South Korea, and Cuba—and would be played in three different cities over eight days. Our first game, in a place called Haikou, was against Cuba, our opening opponent in the Olympic Games. We had played Cuba in the World Championships qualifier in Brazil, and it had been such a tough game that I toasted our victory with a drink afterward, and I don't drink.

We beat them in Haikou by 13 points. There was something about the Cuban team that clicked with us. Maybe it was because Cuba was the only other team at the tournament that had black players. Or maybe it was the respect we felt for how well they played despite such meager resources. They didn't play dirty as some other teams did. They had one great player, their six-feet-six-inch center, Yamilet Martinez. They were very quick, very athletic. But they didn't seem happy. Their coach, I gathered, was pretty harsh. He didn't want his players fraternizing with ours, but he soon gave that up as useless. Lisa talked to their players in Spanish and found out how little clothing they had. Our players gathered up extra T-shirts, sweats, shoes, and even jog bras and delivered them to the Cuban players.

We had to play China next. A Chinese television crew came to our practice and videotaped me holding a broomstick high in the air near the basket. I was simulating for our players what it would be like to face China's six-foot-eight-inch, 220-pound center, Zheng Hai-Xin, and apparently the Chinese crew got a kick out of it. In the game, Katrina played great against Zheng, and we won by 12 points.

Everywhere we went in China, I'd run with Carol and Nell. People on bikes would stare as we passed. One time I saw a police car speeding down a country road toward us with its siren blaring.

"That's our escort," I joked.

But sure enough, he passed and made a sharp U-turn right behind us. He doused the siren but kept on the flashing lights. He stopped traffic at every intersection so we could pass without stopping. If we weren't attracting enough attention as three Caucasian women running in shorts and tank tops, the police ensured that no one in town missed the unusual sight. In the cities, we knew we risked our lives with every run. The biggest vehicle always rules: If you're in a bus, you go where you want. If you're in a car, you go where you want until you come up against a bus. If you're on a bike, you're in trouble. And if you're on foot, say your prayers.

We beat Cuba again, this time by 21 points. Then, against South Korea, Rebecca came up big, scoring 24 points. She would lead us in scoring again—with 19 points—against South Korea two days later. I was excited about Rebecca's performances. We really needed her to step up and play hard, and this was the first time I felt she had really helped us in a game.

Dawn was also playing well in her first games since her injuries. With Sheryl gone, I moved Teresa into Sheryl's slot and started Dawn at the point. Dawn was spectacular in some of these games. She can pass the ball without looking and put it right on the money. She made a huge difference in the lineup, even though her lateral quickness was still not 100 percent.

China played us tough in all three games in which we faced them. During one game, I put Rebecca, Lisa, and Katrina in at the same time. We had been struggling, so I was trying to figure out how to counter China's size. We had never played all three big players together because at practice, if we used all of them on one team, who would play on the other? And when I tried it in the scrimmages against the men, it hadn't been effective. But it worked beautifully against China. Lisa played the "three," or small forward. She could shoot from the outside, so we kicked her out there for three-pointers. And because she's so tall, she could see the floor well enough from the wing to make great passes. Val wasn't in great shape and so she didn't play her best. She hadn't helped her chances of being chosen as the 12th player.

None of the teams in the tournament showed everything it had. There was a lot of sandbagging going on. For example, at the Olympics we would pick up a full-court press, but we hadn't even started to show any of that yet. We would run a half-court trap, but we hadn't started that yet, either. We didn't run many set plays or many different out-of-bounds plays. But in one game against Cuba over in China, we needed a set play to win. Cuba was tearing us up inside, and might have won if they had the physical conditioning, nutrition, and rest that we had. They always looked tired because they never stopped traveling. They played wherever anyone paid them to play. They played us to a three-point game, and only a set play for Teresa sealed the 81–78 victory for us.

Usually, as I said, we showed little of our arsenal. I wanted to make sure that when we unveiled our strategies for a test run against potential Olympic opponents, I could get a video and they couldn't. So when China came to scrimmage in Colorado Springs later in the year, we put in all the tricks we hadn't shown before. We videotaped it, and they didn't.

I figured all the teams were sandbagging when we played them, but at the Olympics, I never saw anything new from China or from Australia. Brazil was a little more crafty, but not a lot. Russia, though, brought in a whole new boatload of players for the Olympics, making it difficult for opponents to prepare.

When we weren't playing or practicing, we kept close to our hotels in China. There seemed to be only two TV stations: one that had sumo wrestling and one that had cricket. We knew we had been there too long when we began recounting matches over meals.

After our last game, Jennifer hung a sign on her hotel room door that read, "Jen Chu's Coffee and Espresso Bar." As teammates filtered in, Jennifer served up vanilla macadamia-nut coffee she had bought in Hawaii. Soon all the players were in the room, the music was playing, and the women were sprawled across the floor and on the furniture, braiding and unbraiding one another's hair.

I knew how tough it would be to drop and add players to the roster. Intellectually, I understood changes were not likely to happen, but I still held out hope. They had become like 11 sisters. In their minds, they had been through hell, and the shared experience drew them closer together. In Hawaii, Rebecca had opened up to Jennifer, sharing all the doubts and hurt feelings she covered so well with her easy smile. Lisa had helped Dawn through her injuries. Instead of getting on one another's nerves, as I had feared they might, they nurtured each other. I didn't know it at the time, but when rumors surfaced later on that one or two players might be replaced, some of the players talked of staging a walkout. If one player was taken off the team, they would all threaten to leave. That was how deeply they felt about one another.

I still wanted bigger, more experienced players at the post, but I admired their loyalty to one another. Everybody on the team would be changed by our journey together, and perhaps I would be changed as much as anyone. I was beginning to believe that their commitment to the team could overcome their physical shortcomings. Nell and Renee had always believed this, and they kept telling me so. But my analytical mind craved numbers and experience and results, quantifiable measurements of success. Heart? Yes, of course, I believed in heart. But heart couldn't make your players tall or fast.

Yet I was beginning to understand the power of feelings and of being positive, of tending to your players' souls as well as their minds and bodies. I'd watch Nell and Renee with the players every day and see how well they communicated. There was a stream of pure energy coming from Nell and Renee all year long. They loved the players so deeply that the players responded in kind. They would have done anything for one another. As important as X's and O's are, the players don't really care what you know.

They just want to know that you care. I'm not so sure feelings are such an important element on a men's team, but for women, how they feel truly matters. I was coming to the belief that how they feel can dictate how well they play.

It's easier, obviously, to be close to the players as an assistant coach. Somebody has to deliver the unwelcome critique sometimes and somebody has to push, and that's always going to be the head coach: "I love you, but get your ass back on defense!" But I knew I was changing, if only by small degrees, during the year. I saw, through Nell and Renee, that being positive and understanding did not necessarily mean you were soft or letting them slack off.

I thought about how I'd be a different coach when I returned to Stanford. Not completely different, but maybe a little lighter, a little more aware of the subtleties around me.

We took our one great outing on the last day of our trip, visiting the Great Wall. I had expected the wall to be out in the middle of nowhere, but you drive down a couple streets and suddenly there it is. Along the wall stood a line of vendors and restaurants, all with proprietors screeching, "Hello-hello-hello!" Several of the players bought fur hats for $2 each (I still regret not buying one). I bought a book about the Great Wall, and over lunch at Kentucky Fried Chicken—none of us could face the duck's feet and other delicacies our Chinese hosts had so graciously served us all week—we talked about whether building the wall was a fair use of manpower for so many years.

Amy picked me up at the airport and said she had bad news.

"Des passed away."

I couldn't speak. I felt a rush of guilt. Had he gotten sick because it was so cold in Colorado? Should we have sent him home right away when Lisa raised her concerns? I broke down. The tears poured uncontrollably. My grandparents had died when I was too young to feel the full impact, so Des was the first person close to me who had died. The players didn't know yet. I would see them ten days later in Charlotte, where we would play the Ukraine (again) on March 28, the night before the Final Four semifinals.

While I was home, Stanford was playing Colorado State at Maples Pavilion in the second round of the NCAA Tournament. Stanford had ended the season unbeaten in the Pac-10 and was ranked third nationally. They had beaten Gambling State in the NCCA first round. At half-time of the Colorado State game, ESPN interviewed me and then kept me on for the rest of the game.

Stanford won and moved on to the regionals in Seattle, where they beat Alabama in overtime to earn a trip to the Final Four in Charlotte. I was so happy for Stanford because even if they lost their next game, they had had a fantastic year. All this was gravy.

For Stanford, the Final Four marked the end of their road. For us, in many ways, it was the beginning. When the college season ended, the focus of the nation's women's basketball fans would shift to us. With our winning streak at 36 games, the press was making us out to be larger than life, some unbeatable force of near mythic proportion. Yet it was the little details, the boring, everyday tasks, that always rose up to humble us—as they did in Fort Mill, South Carolina, in late March.

10

It was 20 minutes before game time in the Fort Mill arena.
I noticed our players weren't warming up. Renee and Nell
tried to distract me so I wouldn't notice.

"What's going on?" I asked.

"Well, there's a mixup," Renee said, "with who was
supposed to pack the socks."

"The players don't have socks?"

"Somebody's out buying some right now."

Five minutes before game time, the socks showed up.
With no real warmup, we played pretty poorly in the first
half against the Ukraine.

These were the nightmarish details that haunted my
thoughts of the Olympic Games. We could work all year
and be thrown off rhythm by a stupid little oversight like
not bringing socks. I remember Stanford's 1992 NCAA
championship game against Western Kentucky. The
higher-seeded team in the tournament always wore white
uniforms, the lower seed wore dark uniforms. We were
the higher seed against Western Kentucky, so we, suppos-

edly, were to wear white. But officials had told us to wear our red uniforms. I asked Amy to double-check. She did.

"We're wearing red," she said.

"Check again."

She did. Red.

When we arrived at the arena for the game, I saw Western Kentucky in red uniforms. I was ready to explode.

"They're wrong," Amy assured me. And they were. But it occurred to me that if we had been wrong, we were dead. Our white uniforms were back at the hotel miles and miles away. From then on, I always made sure we brought both sets of uniforms to every game, just in case.

It was a lesson that would pay off later at the Olympics.

Before the Ukraine game, I had told the team that anyone who drew a foul in the first five minutes of the game was coming out. We couldn't afford to get our starters in foul trouble. The players didn't like that rule at all, but I had noticed in our games against China and South Korea that we were fouling on defense instead of working hard. The Ukraine game was being broadcast on ESPN2, so I knew the rule would get their attention. Nobody wanted to be yanked from a game on national television. And nobody was.

Sheryl was not yet 100 percent, so Dawn continued as our starting point guard, with Teresa in Sheryl's spot. We won, extending the winning streak to 37 games.

Stanford played Georgia in the NCAA semifinals in nearby Charlotte the night after our game, and I watched with my sisters Heidi and Marie, and Marie's husband and their two children. Stanford played well but lost. I went down to the locker room afterward because I wanted to see their reaction to the loss. They had been to the Final Four twice and therefore had high expectations. The players were low, almost angry. The loss had meant a lot to them. They weren't satisfied just to have made it to the Final Four. They had come to win. It was good for me to see that spirit. It was something I could count on when I returned the following year.

We scrimmaged with the Ukraine two days later and nearly lost, managing to squeeze out a two-point victory. I had everyone stay for an hour afterward, and I put them through every defensive drill I knew. Then we loaded up the bus and headed down to Atlanta late that afternoon for a few days of scrimmages against China, and the Ukraine again. We were also playing a national television game against a team of college all-stars.

On the way into the city, a billboard rose from the roadside: "100 Days to the Olympic Games."

A chill went through me. Carol and I always planned the team schedule a couple months in advance, detailing our travel, practices, and appearances for every day. Now we were starting to talk about Atlanta. It was becoming more and more real, like a distant mirage slowly taking solid form as you drew closer.

We practiced at Morehouse College, where we would play our first Olympic game. After practice one day, I finally told them about Des. Ruthie and Lisa took it the hardest; they had been closest to him. The players and coaches gathered in a circle and Ruthie said a prayer for him. We had a very spiritual team, which I had discovered before our first game in October against Athletes in Action. At a brunch with both teams, several of our players led everyone in giving thanks to Jesus Christ. We didn't pray at Stanford. I personally am more comfortable with separating sports from religion. But for the members of this team, religion was a very important part of their lives.

I know it sounds crazy, but as we prayed for Des, I knew we would shoot well at the Olympics. If we needed baskets, we were going to get them. Des would make sure of it. From that moment on, I never worried about our shooting. Even when we shot terribly against Russia in one of our last exhibitions before the Olympics and reporters asked how we planned to remedy the situation, I shrugged. I truly wasn't worried. The shots would drop when we needed them.

The college all-stars had barely practiced together before playing us on April 6. So any time they scored, I went through the roof. Every basket meant a defensive breakdown in my mind. The game was aired by ABC, the first time we had played on noncable television. Also, for the first time, we were playing in front of a home crowd. Against the colleges and in games overseas, we played on our opponents' home courts in front of our opponents' fans. Now we were the home team, finally. With the Final Four over, the focus of women's basketball fans had shifted from the colleges to us. We won, 92–57.

Speculation began about who would be our 12th player. We invited six post players to practice with us in Colorado Springs after the all-star game: six-foot-eight-inch Kara Wolters from Connecticut; six-foot-ten-inch Heidi Gillingham from Vanderbilt; six-foot-three-inch Shanda Berry from Iowa; six-foot-three-inch Val Whiting; six-foot-five-inch Sylvia Crawley from North Carolina; and six-foot-four-inch Venus Lacey.

Right away there was a huge difference in the competitiveness of our practice. Suddenly we had all these centers and forwards challenging our players. It was pretty clear to me that Venus fit our needs best. Kara Wolters was still in college. Heidi wasn't as competitive as I would have liked. Sylvia Crawley played very well—she was quick defensively and ran the floor well, but she wasn't quite strong enough yet for top international competition. I liked Shanda Berry a lot. I had coached her on the World Championships Qualifying team and in the Goodwill Games. I loved her athleticism and her shooting touch. But she wasn't the answer to our problems. We needed a wide-bodied, go-to person on the low block.

We had two purposes for the tryout. One, we needed to choose a player to go to Australia with us. This player would be auditioning, in a sense, for the final 12th spot. We already knew Venus couldn't go because she had a commitment to her pro team in Greece. It was important that we took somebody good. We didn't want Australia, Cuba, or the Ukraine—our opponents in the tournament there—to think we had any weak spots. And two, the USA Basketball subcommittee needed to create a list of alternates. We had to submit a list of 18 names to the International Basketball Federation by May 18. Our Olympic team—and any injury replacements—would have to come from those 18. We'd choose three post players as alternates and three perimeter players.

The committee decided on Sylvia Crawley for the Australia trip. She would join us back in Colorado Springs in about three weeks, after we played China in Philadelphia and gave the players two weeks off.

The Nike mural rose nine stories above Market Street in Philadelphia on the side of a building housing the Le Paradis Beauty Salon on the first floor and nothing else. Dawn's face alone was about six feet tall. In the mural, she was caught in mid-stride, holding the ball as if about to make a pass, her shirt fluttering behind her. On her wrist was a rubber band. No African-American female athlete had ever had a whole building devoted to her image. The mural would be officially unveiled Friday morning, April 12, the day after we arrived. But Dawn drove by it Thursday night. Maybe she needed to see it to believe it was true. When her mother, Estelle, saw it for the first time as she rode the number 33 bus the next day, she broke into tears.

"I never thought it would amount to this," Estelle said later. She had watched Dawn as a child weather the insults and elbows of the neighborhood boys as she proved herself at the Raymond Rosen Housing Project. Boys would tell her to go back to the kitchen. They'd knock her down. But she returned every day. By the time she was 12, she had earned a spot on any pickup team at the recreation center around the corner. As the assistant rec director said, "Dawn had credibility ten blocks that way, ten blocks that way, ten blocks that way and ten blocks that way," pointing north, east, south, and west.

"Words can't really express how I feel right now," Estelle kept saying.

Dawn would talk tough sometimes, about her "peeps"—people—and about guys "packing," or carrying guns. But I never understood what her childhood must have been like until I saw the burned-out buildings and boarded-up stores on the streets that shaped her. She is a survivor, a fighter, which is exactly how she plays.

Dawn still lives in the Philadelphia area and still plays ball at the rec center—now renamed for Hank Gathers—whenever she's home. Nike sponsored a Dawn Staley basketball clinic there the day after we arrived. Neighbors, friends, and old teammates crowded onto the asphalt court to see and talk with Dawn. Some 150 elementary school children, most not born when Dawn left Philly for the University of Virginia, had drawn pictures of her, and six of the drawings were on display that day. Dawn feels a responsibility to the people here, just as Julius Erving did before her. It was his face she saw as a child on a billboard down the block, and it's his example of role-modeling and leadership she has followed, establishing a foundation to help the local children. She is shy by nature, uncomfortable in the spotlight, but she plays a perfect hero: humble, smart, and genuine.

Before the clinic, 200 people showed up for the mural unveiling five miles away. Dawn stood before them and spoke without notes.

"When I see that mural, I see positivity and hope," she said. "Hope for people like me who grew up in the inner city and thought that that was all there was. Life is out there for you. You have to take it."

Later at the rec center, around the corner from the row-house where her mother raised five children, across the street from her elementary school, Dawn tried to articulate what it meant to see a larger-than-life image of herself looking out onto the city she loves so much.

"People look in from the outside and don't understand," she told a *New York Times* reporter. "That's the way of the world. These are my roots. This is all I know: Stand tall, walk the walk, and live the life."

Our game against China at the Philadelphia Palestra was notable mostly for the Chinese coach's tantrums. When their center, Zheng Hai-Xin, picked up two quick fouls and China fell behind 20–9, the coach threw a fit. He pulled his players off the court, claiming the American refs were biased. There were two female officials, and I don't think he was accustomed to that. I heard him make some comment about the women not knowing what they were doing. When he threatened to stop playing, I got a little heated. We had had to put up with horrendous officiating in China. When one of their players fell, we had been called for a foul. Then we'd get knocked down and the refs were silent. Heavy breathing would be a foul for us. But you adjusted. I even told the American officials before the game not to give us any breaks. There were some bad calls, but as a coach you always think the calls against you are bad. The coach for China finally settled down, and we finished the game, an 85–52 victory.

People seemed to be getting more excited about the team as the hype of the Olympics kicked into high gear. The players, if they weren't stars when we began this tour, had become so. They took over a room when they entered. In their posture and their smiles and the almost regal manner in which they carried themselves, they had become the heroines they had never had. At a luncheon for Lifetime television advertisers in the Rainbow Room in New York a few days after the game, the players were introduced one by one. The company executives were like little kids, asking for autographs and posing for pictures. When I flew home that afternoon to attend Stanford's basketball banquet, Sheryl, Rebecca, Teresa, Katrina, and Lisa stuck around to appear on *Regis and Kathie Lee* the next morning. Then they would have two weeks off before leaving for Australia.

I spent most of the two weeks at home in Menlo Park. I tried to relax and rest, but every time I sat down to read a book or watch a movie, a voice in my head told me to get into my office and watch videotape. What if I didn't pick up some out-of-bounds play, some team tendency, some little detail that might mean the difference between winning and losing later on? I did a lot of video work those weeks, mostly breaking down films of Australia.

When the players returned at the end of April, they were in for their greatest challenge of the year, though I didn't know it at the time.

The three Olympic assistants—Marian Washington, Nancy Darsch, and Ceal Barry—were officially joining the team, which meant Nell and Renee were leaving. I was completely unprepared for how difficult the transition would be. Before we left for Australia, we had a party for Nell and Renee, with karaoke music and down-home dishes of macaroni and cheese, cornbread, beans, and ribs. Nikki and Jennifer had scoured the thrift shops for clothes to dress up as Nell and Renee. Nikki walked into the party with a blue blazer and a wig that resembled Renee's hair, and she carried a purse she never set down, just like Renee. Jennifer wore a blond wig, red dress shorts, and a red blazer. They walked and talked like the two coaches, using their catch phrases and imitating their accents and mannerisms. No one laughed harder than Nell and Renee.

As the new coaches watched, the players showered Nell and Renee with funny and poignant gifts. Jennifer gave Nell a miniature red Mercedes, like the one she drove at Louisiana Tech. Teresa and Katrina gave her a mug engraved with the words, "We love you Nellie-poo"—their nickname for her. Teresa also gave her a fifth of vodka to commemorate the Russia trip. They loaded down Renee with hair-care products. They got her every hair-care product you can imagine because she was always giving the players a hard time about how much they fussed over their hair.

I had ordered gold bracelets for Nell and Renee, but they hadn't arrived yet. I get a bit shy in these kinds of situations and so I never shared with the team how I felt. I wanted to tell Nell and Renee in front of the team that my experience with them was one of the most positive things I would take away from the whole year. It was important for the team to hear it from me, but for some reason I didn't step up and say what I was thinking. I was mad at myself afterward. Nell and Renee knew how I felt, but I should have said it out loud, in front of everybody. It sounds like a small thing, but it was one of my few regrets of the year.

When the party broke up, players were crying as they hugged Nell and Renee. I'm sure it wasn't easy for the new coaches to watch, and I didn't envy their position. My intention in having them at the party was to show them what a crucial role the assistants played on the team. But Nancy, Marian, and Ceal must have felt out of place and unwanted, and even by the Olympics, after they had been with the team for three months, I don't think they ever felt completely accepted.

After Nell and Renee left, we practiced for a few days in Colorado Springs. The feel of the team had changed immediately. The players were so accustomed to the nurturing and lightness of Nell and Renee, and here come three head coaches with their steely head-coaching outlook: black and white, bottom line, pull no punches. They were ready to share all their knowledge and observations to help the team, and we wanted their input—that's why they were there. But the team found it difficult to accept outsiders' criticisms right away. The unity we had worked so hard to establish seemed ready to shatter. I was so upset after those first few practices that I was close to tears on the phone back to Stanford. I just wasn't able to communicate to the coaches how I wanted them to be, how I *needed* them to be.

"Talk to them again," Amy said. "Keep talking until you have it the way you want."

We especially didn't need any rifts between coaches and players going into Australia. The last time we had been there, our loss to Brazil in the World Championships had left a tangled mess of misunderstandings and bruised feelings. When you lose, nothing you did as a coach was right, even though you did the same things you always do. That's the nature of coaching. You're a genius if you win and a dolt if you lose. So I was eager to return to Australia to exorcise the bad memories, to show we could win as a united team of players and coaches.

"Look, we've been doing pretty well all year," I told the new coaches, all of whom I respected deeply. It wasn't easy to tell them to do the exact opposite of what they had been doing all year with their college teams. "If we lose, guess who's going to draw the blame? You. Just cheer and clap and encourage. Let people come to you. Don't be out there barking orders and hollering. Get out of your head-coaching mold. If you have criticisms, tell me in private and let me handle it."

After a few more days, the coaching situation had become more comfortable for everybody. One pleasant fallout from Nell and Renee's departure was that I became closer to the players. I was totally invested in these women. You're invested right from the start, but after a year they become your life. I had seen how hard they worked, how far so many of them had come since October. I didn't want to fail them. Every single day, when we came together for a cheer at the end of practice, I pictured them standing on the victory platform with their gold medals. I could hear the national anthem. I knew it would happen, just as we had promised that day on the 50-yard-line of the Georgia Dome.

A while back, Jennifer had printed up gray T-shirts with

the word "Focus" on the front and "Gold medal" on the back. I wore mine all the time, but I worried about taking it to Australia. Did I want to be wearing it in front of our Olympic opponents? Wouldn't that be a little bold? But then I thought, "Hell, yes, I'm going to wear it, because we're going to win it."

In Melbourne, in our first game of the round-robin tournament, Katrina fell down hard against Cuba and had to be carried from the court. Sprained ankle. She couldn't play the rest of the trip.

Against Australia in the next round, we were down by ten points and came back to win, 96–81. Nikki especially played great. Australia had never seen her before, and their players didn't know what hit them. Lisa was unstoppable, scoring 33 points and grabbing 14 rebounds. The Australian coach told reporters after the game that the loss was a fluke, a theory he would cling to all the way through the Olympics.

Then we went to Sydney to play the Ukraine at the site of our World Championships loss. They had brought in a new player, so they weren't the same old cousins, but we still won, 72–50. Then we played Australia again, and again it was a tough game. One of their top guards was out with an injury, which handicapped them a lot. We won by just nine points, 81–72.

Sylvia Crawley, who had joined us on the trip, was struggling offensively, shooting only about 20 percent from the floor. She worked hard, but it was a difficult situation for her to be thrown onto this team with so little preparation. Carla and Jennifer played well, especially in our next game against Cuba. Carla got Cuba's best player into foul trouble while scoring 16 points herself, and Jennifer came off the bench in the second half to spark the team. We won our 44th game in a row.

The tournament moved from Sydney to a place called Townsville, a gambling town. While Nancy Darsch and I were waiting for a bus we went into a casino where I saw a red, white, and blue slot machine. I dropped in a few coins, and it spit out $350. I took that as a good sign, though I tend to be lucky anyway. I've won thousand-dollar payoffs at slot machines in Las Vegas. I got a hole in one though I hardly ever golf. In the 1994 World Championships in Australia, I bought a raffle ticket while I watched the first game of a doubleheader. We played the second game, and during halftime, a little girl tapped me on the shoulder.

"Coach, you won," she said.

"We haven't finished playing yet," I said.

"No, the raffle," she said. "You won."

The prize was a set of drinking glasses, which I no longer have. I smashed each glass on the concrete patio in my backyard when I got home. I wanted nothing to remind me of the tournament.

We beat Cuba in Townsville and moved on to Adelaide for our last two games. In the semifinal, the Ukraine was like a different team. They slowed the game to a crawl, throwing us off rhythm. We couldn't score worth a damn. The Ukraine players were so big, we had trouble scoring over them. And they pushed our shooters so far out that pretty soon we were tossing up shots from eight feet behind the three-point line. We weren't able to pressure them or run on them. We won, but they held us to just 62 points.

I was completely shook up. This was one of those moments when I had to wonder if we could do it. We were struggling against the Ukraine, and the Ukraine wasn't even as good as Russia. They weren't as good as Brazil.

"There's no way we can play like this and win a gold medal," I thought.

We had barely won, and the Ukraine was likely to add better players before the Olympics. The only thing working for us was going inside to Lisa. That was it. Otherwise we couldn't score over their big players. We couldn't win a gold medal with one scoring weapon.

I couldn't eat. Carol asked me to go running, suggesting that maybe that would make me feel better. But I couldn't even do that. I was completely in the tank.

When I checked my answering machine at home, there was a message from my sister Beth. "I can't really tell you too much," she said. "You need to call Mom and Dad."

I got my mother on the phone. Her voice cracked as she told me the news. My father had been diagnosed with level five melanoma on his scalp. Level five is the most serious stage. He had already had surgery to remove it. Starting in June, he would have to undergo daily interferon treatments to kill any cancerous cells left behind. I couldn't picture my father as a sick man; he had always been so strong and active. I wasn't devastated by the news because I knew the cancer wouldn't beat him. My father was angry because another doctor had checked the lesion on his head earlier and had said it wasn't cancer.

"It's a good thing they found it now," I said to my mother. I'm sure I sounded unnaturally calm, but I didn't want to upset my mother any more than she already was. When Beth got on the phone, she was as distraught as my mother.

"Beth," I said, "how is that going to help? Mom and Dad need help, so help them."

As the oldest child, I fell immediately into my role of problem-solver, the one who is logical and practical, which I imagine was sometimes soothing and sometimes maddening to my family. I knew my family was doing everything that could be done for my father, and somehow I knew he'd be OK. I sent him a USA Basketball bathrobe with the Olympic rings on it, which became a great conversation piece at the hospital. All the doctors and nurses asked about it, which gave him a convenient opportunity to tell them all about his daughter the basketball coach. In my mind for the next month, I saw him as the same man who skied and swam and rebuilt our house at Chautauqua. It wasn't until I visited him in late June, a few weeks before the Olympics, that I saw the toll the cancer had taken.

I had to get my mind back to basketball. We were playing Australia in the championship game the next day. Their best player was point guard Michelle Timms, so I put Ruthie on her and then Nikki, but we couldn't contain her. She was quick, put the ball on the floor real well, and had a solid three-point shot. It turned out to be a hell of a game. We played really hard, contending with a crowd rooting against us, an Australian referee, no Katrina, and no true 12th player yet. I took all that into consideration as I calmed myself from the Ukraine game. I was very happy when we won that game 87–78, and could leave Australia with the tournament victory.

On the plane home, I was thinking that in two months we'd be in Atlanta. USA Basketball had named our alternates while we were away. No surprises: Katie Smith of Ohio State; Teresa Weatherspoon of Louisiana Tech; Kara Wolters; Sylvia Crawley; Edna Campbell of Texas; Shanda Berry; and Venus Lacey. From these, we would choose our 12th player.

I was starting to relax when suddenly the plane shuddered violently. The pilot said we were hitting turbulence, but it was unlike any I had ever encountered. We lurched and rocked as if inside a tumbler. All I could think of was the ValuJet plane that had recently crashed into the Florida Everglades. I never prayed so hard in my life. Players moved so they could sit next to one another. For 45 minutes we sat in terrified, prayerful silence until, as suddenly as it began, the turbulence stopped.

Everyone went home for ten days and met again in Providence, Rhode Island, on May 24 for another game against Cuba. I don't know where the Cuban team went between Australia and Providence, but I knew that from Providence they were going on to Japan and then Italy. They were like a team without a country, moving from one place to the next, playing wherever they could get a game.

My spirits rose as soon as I caught sight of Venus on the team bus. Finally! I couldn't wait to see how she changed the dynamics on the court. She was a big, strong player and so tough and eager to do well. If she played well during her stint with the team, she would likely be chosen to fill the final spot on the roster.

The new coaches were helping me get organized for our final push to the Olympics. We were making sure everything was in place: our out-of-bounds plays, transition defense, full-court defense. We were trying to put in new plays and devise new strategies, making sure we could answer every problem our opponents might throw at us, and the new coaches were a huge help.

Cuba showed up with a few different players and, in a scrimmage the day before the game, played much more aggressively, picking us up full-court. By the next day, we were ready. We jumped on them right away, and they seemed to quit early. Venus had seven points and six rebounds, a great showing considering she hadn't practiced much with us. I had told her before the game not to worry about fitting into our scheme.

"Go as close to the basket as you can and call for the ball," I said. "Just get in there and mix it up."

You could definitely feel her presence.

Late in the game, a Cuban player hit Jennifer in the nose with the heel of her hand as they both went after the ball. Jennifer's nose was just smashed. Venus came up to Jennifer as the trainer blotted the blood.

"Did that girl do that on purpose? Because if she did, I'll get her back," Venus said. And she was serious. That's the way she was. She would ask me sometimes, "Just how physical do you want me to be?"

"Very, but not against us. Not in practice. We can't afford any injuries. But against other teams, go for it; we need an enforcer."

The Civic Center in Providence had had a good crowd for the game, which we won by 48 points. When we left to board our buses back to the hotel, people were still waiting outside for autographs. The players signed and signed and signed, inching their way to the bus. As the bus pulled away, several players noticed a little girl near tears because she hadn't gotten any autographs.

"Stop the bus," a few of them hollered to the bus driver.

The driver stopped, and the players piled out and signed the girl's program.

"It didn't take but two minutes," one of the players said, "to turn the saddest girl in Rhode Island into the happiest."

When we scrimmaged Cuba again the next day, I gave the Cuban coach a pair of Nike shorts for his birthday. We had played each other so much, I felt as if we were friends, though we could talk only through an interpreter. I think the gift took him by surprise, but I and the rest of our team felt a special kinship with the Cuban team. I'd get calls from their players at the hotel, wanting to know where Dawn and Lisa were because Dawn and Lisa always hooked them up with clothes. The Cubans were so strapped for cash that when they ate at Burger King, they wouldn't buy drinks. They'd run down the block to buy soda at the supermarket to save a few pennies.

When Jennifer broke her nose, Katy and Rebecca bought her a mechanized stuffed pig because Jennifer loved the movie *Babe*. Before they gave her the pig, they stuck a Band-Aid on its nose. From then on, Jennifer was "Babe." "How's Baaaaabe?" players would ask while Jennifer recuperated, sounding more like sheep than pigs. The pig traveled everywhere with us. When Jennifer missed games because of her nose, her teammates put Babe on the bench, just as they had put a doll's jacket on the bench during Dawn's absence. A few weeks before we left for Atlanta, Jennifer started a fund-raising drive to send Babe to the Olympics. She asked players to write down on the locker room chalkboard what they could contribute. "My boy-friend's credit cards" was a typical response.

Jennifer's doctor back in Colorado Springs said her nose wasn't just broken, it had been crushed. She needed surgery, then bed rest. Her nose was packed with gauze. It was so painful that the doctor kept her sedated. When I visited her in her room after the surgery, she could barely stay awake. She had to breathe through her mouth, and the air was so dry in the mountains that we got her a humidifier so her throat wouldn't dry out. She had trouble eating and lost weight. It was just awful for her.

We left for Canada without her, making a six-day swing to play the Canadian national team twice. In the first game, Venus seemed unhinged. She was trying too hard to impress us and consequently had a bad game, though we won by 14 points. I sat with her on the plane from Calgary to our second game in Vancouver.

"Relax," I told her. "Just play."

I felt strongly that she ought to be our 12th player, though she still had to persuade the committee. I wanted to make sure she didn't play herself out of the position. We talked the whole flight. She told me about her family and her childhood and how she got started in basketball. When the subject turned to food, I mentioned how much I loved brownies.

"I love brownies, too!" Venus said. "My teacher back home makes the best brownies in the world."

"Have her send some," I said.

Venus smiled. "Will it help me make the team?"

"It won't hurt."

Carol and I decided to take a long run in Vancouver. Amazingly (for me), I had kept up my exercise regiment the entire year, running almost every day. We had been going 45 minutes for each run, but I wanted to stretch it out. The Olympics was six weeks away, and I was somehow connecting my running to the games. If I ran hard, we'd play hard at the Olympics. If I overcame obstacles and fatigue and doubt, then so would the team. There is a hill near my house in California I nicknamed Olympic Hill. I ran it every time I went home. Even when my legs burned, I was going to make it up that hill. "How important is this?" I'd ask myself as I ran. "How badly do you want it?" Running was kind of my own individual journey within the team's journey. I kept building up stamina, going farther, getting better, as I hoped the team was.

Carol and I set out on a beautiful morning in Vancouver.

"Carol, today's the day we go an hour," I said.

We ran along the water and into a park and lost track of how to loop back to the hotel. When we stopped running after an hour, we had no clue where we were. All of a sudden I spotted a cab and went racing after it. Neither of us had any money, so at the hotel Carol ran up to the room to get her purse while I waited in the cab as insurance.

I decided not to take our waywardness as a providential sign.

Jennifer caught up with us in Vancouver, though she still couldn't play. We found ourselves down by 12 points to Canada at halftime. Lisa and Venus were in foul trouble. We weren't playing smart basketball.

"All right, here's a good opportunity for us," I told them in the locker room at halftime. "What will we do in the Olympics if we're down by 12? Let's look at the positive things here. Lisa and Venus aren't tired because they got two quick fouls and haven't played much. I know we can beat this team. But people have got to step up defensively for us."

Ruthie, Nikki, and Teresa made some big plays, and we started to catch up. The refs were confused about the three-point line because the college, international, and NBA three-point lines were all painted on the floor. Late in the game, we hit a three-pointer and the refs didn't call it. Dawn jumped up from the bench, sprinted past me, and headed toward the official.

"What are you doing?" I asked her.

"They didn't give us the shot!" Dawn said.

I thought arguing was a waste of time, but hell, I'll get up there and fight if she's going to fight. Sure enough, the ref changed the call and gave us the extra point at a real critical time. To me, that was Dawn being Dawn, always competitive, always smart.

In the last minute of the game, we were down by two points and ran a play to spring Katy free for a three-pointer. She nailed it, which I think was a real confidence-builder for her. In the last 30 seconds of the game, Ruthie slipped and had to come out. Her knee was hurting, but it didn't seem too serious. We ended up winning by seven points.

Teresa had solidified her spot at the point guard, even though Dawn was back. But Teresa was still learning some basic elements that were second nature to Dawn. For example, at the end of the first half against Canada, we had possession of the ball with 30 seconds left on the clock. In that situation, the point guard directs the offense to pass the ball until the clock winds down to the final few seconds, and then to shoot. That way the other team has no opportunity to score. But we shot the ball too soon, so Canada got the ball back and made the final shot of the half. So clearly we still had some work to do. This was why we played these games—to correct our mistakes now, instead of in the Olympics. Dawn was playing 15 or 20 minutes a game, trying to work her way back into top form. She never pouted about losing her starting position. Dawn was always concerned with the team first and herself second. After practice on most days, Dawn and Teresa would play a few games of one-on-one, or horse, in which you try to match your opponent shot for shot.

They were such different players and brought different strengths to the position. Dawn was quick as a bug. She created plays with her dazzling dribbling and her great feel for everyone who was on the court at all times. Teresa was taller and so she had better vision on the court. She would find the open teammate and fire her the ball as if it were shot from a gun. What they had in common were passion and intelligence. They were always talking strategy, dissecting opponents, analyzing various game situations. Both would make great coaches.

The next morning as we left to fly to Oakland, California, for another game against Canada, Ruthie showed up on crutches and with a brace on her leg. Strained knee ligaments. Great. We were going back to the States, to Stanford's backyard, with Ruthie on crutches and Jennifer with a mask on her face, still unable to play.

I was happy to be going home, but when we arrived I saw a story in the *San Francisco Chronicle* that dredged up all the things I had said to *USA Today* about Rebecca, how I wondered if she could help us win or if she was on the team mostly for marquee value. I generally didn't read the papers, but since this was my local paper, I did. I thought, "Here we go again." I couldn't seem to get away from it. And the *Chronicle* story wouldn't be the last on the subject. I talked to USA Basketball president C.M. Newton—I had to talk to someone. I felt that the team dynamic was so positive at that point, I didn't want anything to ruin it. C.M. said exactly what I needed him to say.

"You can't worry about what people are writing," he said. "Just stay focused on what you're doing."

When I walked into the locker room before the Oakland game, I sensed something was wrong, but I didn't know what it was. The players didn't have the kind of enthusiasm I would have expected before a home game. Maybe part of it was the newspaper article. But I found out later they were upset that one of the new coaches was critiquing game videos in the locker room, where the players could hear the remarks as they dressed for the game. They evidently didn't like what they were hearing. Maybe a different coach could get away with doing it, but the new coaches were still on thin ice with the players. The relationships were fragile, and every little thing was going to grate.

At this point, minor annoyances had the potential to become major distractions. For instance, I had discovered that the NBA was going to supplement the men's USA Basketball per diem so they'd get $100 a day. The women would be getting $60. It was a little thing, but I found this disturbing, as I imagined the players would, and told USA Basketball so. It would cost USA Basketball about $20,000 to boost the women's per diem to equal the men's, but they wouldn't go for it. There was still lingering resentment among some women about the double standard they felt had existed in Barcelona at the 1992 games. The men stayed in a luxury hotel while the women stayed in dorms in the athletes' village. At the airport in Barcelona, the women waited for their luggage while the men were whisked away into waiting vans, leaving their luggage for some hired hand to retrieve and deliver to them. The money itself didn't bother me but rather the principle behind the disparity. It conjured up memories of sitting in the stands watching the boys play, of pulling on hand-me-down uniforms, and of living on food stamps for the privilege of being an assistant coach. But since there was nothing we could do about it, USA Basketball Executive Director Warren Brown explained the situation to the players so they could make peace with it before we got to Atlanta. If they were bothered, they said nothing. I think women, even today, expect to get the short end of the stick sometimes. We know that, as high as we have climbed, we're still not breathing the same air as the men. But if we're smart, we learn which battles are worth fighting and which ought to be left for another day. Our players let the money issue slide. It helped that USA Basketball agreed to begin our Olympic per diem—$60 instead of the $30 we had been receiving as the national team all year—as soon as the Olympic team was announced on June 16. The men's Olympic players did not begin receiving their per diem until July 1, the date we originally had been scheduled to receive our increase. It was an acceptable compromise.

Whatever worries and irritations I felt disappeared—at least for a few hours—in the lovefest inside the Oakland Coliseum arena. We had the second-largest crowd of our tour—9,128 people, all screaming for us. Many were Stanford women's basketball fans, and many were fans of Cal and the University of San Francisco, which also have strong women's programs. And many people, I know, were watching the women's game for the first time. The crowd gave me a standing ovation when I was introduced, an incredible feeling that tilts the brain to overload. Getting an ovation is the closest thing to getting a cape and a big "S" on your chest. You feel, for a few moments, that you are capable of everything all these people think you are capable of.

"This is what Atlanta will feel like," I thought as I stood on the court. I related everything to Atlanta. When I was taking a shower on August 4, 1995, I wondered how it would feel when I took a shower a year from then on the morning of the gold medal game. I thought about what I would wear to the games. I wondered how I would feel when it was over.

We started slowly against Canada—the players still seemed in a funk—missing about six open shots in the first two minutes. Once we settled down, we ran out to a 13–4 lead and never looked back. The 80–62 victory was our 50th in a row.

Lisa had a chance to bring the house down with 11 seconds left in the game. She blocked a shot and took off down court. Everyone in the arena seemed to fall silent. No woman had dunked in a game since North Carolina's Charlotte Smith did it in an early-season game in 1994. I had told Lisa not to dunk, but I thought she might here, and I would have been perfectly fine with it. The crowd was anticipating it, the game was live on ESPN, and she was alone at the basket, so had no chance of being undercut. But she rolled the ball in off her fingers for an easy layup. The other players gave her a hard time in the locker room later.

"Why didn't you dunk?" they asked.

"My mind wanted to dunk," Lisa said, "but my legs wouldn't let me. I was just too tired at that point."

And no wonder. She played 29 tough minutes. I thought the team was still relying on her too much down low, and she was getting hammered.

In a week, the official Olympic team would be announced in Chicago after we played the Russians in a Saturday afternoon game. I was looking forward to playing them. To me, they would provide a true test. I was curious to see what they had, how big they were. We hadn't played them when we were in Russia because they weren't together as a team yet. Usually they trained for many months before the Olympics, as we were doing, but money was so tight, they couldn't afford to finance a long-term program.

We would scrimmage them first in Colorado Springs when we returned from Oakland. I gave our players a day off when we arrived so they would be well-rested for Russia. Even in the scrimmage, I didn't want the Russians to get any kind of mental edge on us, to begin thinking they were better than we were. They were big, as I expected, but they were much better shooters than I had thought. If you left them open, they could put the ball down. They passed the ball well. They moved well. Their weakness was depth. If you could tire them out or get them in foul trouble, they struggled. They played us in a zone, one of the few teams to do that. We handled it OK and won by nine points.

In the second game we disrupted their offense with a trapping defense—when two or more defenders rush to the ball handler to prevent her from passing, shooting, or dribbling in an attempt to force her to turn the ball over. We won by about 30. But they had pulled their best players from the lineup early. They throw games sometimes, and they threw this one.

Jennifer and Ruthie were still out. We weren't sure when they would be back at full speed—by the following week, I hoped. I wanted to see our true starting lineup against Russia, especially with the game being broadcast on ABC. As if we didn't have enough worries, the Russians threatened to pull out of the game unless they got a $100,000 payment from USA Basketball for the appearance. But they backed off.

In Chicago, I joined our likely Olympic starting lineup—Teresa, Lisa, Sheryl, Katrina, and Ruthie—for a photo shoot for the cover of the *Sports Illustrated* Olympic preview issue. We were supposed to be on *Oprah,* too, which is taped in Chicago, but it didn't work out. The players were disappointed; they loved *Oprah.* We had interviews with ABC and SportsChannel and a conference call with newspaper reporters around the country. All of us were taking care of ticket requests from friends and family for the Olympics and arranging hotel rooms and coordinating schedules.

In the game, we got into foul trouble early against Russia, partly because of a Russian official the team had nicknamed "Michael the Monster." Even the American official was appalled by some of his calls. So she made a couple of calls of her own to try to level the playing field. It was six against six. They played a zone again, forcing us to take the outside shots. We were awful: We made just one of 15 from the three-point line. Ruthie could have helped us a lot in that category, though I didn't worry about the shooting. We had Des.

At halftime we were trailing 41–38. We traded leads in the second half, and with 17 seconds left, we were up by just two points. Then Dawn sank two free throws to put us up 80–76. But their guard, Irina Routkovskaya, hit a three-pointer to close the gap to one point. We had possession of the ball, and, strangely, the Russians never tried to foul us to regain possession. Time ran out, and by the skin of our teeth, we won our 51st game.

"This is the beginning of what we're going to be experiencing in the Olympics," Katrina told reporters afterward.

We had been on the road for 216 of the last 255 days. We had traveled around the world. All the while, the players could never be sure if they would be Olympians. Until the night of the game with Russia, Saturday, June 14, when they were summoned to my suite at the airport Sheraton, they were the national team. USA Basketball executive director Warren Brown was there. Nell and Renee. Carol. Nancy, Ceal, and Marian. And Karen Stromme, the chairwoman of the player selection committee. She stood in the front of the room and started by talking about the year. Then she pulled a champagne glass from the sleeve of her jacket and held it high.

"Here's to the 1996 U.S. Olympic team!" she said.

The players yowled and hugged. Until that moment, they hadn't known for certain that they all would make it. Venus was standing next to Nell and hugged her so hard that Nell couldn't breathe. "It's like I'm still sleeping and I don't want to wake up," Venus said. She had been an early cut on the 1992 team and had thought her chances of ever playing in the Olympics was over. Everyone was taking pictures. I gave each player a gold necklace with her number on it. I didn't know for sure who would be on the team when I had ordered the necklaces two months earlier, but I knew the numbers would be four through 15—all the international numbers are the same.

A strange thing happened when the team became official. The Horse disappeared, I closed the door on it. From that night on I never discussed my anxieties about our post position again. It was my all-or-nothing nature. The battle to make the team how I wanted it was over. So, just like that, I dropped the issue and moved on.

The next day, we announced the roster at a press conference.

"What if you lose?" a reporter asked Teresa.

She wouldn't even consider the notion. I don't think any of us had thought of losing, not seriously. It was too dreadful a thought to entertain, even as a mental exercise. And we truly believed we wouldn't lose. No team had ever been in such great physical shape. We had—I hoped—considered every angle, confronted every potential problem. We had played all but three of the 12 Olympic contenders. We had spent time in Atlanta and in the Georgia Dome so we wouldn't be intimidated or apprehensive when we got there. We had given the players quizzes on game situations to make sure they had everything down cold. In Kiev, we had played a version of *Family Feud*, having each player come up to the front of the room to diagram a play or answer a question about what to do in certain game situations. Once I asked Teresa a tough one. I thought I would stump her.

"What's the first thing a point guard does when she walks on the court?"

Teresa didn't hesitate. "Shake the refs' hands."

Teresa understood how important it was to ingratiate oneself to the refs. I remember during the World Qualifying tournament in Brazil, one of the referees asked if he could have a "posey" board, the small, erasable boards we use to diagram plays on the sideline. I told him I'd have it for him after the game. Right before the game, he looked over at me and raised two fingers. Now he wanted two, one for himself and one for the other ref. I nodded, then turned to Marianne Stanley, my assistant.

"If he starts making calls against us, take this posey board and break it over your knee," I said. We got a fair game from him.

Even at the Olympics, the referees have no reservations

about asking for things. After an early game, a ref asked one of our players for a signed ball. She said OK but seemed a little casual about it. But Teresa had overheard the exchange. She immediately alerted Carol Callan, who got the players to sign a ball, and then she gave it to the referee. Teresa understood that such requests are not to be taken lightly.

Before another game at the Olympics, an Eastern Bloc ref told me flat-out he didn't like women's basketball. The way it worked in the Olympics was that the top officials worked only men's games. The second tier worked men's and women's, and the bottom tier worked only women's games. This guy was in the second tier. He resented doing the women's games. Usually we give the officials a team pin and a T-shirt, but when I heard his remarks I told Carol to get me a men's team pin and T-shirt, which I gave to him. A few days later I saw him doing one of the U.S. men's games (and asking for Charles Barkley's autograph). When he showed up at another of our games, I shook his hand.

"Saw you doing the men's game," I said as sincerely as I could. "You did a great job."

I wasn't trying to buy the refs so they would give us good calls. I was just trying to avoid getting *bad* calls. I don't like playing the political game, but in international basketball you ignore the refs at your own peril.

We had a month left to smooth the final rough edges, get everybody healthy again, and make sure we didn't wear the players out. We had five days off before gathering again in Colorado Springs. I went home and packed for the Olympics. Though the team would have another break before the games, I wouldn't be going home again. I planned to spend the break in Chautauqua. I figured it would be just the respite of peace I needed, and it would get me on East Coast time in preparation for Atlanta. I packed five game outfits, all of them new. There would be eight games, and I figured I could wear each one twice.

The extra one was in case we lost a preliminary game. I'd never wear an outfit that I had lost in.

When I ran Olympic Hill near my house, I raced. I ran faster than I had ever run it before.

"The next time you run this hill," I said to myself, "the team will have its gold medal."

11

"Always bear in mind that your own resolution to success is more important than any other one thing."
—Abraham Lincoln

Something wasn't right. I could see it in the players' stiff faces and in the way they took a split-second longer to move from one drill to the next, or to pick up a ball for shooting practice. We were back in Colorado Springs for the last time. Afterward, we'd take a short break, go to Orlando to practice at Disney World, then to our last exhibition game in Indianapolis, then back to Orlando, and finally to Atlanta.

The Olympics were one month away, and the players seemed to have lost their edge, just as Bobby Knight and Mike Krzyzewski had warned. They didn't seem excited to see each other. They looked tired, perhaps from the physical exertion, perhaps from the pressure that mounted as the Olympics drew closer. Maybe there was an emotional letdown after the initial excitement of making the Olympic team. Or maybe a month seemed like a lifetime away when you had worked as hard as these players had for so many months on end.

I knew I had to do something.

I called in Teresa, Jennifer, and Dawn for a meeting. They were my point guards, leaders on the team. If they liked my idea, the rest of the team probably would, too. I told them about a nearby ropes course I had read about. It was similar to the Outward Bound exercises that are designed to foster trust and cooperation. It might help pull the new coaches and Venus closer to the team, and it might be different enough from our regular practices to jump-start the players emotionally. Teresa had done a ropes course and was lukewarm about doing it again, but she didn't object. Jennifer and Dawn were enthusiastic and curious.

After explaining the ropes course to the players, I made a second announcement. I was letting them go home three days early. At my request, Carol had changed all their plane tickets so they could have a full week at home instead of four days before gathering in Orlando.

I think the players were stunned. I'm not known for being a soft touch, but I knew they were tired. I had learned from my friend Brooks Johnson, the former track coach at Stanford, that athletes should be well-conditioned but not overtrained. Better to err on the side of pushing them a little too lightly than pushing too hard. We had already cut back on our weight training by this time. And when we practiced against the men, I was particularly emphatic that the men not be too physical.

"No matter what happens when we're playing, if they score on you, if you get elbowed, you cannot put a hurt on anybody," I told the men before every scrimmage.

After practice the day before the ropes course, June 26, the team surprised me with a cake for my birthday. Actually, it wasn't such a surprise. We celebrated everybody's birthday (thanks to Carol, who noted each birthday on our monthly schedule). What the players surprised me with was a watermelon. Growing up, I had spent almost every birthday with my family at our isolated cabin on Saranac Lake. We'd go there the day school let out, spend ten days, then travel on to Chautauqua. The cabin was reachable only by boat. It had no running water and no electricity. We were the only people for miles, so we swam without bathing suits and played music whenever we wanted. But because my birthday fell during the ten days there, I never had a birthday cake. My parents would stick candles in a halved watermelon. I hated it because, of course, I felt I wasn't getting my due. So the players walked in to our meeting room with a watermelon studded with candles. Then they came through with a real cake and a gorgeous black leather bag. It was really touching. They were a caring, thoughtful group.

The camp for the ropes course was 45 minutes away up in the mountains. We gathered under some trees and were asked to talk about ourselves as an ice-breaker. Even though we had been together for almost a year, I saw bits and pieces of the players' lives I hadn't seen before. For instance, I had always thought Katrina was from the South because that's where she went to high school and college, but she talked that day about spending most of her childhood in Baltimore. Since I knew the players saw me as this person who was all basketball, all the time, I talked mostly about the things I love beyond basketball, things like skiing, sailing, and music. I wanted all of us to see one another with new eyes.

But I think it was my own vision that might have changed the most that day. Teresa and I had been chipping away all year at the wall we had built between us in Australia. Now we would let the last fragments of the past drop to the ground.

The exercise was called "Lean on Me." There were two wire cables attached to the trunk of a tree about two feet off the ground. Over the course of about 20 yards, the cable widened to form a V, with the opposite ends attached to two trees about ten feet apart. Wearing helmets in case they fell, pairs of players began the exercise at the tight end of the V, facing each other, grasping both hands, their noses almost touching. Then they moved their feet along the cable, like tightrope walkers, as the distance increased between them. The only way to balance was to lean slightly forward toward one's partner, essentially using each other as a railing to hold onto.

The second set of cables was 30 feet up in the air. We talked about how the lower cables were like the exhibition tour. There was little pressure and we could win without much trouble. The high wires were the Olympics. In those games, we could not make a false step. We would have to count on each other, trust in each other, and not get rattled by the pressure.

When it was time to move to the high wire, no one was eager to volunteer. I'm not real comfortable with heights, but somebody had to start it off. I asked Carol to join me, but then Teresa interceded.

"I'll do it with you," she said.

We strapped on our helmets and hooked our waist harnesses to safety ropes that two other players held in case we fell. We each had a "coach" to advise and encourage us. Lisa was my coach. I was the first to climb up, trying not to look down. The wires were attached to poles that looked like telephone poles. When Teresa came up, neither one of us wanted to let go of the pole and step onto the wires. We were facing each other less than five inches apart, each of us with one arm wrapped around the pole. As our feet felt for the wires, our legs shook.

"T," I said, "let's grasp our free hands. Then I'll move my other hand to the side of the pole, and you do the same. I think we can let go of the pole at the same time and grab each other."

We could hear voices yelling at us from below, but we paid no attention. We were completely focused on each other. My hands were sweating so much I was afraid they might slip through Teresa's. We slid our hands to the side of the pole, then on cue grabbed each other.

"Push me," Teresa said. She felt off balance and needed more resistance.

We inched our way along the wire, leaning in and pushing against each other as our bodies moved farther apart. I was completely dependent on her, and she on me. Mustering the strength we needed to stay balanced was tiring. "I'm not giving up," I thought. "I'm not going to mess this up."

We both realized, however, that we couldn't reach the other side. It was too far. We had been up there for about 20 intense minutes, but it felt like forever. To get down, we had to fall inward and be lowered to the ground by the ropes attached to our harnesses.

"If we ever have a problem at the Olympics," I said to Teresa, "we have to remember what it was like being up on the wire." Teresa didn't have to say anything. We both knew our relationship had changed, the way you know a shot's going in before it reaches the rim. Whatever the ropes course cost, it was worth it for my time up there with Teresa. I knew now I could trust her. It wasn't that I hadn't thought I could, but I didn't *know* I could.

Later, Nancy Darsch gave me a picture of Teresa and me on the wire, and I taped it to my hotel mirror at the Olympics, alongside the photo of the gold medal from our notebooks and a photo of the Georgia Dome.

When the players flew home, I flew to Chautauqua. By that point, my parents were driving four hours round-trip every day to Buffalo for my father's cancer treatment. My father wasn't himself. He looked tired and he had lost weight. He loves to eat; he's the kind of person who sits at breakfast and thinks about lunch. But he had no appetite. I offered to drive him, but my parents wanted me to concentrate on the Olympics. Seeing my father struggling with the cancer put some things in perspective for me. Nothing's guaranteed in life, so you have to seize the day. Instead of diminishing my drive to win the gold medal, my father's illness validated it. I wanted to do the absolute best job I could so I would have no regrets, win or lose.

For most of my stay, I had the house to myself. I was so tired, but I couldn't rest too much. I was afraid that if I closed my eyes for a moment I would sleep all day. I had to stay focused during this home stretch. I'd have time to rest in September.

I spent my mornings there watching videos of our Olympic opponents—I brought three boxes of game films with me. I was also reading *The Power of Positive Thinking* and listening to a series of tapes on peak performance. I concentrated on one Olympic team each day, immersing myself in the scouting reports and videos until I felt I knew every player, every play, every tendency. I divided each tape in half, putting all the defensive plays together and all the offensive plays together. Then I charted the plays, noting what plays they ran in what situations. I watched each of their players to figure out their strengths and weaknesses, their favorite moves. I watched the edited tapes over and over until I felt I could almost predict what would happen in the game. I also had scouting reports on our own U.S. team, which I had asked other American coaches to write up for me. I wanted to see what opposing coaches might do against the team, what weakness they might exploit and what strengths they would try to neutralize. These scouting reports were valuable in planning our practices; we knew what we needed to work on.

My favorite afternoons were spent sailing on the lake. I needed the quiet to calm my buzzing nerves. That was the toughest challenge, keeping the stress from rising up and taking over. It helped to visit with old friends who still returned to Chautauqua every summer, as I did. I listened to the symphony. I went to see *Mr. Holland's Opus*.

On July 4th, Chautauqua held its big Independence Day celebration at the amphitheater with music and readings. During the show, the president of the Chautauqua Institution asked me to stand up in the audience and introduced me as "one of Chautauqua's own." There had been a big story in the local paper about me, so everyone knew I was in town. I looked like a walking flag—I was wearing red, white, and blue with gold stars on my shirt. The whole place stood and cheered. When the band played the national anthem, I nearly broke down. In exactly one month, we would be playing the gold medal game, and I hoped I'd be listening to the anthem again, watching the American flag rise toward the ceiling of the Georgia Dome. I stood there feeling overwhelmed by the emotion of wanting the gold medal for the team. They had done all the right things. Sacrificed. Listened without complaining, whining, or fighting.

"I want that gold medal," I thought, "more than anything I've ever wanted in my life."

Two days later, my father and my sister Beth drove me to Buffalo, where I met my assistant coach Nancy Darsch. We rented a car and continued on to a tournament in Hamilton, Ontario, to scout the Russian, Canadian, and Australian teams, and also Brazil, a team we had not seen since the World Championships two years earlier. It turned out that Brazil had greater depth, having added a big new post player to an already strong lineup. They were still great offensively, and this time their defense was much better.

"Great," I said. "They scored 108 against us in Australia, and now they've improved their defense."

Russia had added three new starters since our one-point game in Chicago. So I could only assume that they had improved themselves. Australia played like pit bulls. No team is more aggressive and tenacious than the Australians. They could give us trouble simply for those two reasons.

We returned to Buffalo, and I flew to Orlando to meet the team at the Disney Institute. We each had our own condo, so friends and family came in to stay. We closed practices so we could be completely focused and keep the distractions away. We practiced hard. I didn't want to overwork them or get anyone hurt, but I wanted us to play with Olympic intensity. We did a lot of time-and-score situations. If there are two minutes left and we're up by two, what do we do? What if there are 20 seconds left? The players needed to know exactly what to do for every possibility.

We put in a new out-of-bounds play, an alley-oop—a high, billowy pass toward the hoop, where Katrina would leap up, catch it, and quickly lay it in for a score. It would end up paying off against Brazil.

When we were scrimmaging against men one day, Venus got popped in the mouth; there was blood all over. A couple of her teeth were damaged and she had to go in for emergency dental work. We had until July 18 to change the roster; if somebody got hurt, we could still make substitutions. So I figured we would train hard until we got to Atlanta. Then we'd lay off.

We flew on Friday, July 12, to Indianapolis for our last exhibition game, this time against Italy. We were tied at halftime and then blew them away in the second half, winning by 35 points. Ruthie was playing again for the first time since she hurt her knee in Canada a month earlier. She looked great, which meant I'd sleep more restfully. She'd be fine for the Olympics.

The next day, the men's Olympic team played an exhibition against Greece in the same arena. The men players couldn't have been nicer. After the game, the men invited the women's team onto the court for high-fives and hugs and they all walked off together, just as we had done for them the day before.

All along, the press kept comparing our team to the men's, and found the men lacking. Writers and broadcasters were saying how much more exciting the women were to watch, which struck me as completely ludicrous and more than a little hypocritical. If the women were so much more exciting to watch than these great NBA men, why didn't we have a pro league? Why weren't the women making even a fraction of the salaries the men earned? I didn't like to be contrasted with the men. We were 100 percent supportive of them, and they of us.

In a way, I felt sorry for the men's team. They were clearly tired and beat up from playing a full NBA season. And no matter what they did, they couldn't win the public relations game. If they beat up on teams, they were bullies. If they didn't beat up on teams, everybody wanted to know what was wrong with them.

The morning of the men's game—Sunday, July 14—I picked up the *New York Times* and found a story about me in the Olympic preview section. A *Times* reporter had interviewed me when I was in Chautauqua, and even then I felt she had her story already written. "The coach of the women's team is about as flashy as beige," part of the story said. It quoted male coaches as saying I resented the players becoming more glamorous and that I wouldn't help promote the sport because of it. "The angry woman, some of her male colleagues call her," the reporter wrote. That's crazy. I wonder why the writer talked only to male coaches and not to Pat Summitt, for example, or Jody Conradt at Texas. I felt a little defensive about my critics taking potshots at me. I didn't understand why anyone would be critical of what we were doing, what I was doing, when we had worked so hard all year for the sole purpose of winning a gold medal for our country.

We flew back to Orlando with the men's team on the Dallas Mavericks private plane. The men's coaches were so relaxed. They were great to talk with. Clem Haskins was the only one who knew much about women's basketball because his daughter had played at Western Kentucky and now is the head coach at Dayton. But the others had no clue, which was fine. We seemed very serious to them, I think. They, on the other hand, were extraordinarily loose. For example, when I ran into Jerry Sloan at the hotel gym in Atlanta before the men's semifinals game, I asked whom they were playing.

"Argentina," he said. I wished him good luck.

Later I found out the team had played Australia. When I kidded him about it later, he laughed.

"I knew it was some team that started with 'A'," he said.

By contrast, we were breaking down every offensive and defensive play our opponents had ever run.

The men teased us in Orlando for practicing so hard. But once we got to Atlanta, we tapered off and they trained hard. So it evened out.

On the flight from Orlando to Atlanta, men's team captain David Robinson was on the phone the whole time, lobbying the other sports' team captains to choose Teresa to carry the Olympic flag for the U.S. delegation in the opening ceremony. She seemed the perfect choice: She was the first U.S. basketball player ever to compete in four Olympics and she was from Georgia. The vote was taking place in Atlanta while we were in the air, and we wouldn't know the results until we landed.

We flew in late at night purposely to avoid the daytime crush of athletes arriving to get credentials. Even among the world's elite athletes, the men's basketball players drew crowds of autograph-seekers. From South African marathon runners to Chinese swimmers, they all know the Dream Team. So we planned our arrival for after midnight so we could check in without causing a scene at the athletes' credentialing area. When we got off the plane, we heard about TWA Flight 800 crashing into the ocean off the coast of New York. The passenger jet bound for Paris had taken off from John F. Kennedy Airport and exploded in the air minutes later, killing all 230 people on board. It was so frightening to think about. You couldn't help wondering if it was a bomb, and if it might possibly be linked to the Olympics. It had us all edgy. We thought of all the flying we had done all year, and I couldn't help thinking back on that horrible flight from Australia, when turbulence had tossed us around. While we went through credentialing, we listened to news reports on the radio, and some players were calling friends on cell phones to get updates. We felt so awful for the victims and their families.

As we waited to get our pictures taken for our Olympic credentials and to pick up our opening ceremony clothes, a USA Basketball official gave us the results of the flag-carrier voting. Teresa had come in second. Wrestler Bruce Baumgartner, also a four-time Olympian, had been chosen.

A hand shot up in the back. It belonged to Charles Barkley, then with the Phoenix Suns, now with the Houston Rockets.

"What place did I come in?" he asked earnestly.

Everybody cracked up. I really enjoyed Charles Barkley. In Atlanta, he would come onto our bus as we waited to drive to practice and ask what we were working on that day. I'd catch a glimpse of him leading cheers in the stands during our games and dancing to "Y-M-C-A" by the Village People during time-outs.

We didn't check into our rooms until after 3 A.M. The Omni was in a great location that allowed us to walk to the Georgia Dome if need be, though we always went by bus for security purposes. The downside was that it stood at the edge of Centennial Park, the large square with merchandise booths, fountains, and several stages for entertainment.

"You want to go to a concert?" Jennifer asked us the second or third day in Atlanta. "Come to my room at midnight." The music from the stages was so loud that Jennifer and several others finally moved into rooms that didn't face the park.

Our first morning in Atlanta, the players went by bus to the Athletes' Village for gender testing, a practice I consider offensive and demeaning to women. A scraping is taken from inside the athlete's mouth and tested for the XX, or female, combination of chromosomes. Of course, not all women have XX chromosomes and not all men have XY. Take, for example, Polish runner Ewa Klobukowska. She won a gold medal in the 4×100 relay in the 1964 Olympics before gender testing was the practice. Then in 1967, the first year any gender testing was administered, she was "verified" as a woman because the tests were done visually—women stood naked in front of gynecologists. But so many women understandably protested that the IOC switched to chromosomal testing. At the 1968 World Championships, Klobukowska was found to have XXY chromosomes, which six in every 1,000 women do. She was stripped of her Olympic medal and no longer allowed to compete, though she was clearly a woman.

She was the first woman to fail the sex test, but during the test's 30-year existence, dozens more have followed. The tests do not level the playing field, as they are supposedly intended to do, because no female has ever been exposed as a male in disguise. It just hasn't happened. Instead, the tests *do* humiliate and unfairly punish women who have genetic anomalies but no biological advantage. Women who have such anomalies have to carry a doctor's verification with them in order to compete. Those caught by surprise when they fail the chromosomal test often exit the competition under the guise of injury. As women progress toward equality in sports, the slights become more subtle. These games were being celebrated as the Year of the Woman, yet women couldn't compete without having to verify their femininity. It's as if people can hardly believe that women can compete at such extraordinary levels, so they're testing them to make sure.

Among the American women at the Olympics, few drew as much attention as our basketball team. A press conference our first night in Atlanta was packed with reporters asking if we were the best women's team in the sport's history. I kept saying we hadn't proven anything yet. We would have to win the gold medal, I said, before our place in history could be debated. I felt we'd win it, but it's not only bad form to say so, it can foster an atmosphere of complacency on the team.

Sometime in those first two days, we chose our team captains. I had each player write her recommendations on a slip of paper. When I had talked informally with players about captains back in October, most mentioned Teresa, Jennifer, Ruthie, and Dawn. No one had suggested Katrina. This time, the choices were clearly Teresa and Katrina, our two Olympic veterans. I knew this time around, I didn't need to check with Teresa first before announcing her and Katrina as captains. They had been playing the roles of captain anyway for the last few months, especially Teresa. She was clearly the team leader, the one others turned to for advice and direction. For example, Teresa told her teammates they might want to wear tights when they checked into the Olympics because they'd have to try on opening ceremony outfits, jackets, shirts, pants, shoes, and official warmups. Teresa had done everything I had asked of her, so I knew she was committed to the team in a way she hadn't been in Australia in 1994. The announcement was anticlimactic. I was giving the players news they already knew. It showed me how far my relationship with Teresa had come that I would introduce her as a team captain with no doubt that she would gladly accept it.

The next night was the opening ceremony, so we gave the players the day off. I remembered that a year earlier I had been on the phone to Teresa wishing her a happy birthday. Now the time was here.

During the day, I went with Nancy, Ceal, and Amy to check out Centennial Park. The most beautiful part was a fountain in the shape of the Olympic rings. The water came on intermittently, so you could walk to the rings while the water was off and then stand inside them while water gushed all around you.

I walked in with a hundred other people, trying to get at least a small taste of the Olympics from a fan's perspective.

"Hey, lady!"

I heard someone yelling through a bullhorn.

"Hey, lady!"

Amy elbowed me. "I think he's talking to you."

"Lady! You can't go in there with no shoes! Gotta get out!"

Kicked out of the Olympic fountain on my second day. Now there was a good start.

The men's and women's basketball teams spent most of the opening ceremony in the baseball suites of Atlanta Fulton County Stadium, next door to the Olympic Stadium. Venus didn't go because her teeth were bothering her. We ate food left for us on platters and took pictures of one another in our opening ceremony outfits. As the 196 other nations paraded into Olympic Stadium, we watched on television monitors. There's something very quaint about the opening ceremony, aside from all the pomp. Despite all evidence to the contrary, the ceremony still holds to the notion that peoples of the world might someday come together as they do at the Olympic Games. On that hot, moonless Southern night, I couldn't help believing it myself. I loved that in the opening ceremony, the lone athlete from Brunei Darussalam walked on equal footing with American track superstar Michael Johnson, and that the 134 athletes from Greece—one of the founding teams in 1896—were no less exuberant than the six from first-time participant Dominica.

As the host country, the United States was the final team to enter the stadium, and the basketball teams were bringing up the rear. The USOC wanted to keep the NBA players hidden until the last possible minute so they wouldn't be a distraction.

After waiting for a couple hours, suddenly it was time for our entrance, and we had to bolt like bats out of hell. We women were wearing low heels and hose, and I could just picture one of us breaking an ankle.

"I'm going to get to the opening ceremony and these

thigh-high hose are going to be around my ankles," Ceal Barry cracked.

A guy on a bullhorn kept hollering at us to speed it up as we chugged up the ramp that would take us to our descent into the Olympic Stadium. When we reached the top and looked down into the stadium, it was like catching the first glimpse of Oz. Suddenly before us was a vast sea of lights and flashbulbs and color and thousands of people. It was so stunning that I don't quite remember walking around the track. I do remember seeing Demi Moore and Bruce Willis off to the side, and it was almost comical how the athletes seemed more excited to see them than President Clinton.

I knew that up in the stands, Nell and Renee were watching. I hated that they couldn't be down here with us. They belonged as much as anybody. If this team won a gold medal, they owned a piece of it.

The infield where all the athletes were gathered was packed by the time we arrived. We marched around the track, then lined up next to the rest of the American contingent. Athletes from other countries were pushing and jockeying to get close to the basketball players, so I moved away to talk with the U.S. swim coaches, Skip Kenney and Richard Quick, who also coached at Stanford. We watched as Atlanta boxer Evander Holyfield entered the stadium with the torch. He was joined partway around the track by Paraskevi Patoulidou, a 1992 gold medalist from Greece, who had emerged magically from the infield. Then they handed off the torch to Olympic swimmer Janet Evans—who went to Stanford. Janet ran up the long ramp toward the Olympic cauldron. From the shadows at the top of the ramp emerged a figure with a torch in his shaking hand. We gasped. It was the great Muhammad Ali, his arm shaking from Parkinson's syndrome. He lit his torch from Janet's, then turned and touched the flame to a fuse that, when lit, sped along a wire up to the Olympic cauldron, which burst into flames to begin the 26th Olympiad.

A spotlight focused on a platform in the middle of the infield. Alone on a platform stood Teresa. An estimated 3.5 billion people were watching the ceremony around the world. And Teresa stood as calmly as she did when speaking to high school classes and basketball clinics during the year. She had been chosen to speak for all 10,800 competitors in reciting the athlete's oath. I prayed she wouldn't freeze. I couldn't imagine doing what she was about to do. But Teresa was perfect. Her steady voice boomed through the stadium.

". . . I promise we shall take part in these Olympic Games respecting . . . the true spirit of sportsmanship."

....

In the crush of people I was pushed farther and farther away from the basketball teams, and so I didn't notice when they left. I had no idea where our buses were parked to return to the hotel. Just as I began to worry, a basketball security guard took me by the hand and we ran through the crowd and up a ramp. Huge floats were descending the ramp at the time and we were nearly flattened to the wall trying to slip by. I was the last one on the bus. The incident struck me as a metaphor for how enormously overwhelming the games can be, and if I didn't watch out, I could become distracted by the excitement.

The next day, we focused on Cuba, our first opponent. We had reams of scouting reports broken down for each player. My sister Heidi, also a coach, was in my suite with some friends one afternoon.

"Hey, want to see one of our scouting reports?" I asked.

"Yeah!" Heidi said.

I knew they were expecting to see some top-secret plan. I turned to a large easel and lifted the cover page of a paper pad to reveal Nell's report.

In bold black letters were the words, "KICK THEIR ASS!"

There wasn't a whole lot left to do at this point. We knew our opponents so well, even Brazil, which we watched on videotape endlessly. It was a matter of keeping our focus, executing the game plans we had been polishing for nearly a year, and not cracking under the pressure. So much was expected of us.

Our journey to a higher level of women's basketball had dovetailed in Atlanta with an overall celebration of female athletes, a development that could never have been predicted when the Olympics were revived a century ago. Olympics founder Pierre de Coubertin barred women from competing in the first Olympics in 1896, as the ancient Greeks had done. But de Coubertin soon gave way to the progress of modern times. Nineteen women broke the gender barrier by competing in 1900. In Atlanta, about 3,800 women were among the 10,800 athletes who competed. The American women's softball, soccer, and gymnastics teams were predicted to win gold. We also had strong women's teams in beach volleyball, field hockey, swimming, volleyball, cycling, archery, track, fencing, and synchronized swimming.

The great sportswriter Frank Deford devoted an essay to female athletes in *Newsweek*'s Olympic preview issue.

"What has happened in the last generation to women in sports has been nothing short of revolutionary—and those who would seek to understand the 21st-century woman dismiss fun and games at their peril," Deford wrote. "Indeed we have actually come to this pretty pass: [Women] can play so well that this summer's Centennial Olympic Games fairly promise to be dominated by women athletes . . . Our men are assured the greater success only in basketball, but even there, the women might also win a gold, should they be able to beat China."

And Cuba and Australia and the Ukraine and Brazil.

In this year of the woman, no women's team had invested more or had more riding on its success than we did. No team, with the exception of gymnastics, loomed larger than ours among the emerging women's teams. With the help of NBA marketing, it had caught the attention of an American public that historically had not embraced women's sports. Of course, I wasn't thinking about any of this at the time. My vision had narrowed to Morehouse College and the Georgia Dome and my suite, where I met with my coaches every morning to update scouting reports and review tapes.

One day, I was in my hotel room watching the Olympics on TV with my mother, who had flown in for the second week of the games.

"Would that be great, to go to the Olympics?" I said absently.

"Tara, you *are* at the Olympics," my mother said.

But I wasn't at the same Olympics the fans were. I had no idea what else was going on, what other people were doing for fun, how the other U.S. teams were faring. I rarely left the hotel, except to take a run early in the morning and to go to practices and games. At the last minute, Nike, with whom I have a contract, asked me to appear at a press conference for them, and I declined. I got very rigid about how I was going to spend my time. It wasn't going to be at press conferences and Centennial Park concerts.

"All this is lost on me," I kept telling Carol during our runs.

I wanted the games to begin. Nothing else mattered. We had won 52 straight games. But they would mean nothing if we didn't win the next eight.

12

*It is the last step that counts. It is the last stroke on
the clock that counts. Many a prize has been lost
just when it was ready to be plucked.*

The journey of a hundred thousand miles, from coast to coast of the United States to China to Russia to Australia, had finally brought us to the Morehouse College gym on the afternoon of July 21, a Sunday. Our first game of the Olympics was 90 minutes away. I watched Sheryl sinking three-pointers on one end of the court as fans began to file in. Jennifer was on the other end catching passes from a ballgirl, stutter-stepping past an invisible defender and hitting jumper after jumper. They looked nervous, and I understood. A year of their lives, a country's hopes, a professional league's future—the time to deliver had arrived. We could lose one game in the preliminary round and still reach the gold medal game, but a second misstep would likely eliminate us.

I kept waiting for my own nerves to buzz, but they never did. I felt only the excitement and anticipation of watching our chess pieces, after careful maneuvering, close in on the king. To reporters, I had been saying we had proved nothing yet with our 52–0 record, that we weren't the indomitable Dream Team they made us out to be. But, deep down, so far that I would barely acknowledge it to myself, I knew we were. This was a phenomenal team, and I couldn't wait to see how the players would distill the hundreds of practices, scrimmages, and meetings into these next eight games. I felt as if I were about to take a test for which I had studied harder than I ever had before in my life. I knew the material cold. You're not nervous before a test after all that. Just the opposite. You feel almost euphoric.

"The players have taken on your focus," Ceal said to me one day during practice. "There's no way they're going to lose."

We had played and beaten Cuba six times in the past year and won the final three by an average of 35 points. No matter whom we played, we'd be ready. The coaches and I had scouted our opponents almost beyond reason. And as the games continued, we would have the benefit of watching tapes of all our opponents' games at the Olympics. A USOC video center recorded every competition in every sport at every venue and made the tapes available to the American coaches and no one else. Every day, Nell and Renee would break down our opponents' games on editing machines we had set up in their rooms. The players and coaches would spend about 45 minutes before practice watching the edited tapes. Back in the fall, each of our 11 players had been assigned to study one of the 11 teams we might face in the Olympics. The day before a game, the player assigned to that team would share what she remembered from playing them in previous games and what she had gleaned from the scouting tapes. I had not done this with my Stanford teams or other national teams. But with this team, it was crucial that every woman felt completely invested in our success. I wanted them to take responsibility for getting us prepared to play. (Because Venus joined us late, she wasn't assigned a team. She had enough to do just learning our own plays.) The three assistant coaches—Ceal, Marian, and Nancy—were assigned three and four teams each to study in greater depth. They would prepare one-page prescouting reports, then expand the reports to three or four detailed pages the day before a game. They would also prepare edited tapes of individual players on opposing teams so we could study their strengths and weaknesses.

Cuba was Teresa's team. She knew better than most how dangerous Cuba could be despite our success against them in exhibition games. Teams had been sandbagging each other in these games, so we couldn't be sure that the team we had beaten so many times in the past year would look the same on the floor of Morehouse gym. Teresa also didn't let us forget that Cuba had come within three points of beating us in China a few months earlier and had beaten the United States in the 1991 Pan Am Games in Havana— a loss Teresa had witnessed firsthand.

As our players warmed up on the court before the Cuba game, security guards suddenly ordered them into the locker room. They had found an unattended bag in the arena and had called in the bomb squad. It turned out to be a false alarm, but for 20 minutes the players sat around the locker room with no way to expend their nervous energy. Before we returned to the floor, we held hands in a circle and bowed our heads. We could hear the muffled pounding of the fans in the gym, but we were silent. We prayed like this before every game the entire year, each of us speaking to her God. I always offered up a separate prayer for each player as I visualized each receiving her gold medal. Then we closed in tight and touched hands high in the air in the center of our circle.

"OK!" I said. "This is it! The goal is gold!"

"The goal is gold!" they shouted back. They broke for the locker room door and emerged on the Morehouse court to thunderous cheers from the capacity crowd of 4,869 fans, among them Chelsea Clinton, Magic Johnson, Scottie Pippen, and George Steinbrenner.

Our starters—Teresa, Sheryl, Lisa, Katrina, and Ruthie—got off to an awful start, clunking shots off the rim and backboard. Five minutes into the game we were behind by seven points.

Cuba wasn't going to leave quietly.

A Cuban player yanked Venus to the floor, but no foul was called. So Venus retaliated by barreling between two Cuban players who were trying to block her from reaching the Cuban shooter. She nearly sent the two women flying—also no foul. Lisa lunged for a loose ball and smacked her head against a Cuban player's head, hitting her hard enough to force Lisa to leave the game. But before she left, she snapped a pass out to Dawn on the three-point line. Dawn drained it to put us ahead 23–20 midway through the first half.

Dawn was a joy to watch. Later, when Lisa returned, she passed the ball to Dawn and then cut quickly to the hoop. Without looking at Lisa, Dawn flipped the ball right back to her, and Lisa had an easy two. Then Dawn threw an over-the-shoulder, no-look pass to Katy for another two. Both plays pulled the crowd to its feet.

We had just a two-point lead when I took most of our starters out. I was counting on the reserve players to snap us out of our nervous funk, and that's what they did. Dawn and Katy in particular energized us off the bench. We knew, if we hadn't known before, that no one was going to hand us the gold medal simply for showing up. The starters, I think, drew inspiration and confidence from the reserves, who gave us an 11-point lead at halftime.

"We need to rebound," I told them in the locker room. "We need to play better defense. But we're doing all right. Our bench gave us the spark we needed, and now let's keep it going in the second half."

Lisa scored 17 points in the second half and did a better job of defending Cuba's center. The starters became more efficient and businesslike, the way they had been most of the year. We played well but not great in the 101–84 victory. Teresa, officially making history by playing in her fourth Olympics, had nine assists and five rebounds, and hit three of her four shots. All 12 players not only got into the game but scored. We couldn't hit anything from three-point range, however, sinking just three of 14 attempts.

Afterward, Katy spoke for all of us when she told reporters, "We're 1–0 in the biggest eight-game season we'll ever play."

Two days later, we played our cousins, the Ukrainians, in front of another sellout crowd at Morehouse gym. Our last game against the Ukraine had been in the tournament in Australia. We had won but played so poorly that I had plunged into a funk and wouldn't even go running with Carol. I told our players before the game they'd have to do a better job taking care of the ball, forcing turnovers and hitting outside shots. Despite the Ukraine's new starting point guard, our quickness and speed overpowered them, and the outcome was the same as in our previous 17 or 18 meetings during the year. We won by 33 points.

Two games down. Six to go.

Between games, I kept to a strict schedule: run at 7:30, work out in the gym, meet with the coaches at 10, meet with the players for a scouting session at 1, practice from 2 to 4, eat dinner, then scout other games. The assistant coaches and I would make friendly bets on the outcomes of these games, and we'd use the pagers the USOC gave us to inform one another of our own brilliant picks or of their poor ones.

We seemed to have conquered our nerves, and even though we were going to play our next game in the much larger Georgia Dome, I felt we wouldn't be awed by the scale and majesty of the place. Plus, the game was at noon on a Wednesday against Zaire. Spectators probably wouldn't be beating down the doors. I figured on 6,000, maybe 10,000 fans in the arena.

Some 31,000 showed up, the most ever to watch a women's basketball game. It was almost too much to absorb, all those people, sitting row upon row as far as we could see, cheering for us, waving American flags, holding up signs that read, "The REAL Dream Team." We were absolutely shocked when we walked into the arena. In that moment, all the work we had put in all year was worth the effort and sacrifice. To me, the incredible turnout for the game seemed proof that women's basketball was arriving—perhaps had arrived—as a major, mainstream sport in the United States.

I said a little prayer of thanks that we were playing Zaire. Australia or Russia might have been able to take advantage of our being overwhelmed by the scope of everything: the arena, the crowd, the noise, the attention. But the players from Zaire had no chance. Two days before playing us, they had lost by 46 points to Australia. They weren't skilled in the fundamentals, though they had talent and played extremely hard. They're the kind of team that would be fun to coach because you could absolutely transform their performance. Part of the problem was that the team had so few resources. Just a few days before the Olympics, NBA player Dikembe Mutombo gave his countrywomen money to buy uniforms and good basketball shoes.

Our main goal going into the game was to rest some players while giving others experience. Our starters played very little; among them, only Sheryl played more than 20 minutes. Lisa, whom we would need to depend on in later games, played nine minutes, three in the first half and six in the second. This game belonged to the reserves. Jennifer, who had scored just three points in the first two games, led the team with 18 points as we won easily and with absolutely no drama by a score of 107–47, the largest margin of victory for any U.S. women's Olympic basketball team.

The win assured us of a spot in the medal round.

In the meantime, Australia beat Cuba to set up something of a showdown against us in the next round. Like us, Australia was undefeated. Whoever won our game would own the top spot in the pool and would be rewarded in the first game of the medal round by playing the team with the worst record, theoretically giving the victor an easier path to the championship game.

President Clinton was supposed to come to the game against Zaire, but he was visiting the families of the TWA plane crash victims in New York. His aides said he'd like to see us after the game, so we waited for two hours in the locker room. I went into the trainer's room and fell asleep on one of the treatment tables as the players ate hamburgers somebody had fetched from a nearby Wendy's.

When the President and Mrs. Clinton arrived, we weren't sure what to say or how to act because they had had such a tough day. But they couldn't have been more enthusiastic about our success so far. They posed for pictures with all of us. As we set up for one photo, Venus massaged the President's neck. Only Venus would have the nerve.

"We're so proud of all of you," the President told us. "We're behind you 100 percent."

Once they left, I went back to the hotel to rest for a bit, then returned to the Georgia Dome to scout another game. But I couldn't get back in. The President was leaving the gymnastics arena, so no one was allowed in or out of the Georgia Dome until he was safely in his car. Here I had been standing inches from him just a few hours earlier and now I couldn't even be in the same building because security was tight. I groaned at the time, but what happened two days later stopped me from questioning even the most inconvenient safety precautions.

I woke up the morning of July 27, the day we were to play Australia, without knowing that the Olympics had been thrown into chaos. A bomb had exploded in Centennial Park within sight of our hotel around 1 o'clock in the morning. It had killed two people and turned downtown

Atlanta into a war zone of police in riot gear and panicked fans. Most of the players, who were staying on the 14th floor, had gathered in the hallway after the blast. Katrina's room had the best view of the park, so the team crowded by her window to watch the scurrying of ambulances and police cars and listen to CNN on the TV.

In my room on the tenth floor, I slept through it.

I didn't know anything until I got up in the morning for my jog and was told not to leave the hotel without a picture ID—I'd need it to get back in. Security had been tight from the beginning of the Olympics. Just as at the Athletes' Village, everyone staying at the hotel had to carry special credentials to enter and had to verify one's identity by placing one's hand on a scanner that matched the hand-print with the bar code on the credential. All guests and visitors had to scan purses and bags through a metal detector set up in the lobby. The men's and women's basketball teams had been assigned extra security from Olympic officials and also from the NBA's own security forces. But we often left the hotel with only our Olympic credential and not our hotel ID. Now the guards were cracking down. We had to carry every ID with us at all times. Bags going into the hotel were searched more thoroughly, as they were at the Olympic venues, after the bomb.

We met with the players in the morning to see how shook up they were. But like nearly all the athletes at the Olympics, they felt that quitting would be the wrong response to this act of cowardice. As Charles Barkley put it, "We shouldn't allow some knuckleheads to ruin it for everybody."

Despite speculation that the bomb would chase fans away, 33,952 showed up for our game against Australia that day, breaking the attendance record set two days earlier. Anyone who knew women's basketball knew this would be a great battle. All three games against Australia on our tour had been competitive. The Aussies were dogged if nothing else, and they had a great star in point guard Michelle Timms, one of the cagiest players in the world. Even Ruthie couldn't shut her down. She was fast, smart, competitive, and a great outside shooter. She played at all-out speed at all times, wearing out her defenders.

I didn't have to say much in the locker room before the game. We had been down by ten points against Australia in one game months earlier. We had been down by seven in another. And the Australian coach gave us wonderful incentive by popping off in the newspapers about how our team was overrated, how we were ripe for the taking and they were just the team to do it. What he failed to mention was that when we played them in Australia, we didn't have Katrina because she had been hurt. We didn't have Venus yet. We didn't have two neutral officials. And we didn't have a home crowd. From where I stood, it looked like the pendulum was swinging our way.

We didn't feel much pressure going into this game because losing one pool-play game wasn't the end of the world. But I knew we wouldn't lose. The Australian players came out running, as always, and led by six points early on. I was grateful that we had been able to rest our starters against Zaire because we needed everything they had. When Australia scored eight unanswered points, I sent in Venus, who was bigger and stronger than most of their players, and she muscled out eight points. At halftime, we led by three.

Australia prided itself on its defense. They felt they worked harder than any other team, and they had suggested in the past that the Americans were fat and lazy and got by on sheer talent. If that ever was true, it certainly wasn't now. We came into the second half focusing on our defense. We were relentless. We trapped them, forcing turnovers and then rocketing down the court for breakaway layups.

Timms tried to carry the Australian team on her back, hitting three consecutive three-pointers and then a layup to tie the game at 56 with 16 minutes left. This was when

Teresa and Katrina showed why they're the best in the world, and why their teammates had chosen them as captains. They took hold of the game as if taming a wild horse. Katrina scored 16 points in the second half, 24 overall. She missed just two shots all night. And Teresa played one of the most inspired games I've ever seen.

She was awesome, and I don't use the word casually. She seemed to see all the players on the court as if they were in slow motion. Timms, who had the sorry task of defending Teresa, found herself watching the older player stutter-step around her, whip passes by her, and shoot jumpers over her. In one play, Teresa was dribbling the ball with her right hand full speed down the court. Timms stood between her and the basket, so Teresa switched the ball to her left hand, causing Timms to shift in the same direction. Then in a blink, Teresa had switched the ball back to her right hand, leaving Timms rooted to the court, unable to change direction fast enough. Teresa drove straight to the hoop for a spectacular layup. The crowd let out a low "ooooh" in unison.

"Edwards just absolutely kicked my butt tonight," Timms said afterward.

Teresa scored 20 points, two more than she had scored in the three previous games combined. She missed just one shot, which gave her three missed shots so far at the Olympics. Even more impressive than her scoring were her smart, veteran instincts at the point. She found virtually every open player. By game's end, she had *15* assists. And seven rebounds. Any kid who wants to learn how to play basketball ought to find a tape of that game and study Teresa. You can't play much better than she played that night.

We won, 96–79.

"I didn't think *I* did it," she said in the press conference afterward. "Our team did it. Everything just fell into place for me."

But in our locker room, all the talk was about Teresa.

"T-money!"

"T-Bone!"

"T showed out!"

But Teresa didn't luxuriate in the moment. She knew, as we all did, that until we won the gold medal, we couldn't let our emotions run free. There was too much work left to do.

We had one game left in the preliminary round, against Korea. But instead of practicing for the game, I gave the team the next day, Sunday, off. I told them to bring whatever memorabilia, pictures, programs, and balls they wanted their teammates to sign and meet in my suite that afternoon. We had signed autographs for fans all year but had not signed for one another. I felt it was important to energize the team with something fun, something outside the gym and beyond the glare of the media and fans, something that would pull our tight-knit group even tighter going into the second week of the Olympics. For three hours we signed one another's souvenirs.

But before we started, I made an announcement. "I have a tape I want you to watch," I said. I could hear the groans. They figured it was a scouting report on Korea. But I had asked NBA Entertainment for the video they had just finished making that chronicled our year together. None of us had seen it yet. We howled and laughed and needled one another as we relived our first practice together in Colorado Springs, our trips to Russia and China and Australia, the late nights on buses traveling from one college town to another, our appearances in parades, malls, and classrooms. At the end, I handed every player her own copy of the tape. Little treats like this, I thought, would help keep the players energized and loose as the pressure mounted.

Korea stayed close for 20 minutes; we were ahead by just three points at halftime. Korea was much shorter than we were, but compensated with quickness. We were quick, too, but we were having a tough time chasing them all over the court. They'd bring their big players away from the basket to draw our big players away with them, thus giving their teammates a clearer shot at the hoop. So I had the team start the second half in the zone defense Don Monson had helped us learn back in October. It was a risk. The Koreans were good shooters, and if they could hit their outside shots, we were dead. But they couldn't. The zone absolutely stifled Korea. They apparently hadn't prepared for a zone defense because we weren't known for running it. We went on a 24–2 run early in the second half and won 105–64.

My mother, brother Nick, and sisters Beth and Heidi had arrived for the final week. My father stayed at home, but not only because he was sick. He had never intended to come. He gets so nervous he can barely watch my games. Nick is just like him. The two of them would wander the arena hallways during big games, their stomachs too knotted to sit.

My family immediately fell into the rhythm of Atlanta. They went to gymnastics, swimming, tennis, and boxing competitions. They stocked up on souvenirs for the folks back home, went out to dinner, and figured out the MARTA transport system. I, on the other hand, saw very little of the city beyond my hotel and the Georgia Dome. I crave routine, so I didn't want to disrupt my schedule by sightseeing or watching other competitions. Every day I'd meet with the coaches at the same time in the morning, have practice at the same hour, and go over scouting reports and videos with the players at the same time in the afternoon. I had little idea of what was going on in the Olympics beyond my narrow slice of it. And now that we were in the medal round, my focus narrowed further.

The year had come down to three games. Unlike the preliminary round, there were no second chances this time. This was the high wire. One loss and we were gone. But as with our first game, I wasn't nervous. I had been reading *The Power of Positive Thinking* before I fell asleep every night. So I had turned my nervousness into excitement. I looked forward to the final three games rather than feared them. Plus I knew that if I was uptight, our players would likely follow suit.

Our quarterfinal opponent was Japan, a team we had not played since scrimmaging against them before the 1994 World Championships in Australia. They had surprised everyone by beating China to reach the medal round. Japan was fascinating to watch because the team knew itself so well. Their obvious shortcoming was height; they had no player over six feet tall. The players couldn't do anything about that, so they nurtured the parts of their game in which they excelled: three-point shooting and defense. That was a great lesson. Identify what you do best and do it as well as you can. They were so disciplined and passionate that you knew they weren't going to let themselves down because of lack of preparation, lack of focus, or laziness, as some teams do. Their coach squeezed every drop of talent and skill from his players, more than any team I saw at the Olympics. Japan had beaten China and Canada to qualify as the fourth team in their pool, so I wasn't surprised that they challenged us.

Japan tossed up three-pointers at every opportunity, knowing that was their only chance to beat us. They tried 32 three-pointers and made 13. We went inside to Lisa and Katrina, using our size advantage to score and rebound. We had a 28-point lead in the second half, but Japan kept chipping away and cut the lead to 13 with seven minutes left. I think we had become a little complacent, and Japan's comeback was a wake-up call that no game, not even a portion of a game, could be taken lightly. Lisa and Katrina led a scoring spurt that widened our lead to 21 points, and we ended up winning 108–93. Lisa scored 35 points, the most ever by an American woman in the Olympics. And Katrina had 16 rebounds, another U.S. Olympic record.

After the game, I asked track star Jackie Joyner-Kersee

into the locker room to talk with our players. Our players and I had met her in New York the previous October at the Women's Sports Foundation's annual awards dinner. She had played basketball for four years at UCLA, and there were rumors that she would play in the ABL. When I spotted her at our game against Japan, I remembered how impressed our team had been with her at the dinner and knew her words would carry weight with them.

"All of this is nothing," she told us in the locker room, "unless you win the gold medal."

In the other quarterfinal on our side of the draw, Australia had upset Russia by four points in an overtime thriller, setting up a rematch with us in the semifinals. I wasn't sure which was a better matchup for us, Australia or Russia. We had beaten Australia four times in the previous three months, but the only time we played the Russians, in Chicago, we barely escaped with an 80–79 victory. So on the surface Australia seemed an easier foe. But we were tired of playing Australia. We wanted to be done with them. If we were the least bit complacent, Australia could rise up and surprise us. Russia, on the other hand, would keep us sharp. We knew we would have to play our best to win, and great teams draw energy from such challenges. So I think we were a bit disappointed to be facing Australia yet again.

Even against Australia, however, we couldn't take anything for granted in a semifinal game, where we had met our downfall in recent years. We had reached the semifinals of the 1991 Pan Am Games, the 1992 Olympics in Barcelona, and the 1994 World Championships and lost all three times. These last two games of the Olympics would either justify USA Basketball's investment or render it a failure. We could beat most teams with just a few weeks of training—we had proven that in the past. Our year of work was solely to win these last two games of the tournament.

In the other semifinal, the Ukraine would play Brazil.

The winner of our game would play the winner of theirs for the gold medal. I prayed Brazil would win. We had played against the Ukrainians so often that playing them yet again for the gold medal would be anticlimactic, and we had come too far to be cheated of the emotional payoff we had anticipated for so long. After the championship game, I wanted to feel the most extreme of emotions. I wanted to feel the pure joy of accomplishment, the rush of adrenaline that winning brings. But I also wanted to feel the sadness of coming to the end of the most exciting challenge of my life, of leaving people I had come to love. On that day, in the last hours of the Olympics, I wanted all of those feelings to collide inside me. Only playing Brazil could give that to any of us.

Playing Brazil for the gold medal would be like a *Rocky* movie, with flashbacks of the near-riot in Brazil after we won the World Championships qualifier in 1993, our loss to Brazil at the World Championships in Australia in 1994, the sight of their wildly exuberant players ruffling their coach's hair on the bus as they teased him about his promise to shave it off. I remembered, too, how Brazil's star players, Hortencia Marcari Olivia and Maria Paula Silva, swept onto the bus we shared with them from the airport to the hotel in Australia and how they took the two front seats as if they were queens. Outside the coach's hotel room in Australia, he had posted comments after every game. Even after they lost by 40 points to Australia in an early round, he wrote about the "Great Hortencia" and the "Great Paula." They possessed a real cockiness that piqued our competitive juices. It was our loss to the Brazilians that had set us on this course to recapture our place atop the basketball world. It was only fitting that we end the journey with them as well.

In the paper the day before our semifinal against Australia, I saw that the Australian coach had taken another shot at us. "There's no way they're going to beat us twice," he said. "OK, buddy," I thought, "we're going to kick your ass worse." Maybe I was wrong, but I sensed that the Australian coach's distemper came in part from losing to a woman coach. I was the only female basketball coach at the Olympics. I think losing to my team bothered the Australian coach and the coaches from Russia and Brazil. They never gave credit to our team or to me after we beat them. The Russian coach didn't shake my hand after we beat his team by a point in Chicago. Their dislike and resentment was something I could just feel, though it was difficult to put my finger on exactly what it was. I felt they didn't respect me, unlike the coaches from Japan, China, Cuba, and the Ukraine. I had become friends with those men, even if only in brief conversations through interpreters; there was mutual admiration. But the others seemed to take losses to my team personally. They always had excuses for losing.

In Friday's semifinal doubleheader, Brazil played the Ukraine in the first game. Our team dressed early and sat in the stands to watch. When the Australian team walked into the arena to watch the last part of the game, I saw they were wearing their white uniforms. We were also in whites. I looked at Carol, and she looked at me.

"Who's wrong?" I asked.

Carol checked with an international basketball official and returned.

"We are."

Because of what had happened when I went to the 1992 Final Four with Stanford, when Western Kentucky gave me a scare by showing up in the wrong uniforms, I made sure we always brought both sets to every game. I walked over to Jennifer and quietly told her the team needed to change uniforms. "No big deal," I said. "Just go and change." She tapped her teammates on the shoulders and ushered them back to the locker room. I shuddered to think about scrambling back to the hotel minutes before our semifinal game in the Olympics.

"This is why you're successful," Carol said. "Details."

Brazil beat the Ukraine by 21 points.

Now we had to beat Australia.

This game was do or die. We had beaten them and beaten them. Did we have it in us to beat them one more time? Australia had defeated us in a scrimmage before the 1994 World Championships, and they carried that victory like a talisman, drawing strength and confidence from it. But we knew Australia has few weapons beyond Timms. And I felt fairly certain their coach wouldn't change their strategy from previous games to try to catch us by surprise. He had his game plan and, whether it was arrogance or a belief in consistency, he was sticking with it, even if it had failed against us before.

"All those other times we've beaten them," I told our team in the locker room before the game, "they meant nothing. This is the one we've worked for."

When we fell behind by eight points early in the game, I felt a twinge of anxiety but it quickly disappeared. It was almost as if I had done a brainwashing job on myself. I had convinced myself we would not be beaten, though my family and friends were nervous wrecks in the stands. My brother Nick told me later that he paced behind the top rows of the arena, unable to watch. But I had worked all year on learning how to control my nerves. I had to believe with all my heart that we would win. I couldn't let a doubt creep into my mind. If a coach doesn't believe in her team, how can she expect her players to believe? Plus, panic clouds the eyes and muddles the mind.

We went into a zone defense, which Australia didn't attack well. We had never used it against Australia, so I guess they thought we wouldn't in this game, either. We shut them down. During one stretch in the first half, we kept them from scoring for ten straight possessions while we scored 15 unanswered points. Timms, trying to do everything, got into foul trouble in the second half and wasn't much of a factor. Ruthie and Nikki held her scoreless for

13 minutes early in the second half, though she still scored 27 points by game's end.

The Australians had no answer for Lisa or Katrina inside. Of our 38 field goals, we scored 32 in the paint (near the basket). We outrebounded them, 48–25. Katrina had 18 points and 15 rebounds. Lisa had 22 points and 13 rebounds. We dominated. The final score: 93–71.

In the press conference afterward, the Australian coach predicted we'd lose to Brazil.

"Their horses, McClain and Leslie, are the difference, but this team is beatable," he said. "They have two big players and three good perimeter players—three star perimeter players. Edwards has been sensational. To beat them, you have to beat that first group.

"Brazil can do it. Brazil can't defend the U.S. as well as we can. But the U.S. can't defend Brazil as well, either."

Katrina also spoke at the press conference. She put the championship game in perspective. "If we don't win," she said, "to me the whole year has been a waste."

The journey that had started 14 months earlier had one game to go. "There's 40 minutes between me and that gold medal," Ruthie said to me.

We kept to our regular routine on Saturday, the day before the championship game. I met with the coaches in the morning, held practice in the afternoon, and had individual editing sessions with each player. We put together five-minute videos of Brazil's three star perimeter players—Paula, Hortencia, and Janeth Arcain. I had watched the video of our World Championships loss to Brazil so many times, I had each frame committed to memory. In our last practice on Saturday before Sunday's game, I knew we would be OK. We had reached a peak. We were so prepared and so ready to play. I'm not sure we could have lasted another week—such intensity is impossible to sustain for long. But we were primed right then.

As we inched closer to the moment we had worked for all year, a sense of loss crept into my excitement. After

Sunday night, I would never coach these women again. When I was finished, it would be somebody else's turn to take over the national team. The players would be going on to the pros; I'd be back at Stanford. I thought about how much I had enjoyed the work every day. For an entire year I was able to give my all to the team, and the players gave theirs to me. I knew, as the hours slipped by, I would never again feel this depth of satisfaction.

That afternoon, I played bridge with my mom, Heidi, and Beth, but it wasn't quite like the old days. They were nervous, and I was distracted. I was usually ready to annihilate my opponents, but that day I was merely holding the cards. My mind scanned every detail for the upcoming game as if on a ticker tape through my brain. I had to remind Lisa to protect herself from the Brazilian center's elbow on the opening jump ball. She always elbowed Lisa in the neck. I replayed their favorite out-of-bounds play. I recalled how they liked to bounce free throws off the backboard to set up three-point shots.

"Look, we're 59–0," I said to my family. "We've got one game left. We're not going to let up now."

I was in a "zone," as they say. My focus was so complete, it was as if I could almost see the game before it happened. We were healthy for the first time all year. We were calm. Our game would be the last competition of the Olympics. By the time we took the court, there would be only 12 unclaimed gold medals of the hundreds awarded during those 16 days in Atlanta. They were ours.

The morning of August 4, the day we had targeted on our calendars for a year, I set out on my usual 45-minute run with Carol. We headed down Martin Luther King Drive past the Georgia Dome, past the restaurant that promised "The Best Soul Food in Atlanta," past the field hockey venue, and into a little park. We usually turned around at a particular telephone pole and headed back to the hotel. But when we got to the pole, I said, "Let's go a little farther just in case we go into overtime." On the return loop, there were three hills. In my mind, the first one represented the quarterfinals, the second the semifinals, and the third the final—the gold medal game. That Sunday, we sprinted up the last hill.

While I was jogging, my mother and brother Nick had taken the MARTA underground train to an Episcopal church for mass.

"I prayed that whatever is supposed to happen is in the hands of the Lord now," my mother said to Nicky on their ride home. "If they need to be humbled, they'll be humbled. If they're meant to win, they'll win."

"I'm more selfish," Nick said. "I said, 'Lord, let them win.'"

When I showered after my run, I thought back to my question of exactly a year earlier. How would I feel taking a shower the day of the championship game? I felt no different. It was just another shower, as it would be just another game. That's what I told the players in the locker room later. Don't do anything different from what you've done all year. The court is the same as always. The ball is the same as always. And you'll win the same as always.

Later in the morning, the team gathered in my suite to watch another video. Nell had edited together snippets of every other American gold medal winner. No silver. No bronze. We watched Michael Johnson win the 200- and 400-meter sprints. We saw the women's soccer and softball teams, the gymnastics team and the synchronized swimmers. We laughed and cheered. The video both inspired and relaxed us, breaking whatever tension might have been building as game time approached.

As I got ready to leave for the Georgia Dome that afternoon, I looked at my hotel mirror with the photos of the dome, the gold medal, and Teresa and me on the high wire. I spoke to the Brazilian coach.

"There's no way you're coming between this team and a gold medal," I said out loud.

When I arrived at the arena, I went into the coach's

locker room to be by myself. I thought back to the first time I had ever played basketball as a little kid in the neighbor's driveway. I remembered the afternoons I spent shooting by myself or with the boys. I saw myself on the living room couch charting the Celtics game with my dad. I thought about playing at Indiana and coaching at Ohio State and Stanford. I took this slow trip in my mind and thought of how far my basketball life had come. All the bits and pieces were coming together on this one day. I shook my head.

"This is the gold medal game," I had to tell myself. "And you are the coach."

Out in the players' locker room, the women were listening to music on headsets or talking quietly. Australia was playing the Ukraine for the bronze medal on the court, so I wandered out to watch just to occupy my mind for a while. I saw Kay Yow, who had been the 1988 Olympic coach and headed the selection committee that had offered me the job.

"You'll do it," Kay said. "You're ready."

It meant a lot to know how completely she supported me and the team.

When the team joined hands for our final circle, I felt a sense of mission in the room. No one said anything. We bowed our heads in silence. I once again visualized the gold medal ceremony. Then we pulled in tight for a cheer. I told them about the shower, which got them laughing. Then I got serious. "The outcome of this game won't determine what a great team we have," I said. "Regardless of what happens, you've been a special team. And this has been a special year.

"All right! The goal is the gold!"

"The goal is the gold!" they repeated.

We marched into the arena to deafening noise—music, cheers, announcements in English and French. The huge Jumbotron screen flashed our pictures. I noticed little else.

I didn't see my family in the stands. I didn't see any of the signs people waved. I was just thinking about basketball.

Each team warmed up in front of its own bench, so I didn't watch Brazil much. But every now and then I'd steal a glance their way and think, "We're going to kick your ass."

Brazil was 7–0 in the tournament, as we were. By beating the Ukraine to reach the final, they had assured themselves of their first Olympic medal. The Brazilian women had not competed in Olympic basketball until 1992, when they finished seventh. Since then, they had set the standard internationally and came into the games as reigning world champions. Nearly all their top players were back from their world championship team. Thirty-four-year-old Maria Paula Silva—"Magic Silva," she wore on her headband—was a deadly shooter. She hit five of nine three-pointers against the Ukraine in the semifinal. Hortencia Marcari Oliva was probably their most famous player. She was 36 years old and had left the team for a year when she had a baby. Now she was back and as dangerous as ever. She scored 20 points against the Ukraine, making eight of her 13 shots. In the 1994 World Championships, she scored 32 against us.

With the crowd roaring in our ears, Katrina, Ruthie, Sheryl, Teresa, and Lisa took the floor. Sheryl fouled their center, Marta Sobral de Sooza, who hit one of two free throws for the first point on the board. Then Ruthie hit a 25-foot jump shot for three points as soon as she touched the ball. Defensively, she and Sheryl were relentless on Paula and Hortencia. So it was Brazil's post players who began to give us trouble.

"Maybe we should have done edits on the post players, too," Nancy said to me on the bench.

They kept pounding us inside, and Lisa seemed in a funk, as if she were afraid to draw a foul. I took her out and put Venus in. Venus earned her spot on the team right there. She went right after Marta, bumping her, leaning on her, taking a charge. Lisa sat out just a few minutes, but they were pivotal. She had time to collect herself, and when she went back in she was great. The offense began to click as it never had before.

We made an amazing 72 percent of our shots in the first half. Lisa hit six of seven baskets and sank three free throws for 15 points. Paula, so dangerous in past games, made just one basket in the half.

We went into halftime up by 11 points. That was good and not so good. Shooting 72 percent from the field, you'd think we'd be crushing them. And 11 points was nothing for Brazil. They had been down by 20 to us in the Qualifiers and had rallied to win.

"We're 20 minutes away from what we've been working for all year," I said to the players in the locker room. "We're not rebounding worth a damn. We're letting them get second and third shots. How important can this be if you're not putting bodies on them?"

We scored the first eight points of the second half to build our lead to 19. Lisa capped the scoring run with a drive to the basket along the baseline, and as she ran back on defense, she pumped her fist in the air and yelled. It was as if we could feel the pent-up emotions ready to explode. We had looked pretty dominating in other games during our 59–0 run, but no game matched this one. We scored on 11 of our first 12 possessions. There were no-look passes, bounce passes, steals. There were Lisa stretching for the hoop, Ruthie hitting threes and diving for loose balls.

After a time-out, we took the ball out of bounds under our own basket. I called our "Florida" alley-oop out-of-bounds play, which we had never tried in a game. Teresa floated the ball up toward the basket, where Katrina grabbed it and laid it in for two points. They executed it perfectly.

The players looked bullet-proof, the way athletes do in those rare slices of time when their minds and bodies are working in perfect concert with their teammates' minds and bodies. We felt such an adrenaline rush, even on the bench, that I completely understood mothers lifting cars off babies. There is such power in the passion that runs through your body at certain peak moments in your life. This was what I was seeing now with these women. Since I had been at Indiana, I had always carried in my mind a vision of how basketball should look, as if it were art or a mathematical equation. There should be balance and logic, a little bit of raw genius, some surprise and beauty, and a seamless energy infusing it from beginning to end. This was it.

As our lead stretched to 20, 25, 30, the reserve players who had not been in the game yet began to grow restless. They wanted a piece of this championship game, and I understood that. But even midway through the second half, I wasn't comfortable pulling all the starters. In international ball, teams can't call time-outs whenever they want. So I couldn't substitute players the way I can in college. What if Brazil, an explosive offensive team and great three-point shooters, went on a scoring tear with the reserves in there and I couldn't get my starters back in to stop the damage? I couldn't worry about players' feelings at this point. This game wasn't about playing time. It was about winning the gold medal. After 59 games and a year of work, I wasn't willing to accept even the slightest risk.

With six minutes left, I put in Jennifer, Katy, and Rebecca. And with three minutes left, I put in Carla. Every player scored at least two points. Lisa was already crying on the sideline as the final minutes ticked down. Teresa knelt and raised her eyes to the ceiling. She was about to become the oldest player—at 32 years and 17 days—to play for a gold medal team. Twelve years earlier in Los Angeles, she had become the youngest basketball player to win a gold medal. She had ten assists in the game. Lisa scored 29 points. Hortencia and Paula, who had combined for 61 points against us in Australia, scored 18 between them.

With 17 seconds left, Jennifer—the last player cut from the 1992 Olympic team—tossed in a layup for the final basket. I looked up at the scoreboard: 111–87. No women's Olympic team had ever scored more points in a gold medal game. Ruthie stood next to me in the final moments. Her sister Mae Ola, who had missed making the 1988 team, sat next to her father behind our bench. Both wore USA Basketball jerseys with Ruthie's number on them. Ruthie's father, stoic, almost expressionless, held a framed photograph of his late wife.

"I did this for two people," Ruthie said, her arm around my shoulders. "My dad, and you."

As the clock ran out and the players collapsed into a knot on the court, I hugged Nancy, Ceal, Marian, Carol, Nell, and Renee. I finally allowed myself to look up in the stands at the American flags waving from every corner of the arena, people cheering and chanting, "USA! USA!" From the sea of people I saw my mother rushing down the aisle, screaming at the top of her lungs.

"TARA! TARA!"

A security guard tried to stop her. "Lady, you can't be down here."

"That's my daughter!" my mother cried.

So the security guard started yelling for me, too. When I saw my mother crying like a baby, I began to cry, too. I had been in complete control until then because I had pictured this moment in my head almost every day for a year. I saw us rushing onto the floor. I saw the gold medals hanging from each player's neck. The visions in my head were now simply playing out in three dimensions.

But I hadn't seen my mother in all those daydreams of our victory. Catching sight of her instantly transported me to the neighbors' driveways in West Hill and the junior high gym in Albany where I sweated inside the mascot costume; to the Indiana bleachers where I sat with a notebook on my lap watching Bobby Knight's practices; to the trailer in Columbus, Ohio, where I lived on food stamps to survive my first job as an assistant coach; to the wind-swept track in Colorado Springs, where half the players couldn't make their two-mile times; to the sleepless nights wondering how we would win. The journey to this moment rushed through me like a time-lapse video. Even now, I have difficulty putting words to the feelings that rumbled and swirled inside me. More than anything, I think what I felt was pride. I was so proud of how the team played. They deserved every cheer that was raining down on them. They had scored 100 points or more for the fifth time in the eight Olympic games. They had made 66 percent of their shots for the game. Lisa had scored 29 points, making 12 of her 14 attempts. Katrina scored 12 points, making six of eight shots.

The people in the arena who saw what might have been the best 40 minutes of basketball ever played by the best women's team in history couldn't know what had gone into those 40 minutes. It was not only a year of grueling workouts and exhausting travel, but decades of women—and men—selling cupcakes to buy uniforms, hounding athletic directors for scholarships, refusing to accept second-class status, believing in the game and in women when there wasn't even a national tournament, much less an Olympic one.

As the tears welled in my eyes, the players ran victory laps around the court as the speakers blared the song "Celebration." Some danced. Jennifer did a cartwheel. Then they hustled into the locker room to pull on their warmup uniforms for the medal ceremony. A few minutes later, they marched back out, sandwiched between the Brazil and Australia teams. I noticed the tears on the Brazilian coach's face, but his players took the game's outcome well. They shook hands and hugged us, happy to win their country's first medal in women's basketball.

As our players stepped up to the top platform of the

victory stand, I watched from in front of the bench. They held hands in one long unbreakable chain. One by one, starting with Teresa, they bent forward to receive their gold medals, as they had that October morning in the empty Georgia Dome.

When Ruthie stepped down from the victory platform, she walked to the stands, where her father and sister were still clapping and crying. Ruthie lifted the medal over her head and held it up for Mae Ola. Mae Ola leaned forward, and Ruthie draped it around her sister's neck. As Mae Ola sobbed, her father stood next to her, one hand on his wife's photograph, the other patting his daughter's back.

I walked over to Ruthie and slipped my arm around her waist. She draped her arm over my shoulder, and we walked off the court together for the last time.

"Great, great game," I told the team in the locker room. "This was about more than a gold medal. I appreciate all the hard work and all the sacrifices each of you made to make this happen—"

Suddenly, I felt a rush of cold water on my head. Jennifer had crept up behind me and dumped a bottle of water on me, a substitute for the huge tubs of Gatorade football players traditionally dump on their winning coach. I didn't bother to stop the flow of water onto my new suit. I'm not sure I was feeling much of anything at that point. When the laughter died down, the team drew together for a prayer. We held hands and bowed our heads.

"Thank you, Lord, for what we've had together," Ruthie prayed out loud.

Afterward, the players draped their medals around the coaches' necks and we took pictures. I congratulated and thanked every player individually. When I got to Teresa, I gave her a hug.

"We did it, T," I said. She smiled. "We did," she said.

Then we went into the press room for the postgame interviews. I sat there with wet hair and clothes, answering questions and listening to the players.

"This is what we've been shooting for," Jennifer told reporters. "You can't imagine the workouts we've been through. The things no one ever saw. Eating dinner in China, traveling in Russia, pushing through intensive workouts. The relief and the joy are indescribable."

"This is a great day for women's basketball," Sheryl said. "It doesn't get any better than that. I think we all were feeling it."

"It's the greatest feeling in the world," added Dawn. "I could stop playing basketball right now. That's how good it feels."

Then Dawn was asked about everyone going her separate way, some to the ABL, some to the WNBA, some overseas. The question made Dawn already begin to miss her teammates. "It's really sad. We're not feeling the effects of it yet because we're coming off the floor with a gold medal."

Katrina, who had been the last player to commit to trying out for the team, talked about what she drew from her teammates.

"A lot of time, a lot of sacrifices went into winning this gold medal," she said. "We got to know each other well. There's a lot of love on this team. It's going to be missed. But we're back on top. We beat the best team in the world."

Brazil's players were gracious in defeat. "We did what we could," Hortencia said in the press conference. "We still scored 87 points. It is not our team that lost it, but the United States that won."

USA Basketball hosted a huge party at our hotel afterward. I went up to my room first to shower and change clothes. Then I called my dad in Chautauqua. He had had some friends over to watch the game, but I could picture him reading a book in the back of the room, refusing to torture himself by watching too closely. He told my sister Marie to call him only if we were up by 30 points with five minutes left. He actually ended up watching the last ten minutes, enough to throw in his usual two cents' worth of analysis.

"How are you feeling?" I asked.

"Congratulations! Make sure you tell those players your father sends his best wishes."

"I will."

Pause.

"You know you could have played a little better defense."

I laughed. He really doesn't know that much about basketball, but it's a little joke between us. He always has to say something, as if he's Red Auerbach or somebody.

The party was in full swing when I arrived around 11 o'clock. The players were having a ball, hugging everybody in sight. I was so spent that I mostly sat in a corner with my family and Amy and a few friends as they told jokes and relived the highlights of the game. I didn't say much. I had given everything I had every day for so long, and I think there was nothing left. I went up to my room around 1 o'clock, and my sister Heidi helped me pack. All the players, coaches, and USA Basketball people were leaving in the morning. We had been together for so long, and just like that everyone would be gone. We were flying home in a dozen different directions to pick up our lives where they had left off. No, that wasn't true. Nobody's life was the same as it had been when we began this trip together a year earlier. The ABL was waiting for Jennifer, Teresa, Nikki, Katy, Dawn, Venus, and Carla. Lisa, Sheryl, Rebecca, and Ruthie would sign with the WNBA. In fact, Lisa would land a $1 million contract with the WNBA, reportedly the largest contract ever for an American woman in a team sport. Katrina would return to her $500,000 contract in Turkey. They were stars now. Olympic gold medalists. Basketball had changed, too. Attendance at college games would continue to rise. More games would land on television. Newspapers would run more stories on the college women and the ABL teams. Women had arrived.

A month after the Olympics I got a letter from Ruthie postmarked from Istanbul, where she was playing in a pro league, waiting for the WNBA to begin the following summer.

"Dear Coach VanDerveer,

"Excuse me for waiting so long to write you a thank-you note for all you did and have done the past five years. You are truly my *Number One* coach. You'll never know the impact that you've made on my life. You were the first coach to truly believe in me, and for that I owe you so much. As long as I live you will always remain a very special part of my life. Take care, and I wish you all the success this season. Love, Ru-Ru Ruthie."

Hundreds of letters arrived at my Stanford office from fans and colleagues. I answered every one of them. Ruthie's was special, and so was this one, from Bobby Knight.

"Your team was a pleasure to watch as they played basketball the way the game was meant to be played," he wrote. "There are not many teams that I enjoy watching play but yours was certainly one of them. The teaching, discipline and enthusiasm that you instilled in your players was evident in all that they did. The teamwork that your kids had was a further testimony to your ability to teach.

"Best wishes and again congratulations on what was a magnificent job of teaching and leading."

My basketball camp for kids was starting at Stanford soon after I arrived home. In the middle of one of the drills, a 12-year-old girl sighed heavily.

"What's the matter?" I asked.

"This drill is too basic," she said.

This was a drill we had done with our Olympic team. I thought back to when I was 12 and had to wear a bear costume to get near a basketball. Now 12-year-old girls were so advanced and cocky that drills we ran with our Olympic team were old hat. I smiled. On the one hand, the girl's complaint went against every tenet I hold about hard work, discipline, and the importance of fundamentals.

On the other hand, it made my day.

Epilogue

What your desire is, so is your will.
What your will is, so is your deed.
What your deed is, so is your destiny.
—*Deepak Chopra*

For months after the Olympics, I'd sometimes dream I was still coaching the Olympic team. But the floor was tilted, the lights wouldn't come on, and we were playing with a Nerf ball. Or I'd dream we were playing Brazil again and again and again. I'd wake up in a cold sweat. I had never allowed myself to consider the possibility of losing. At least, I had never allowed the thought to rise to the surface of my consciousness. Now it came bubbling up. Even while awake—in the car, sitting at dinner, writing letters— I'd be gripped with a flush of panic, then remember the Olympic Games were over. We had won the gold medal.

The morning after our championship game, I flew from the Olympics back to Stanford, where our annual girls' basketball camp had already begun. No time to take a breath. After the camp, I traveled to Italy with the Stanford team and spent the flight and every spare moment answering 200 letters of congratulations. We played games for two weeks in Italy, in some of the same cities I had traveled with the Olympic team. A waiter I had met the previous year congratulated me on the Olympic victory. From Italy, I went on the road to visit recruits. Then practice for the new season at Stanford began in October.

Every morning when I arrived in my office, my desk would be a patchwork of "While you were out . . ." phone messages from TV stations, fundraising organizations, coaching clinics, corporations, journalists. They were a daily reminder that the life to which I returned wasn't the life I had left. In the supermarket, men and women would look at me closely, then blurt, "Are you Tara VanDerveer?" People who I suspected knew little about women's basketball a few months earlier now wanted autographs and pictures with me.

My focus had to stay with basketball. We had ten players returning from the previous season's Final Four team, including all five starters, and we had three freshman guards who were good enough to challenge for playing time. The players made my adjustment back to college ball easier because they were so motivated and excited about the new season. I fed off their energy as much as I could because I was exhausted—but stubbornly refused for a long time to acknowledge just how exhausted I was.

I had coached games in each of the previous 12 months, and now there were five more months waiting for me at Stanford. I felt I was running on empty, but how could I slow down? I wanted to give our Stanford players all the time and energy they deserved. My friend Brooks Johnson, the former Stanford track coach, sent me a note. In capital letters, he wrote, "REST IS NOT A FOUR-LETTER WORD." Amy was telling me, too, I had to allow myself some down time or I'd burn out or get sick. I began coming into the office less and turned down most speaking engagements. At Christmas I spent four restful days with my family in Florida. I brought no basketball work with me. It was the first time in nearly two years that I allowed myself to be completely free of basketball—no scouting reports, no tapes.

I returned to Stanford for the second half of the season feeling refreshed. We were ranked No. 3 in the country after losing to Old Dominion. It would be our only loss of the regular season. I think it was difficult for some Stanford players to readjust to me after spending the previous season with Amy as head coach. Things were more relaxed under Amy, a reflection of her more laid-back nature. I had returned to Stanford on a mission, eager to continue the success I had just enjoyed with the Olympic team.

"All right," I told the team. "You had a great year last year. You reached the Final Four. Now we want to do better."

I took the players out of the comfort zone they had established with Amy. Bill Walsh, the former coach for the San Francisco 49ers and for Stanford, believed in keeping his players on edge, making sure they always felt they had to prove themselves. I put a quick stop to the players' newfound practice of "belly-bumping," in which they smacked bellies instead of high-fiving after big plays. I felt it was showing up the other team and wasn't in keeping with the image of Stanford.

I wouldn't have tolerated the antic any year, but I especially wasn't open to it when I returned from the Olympics. Working with the pro players was all business. And I expected a similar attitude from the Stanford team. I had such high expectations after coaching some of the world's best players that I was difficult to impress. Amy had to remind me, "You're dealing with 18–, 19–, and 20–year-olds. They make mistakes, they forget plays, they leave things at home." She was right, of course. I had to make concessions not only for their youth but also for their commitment to school. Once I got some rest and felt like myself again, I relaxed a bit more.

As the season went on, I saw how I had changed as a coach. I had become a better teacher during the Olympic year because I had to tailor my teaching to such a variety of personalities. I was also a better tactical coach. I had been exposed to so many different teams and styles of play that I had greater confidence in my ability to make adjustments to whatever an opponent might throw at us.

And as much as anything, I learned how to deal with pressure. Shouldering the pressure of trying to win a gold medal for my country put all other basketball pressure in perspective. The pressure of trying to get back to the Final Four didn't weigh on me as heavily as it had in years past.

I found, too, that for as focused as I was on winning the national championship with Stanford, my world had grown much larger than college basketball. Going to the Olympics, I felt as if I had been to the moon, and once you've been there, the view on earth is never the same. There were the pro leagues now that offered potential opportunities. There was broadcasting. Motivational speaking. Perhaps there were opportunities with international basketball. I want to start a coaches' academy to share what I've learned. Many colleges have dropped physical education as a major, so there is not the development of coaches that there used to be. I feel very strongly about my responsibility to help the next generation of coaches, particularly women.

The weekend of my first game back at Stanford, Carol Callan called me with an invitation to fly to Orlando. I had been voted the United States Olympic Committee's Coach of the Year. The award, along with other USOC team and athlete awards, would be presented at a gala dinner in Orlando. I was stunned by the honor, but I couldn't go to a dinner across the country the day before our season-opener.

I've seen Jennifer at many of our Stanford games, watching from up in the press section. She played for the San Jose Lasers of the ABL but dislocated her shoulder after eleven games and was out for the season. Before she was injured, she was averaging 16.6 points a game, making 57 percent of her shots.

Several of the Olympic players struggled with injuries during the ABL season. Carla's playing time was limited for the Atlanta Glory because of ankle problems. She played 26 games in the 40-game season, and she started just 14 games. Venus was bothered with a knee injury from the pre-season and played in just 13 games for the Seattle Reign before having surgery. She missed the rest of the season. She was also involved in a car accident in Louisiana, which, I'm told, affected her memory.

Katy started 29 games and played in all 40 for the Portland Power, averaging 8.4 points and 4.4 rebounds. She was married in May.

Teresa, Nikki, and Dawn turned out to be the top stars in the ABL. All three were named to the inaugural All-ABL First Team, selected by a national media panel. Nikki was named Most Valuable Player. Teresa finished second in league scoring, averaging 21.1 points a game for the Atlanta Glory. She led her team in scoring, rebounding, and assists. Nikki finished third in the league in scoring with 19.9 points per game for the Columbus Quest. Dawn led the league in assists, averaging 8 per game for the Richmond Rage.

The ABL got off to a fairly strong start in its first season. The New England franchise averaged a league-leading 5,008 fans per game, despite finishing last in the Eastern Conference. Columbus, on the other hand, finished first in the conference and attracted a league-low 2,682 fans per game. Overall, the league averaged 3,536 fans per game, rising to more than 4,000 for February, the final month of the regular season.

Yet I was disappointed in what I saw at the games I attended. I felt in some ways the women were trying to emulate the men. They were acting like something they're not, meaning they were not big enough stars yet to get away with the bad habits and bad attitudes many of the men in pro basketball have. I saw women out of shape, women who didn't hustle, women who in their body language conveyed that they weren't giving the fans a full effort. I felt our USA players had been tremendous role models. They trained hard and played hard. They ran to the bench during timeouts. They played 60 games in a year—20 more than the ABL regular season. So the USA players had plenty of excuses to slack off, but they played 100 percent on the court every night.

But watching the ABL games, I wanted to go out there and shake some people and say, "Look! You don't get a second chance to make a first impression. There are people here watching your league for the first time. You want to do everything you can to communicate to the fans, 'Come back again, and bring your friends.' "

Teresa, Nikki, Dawn, and Jennifer were among the biggest stars in the ABL and still the hardest workers. They had the least to prove and yet every night put out the greatest effort. I hope the rest of the league takes the cue.

Ruthie went off to play in Turkey. She was assigned to the Sacramento Monarchs of the WNBA. Sheryl was assigned to the Houston Comets but may miss the first season because she is pregnant. Rebecca went to the New York Liberty. Lisa signed a multi-year contract with the Los Angeles Sparks for huge money. She also spent time modeling for the Wilhelmina Modeling Agency, appearing around the country for Nike and working as a color commentator for FoxSports West on USC women's basketball games.

Katrina played in Turkey but returned when she ran into problems with her contract.

I'm looking forward to the first WNBA season this summer. The league signed some of the top international stars, such as Australia's Michelle Timms, China's six-foot-eight-inch center Zheng Haixia, Brazil's Janeth Arcain and Russia's Elena Baranova. It also signed such legendary favorites as Nancy Leiberman-Cline and Lynette Woodard. Nancy is already inducted into the Basketball Hall of

Fame, perhaps making her the first Hall of Famer in any American sport to be on an active roster.

Renee is loving her job as WNBA director of player personnel. Nell Fortner coached her Purdue team to a tie for the Big 10 title—she was carried off the court by her players after clinching the tie. Nancy Darsch accepted a head coaching position with the New York Liberty of the WNBA. Marian had a good year with Kansas, as did Ceal with Colorado. Both earned berths in the NCAA tournament, as did Nell and I. Stanford lost to Old Dominion (again) in the semifinals. My friend, Pat Summitt of Tennessee, won the championship yet again.

As I reflect on the year with the Olympic team and the changes that have come in its wake, I'm excited about the opportunities for women in basketball. But what I've seen in my own sport seems a reflection of the larger community of women. We're taking longer, more purposeful strides, not content anymore with the baby steps that defined our early progress. The playing field still isn't level, but it's getting closer all the time because, as they say, nothing succeeds like success.

What I have discovered over the years is that success is rooted not only in confidence and hard work but in joy. Passion produces its own energy. Women in sports are free now to embrace their passion for basketball and volleyball and track and field without reservation, without fear of being considered strange. We can throw everything we have into coaching and playing, which is the only path to excellence. I'm reminded of a remark the writer Pearl S. Buck once made.

"The secret of joy in work is contained in one word—excellence," she said. "To know how to do something well is to enjoy it."